REGNUM STUDIES IN MISSION

When Women Speak…

Series Preface

Regnum Studies in Mission are born from the lived experience of Christians and Christian communities in mission, especially but not solely in the fast growing churches among the poor of the world. These churches have more to tell than stories of growth. They are making significant impacts on their cultures in the cause of Christ. They are producing 'cultural products' which express the reality of Christian faith, hope and love in their societies.

Regnum Studies in Mission are the fruit often of rigorous research to the highest international standards and always of authentic Christian engagement in the transformation of people and societies. These are for the world. The formation of Christian theology, missiology and practice in the twenty-first century will depend to a great extent on the active participation of growing churches contributing biblical and culturally appropriate expressions of Christian practice to inform World Christianity.

REGNUM STUDIES IN MISSION

When Women Speak…

Edited by Moyra Dale, Cathy Hine and Carol Walker

First published 2018 by Regnum Books International

Regnum is an imprint of the Oxford Centre for Mission Studies
St. Philip and St. James Church
Woodstock Road
Oxford OX2 6HR, UK
www.ocms.ac.uk/regnum

09 08 07 06 05 04 03 7 6 5 4 3 2 1

British Library Cataloguing in Publication Data
A catalogue record for this book is available from the British Library

ISBN: 978-1-506475-96-7

Typeset by Words by Design

Distributed by Fortress Press in the US and Canada

Contents

INTRODUCTION

Moyra Dale and Cathy Hine

Women's voices are often unheard and unreported; and their place can be controversial. This book brings together the voices of Christian women scholars and practitioners at the nexus of Christianity, mission and Islam. It comes out of the colloquium of the same name, held in Melbourne, Australia in 2015, when twenty-eight women from different nations and nationalities, different ages and theological perspectives, and different religious backgrounds met together – those of Christian background, and also first and second generation Christians of Muslim background. The colloquium grew from a recognition that women's voices are underrepresented to such an extent that they are almost not present in much of the discussion around missiology and Islam, despite the numbers of women with both significant practical experience, and engaging in higher research and scholarship in the area.

Many missiological books on Islam are written by a single author based on the particulars of their context and experience. While these books offer useful insights and raise awareness of issues, the size and breadth of the Islamic world means that almost everything that is stated for one situation will be different and perhaps even opposite elsewhere. Texts find different interpretations, and cultural patterns vary broadly. This contrast between different regions is evident in this book, with the respondents speaking from their very different experiences (for example, South East Asia versus Central Asia). The writers also vary in style: some are more academic, others more conversational. They come from divergent theological places, even within the evangelical spectrum. And these different voices invite the reader to join the conversation, bringing their own experience on which to reflect.

The book offers six keynote papers. Each paper has two respondents, building on and sometimes challenging the keynote perspective. In these pages you will find people paying attention to each other's voices, rather than competing to be heard. At the same time, this attentiveness to one another's voices is not inimical to but rather frees the space for robust discussion and different perspectives.

Speaking from a variety of nationalities, some of the writers also challenge prevailing views and practices in western missiology. In particular, they question understandings of universal oppression of women in the Muslim world. So Dwi quotes her Muslim cousin saying that "the real oppression that I feel is the western perception of Indonesian Muslim women who are wearing hijab." Bassma also points to the "strong intellectual women" within Islam. Miriam cites examples of the phenomenon of gifted women blocked from ministry among Muslims by western male missiologists with a culturally gendered view of ministry.

Cathy Hine's initial paper challenges this view as it is expressed in prevailing strategies of mission, particularly the family networks and the insider movement, showing how rather than allowing gospel challenges to cultural views of women (such as the pervasive *hadith* that women are 'lacking in religion and intelligence'), some missiologies reinforce the marginalisation of women's contribution: and therefore the marginalisation of Muslim women from access to the good news of Jesus. Dwi Handayani draws on her context in South East Asia to respond, including the place of Muslim single women. Karen Scott reflects on the place of women in holistic community development in South Asia.

Kathryn Kraft asks provocative questions about women whose lives and faith do not fit into easy categories of experience or identity. She raises the questions around marginalization for women who are childless. Kathryn uses the categories of the 'Together towards Life' 2013 World Council of Churches statement to shape her paper about Um Muhammad, and her relationship to Christ and to Christian community. Bassma Jaballah reflects on her experience in North Africa and the Middle East to extend some of Kathryn's conclusions. Jenny Taylor brings a wide range of readings to respond to the description of Um Muhammad's situation.

The next cluster of papers asks about identity formation. Moyra Dale describes the place of communal allegiance, models, different texts and (perhaps surprisingly) music in shaping people's identity, and asks how people may take opportunities to retell their stories of who they are. Sarah Yoon takes examples of women of Muslim background who have become Christians, and the place of worldview, Islamic society and perceptions of 'Christian' and western behaviour. Iris Funk brings her involvement with women in the wider North Africa and Middle East to look at the place of relationships, and shifts in the sociological and political landscape and the possibilities they offer women. Like Karen Scott, she mentions the importance of work and microloans for marginalized women, as well as the place of oral Bible story telling.

Miriam Adeney takes the question from Lila Abu-Lughod's book of that name, to ask 'Do Muslim women need saving?' She focuses on Muslim women as decision-makers and initiators in different cultures, and asks how different cultural patterns may be bridges to truth in Jesus Christ. Farhana Nazir notes the restrictions faced by women in some countries and communities, and therefore on whether women are able to share their faith. Ruth Nicholls also comments on how the place of, and possibilities for women, varies widely in different cultures. She notes that 'salvation' is more about an ongoing relationship with Jesus Christ, and a missional response calls us to make disciples. She suggests some ways to help women, in their unique contexts and identities, in the way with the Messiah.

In her paper, Ida Glaser draws on her own personal experience to ask what it means to voice our trauma before God, and to develop a theology of the pain of God. The Bible offers us a mirror to see our own pain, particularly through the lives of women in the Bible. Does worship help the person experiencing pain to find a place of safety? And how does our experience of pain take us out into God's mission? Guli Frances-Dehqani responds from her family's lived experience to explore further dimensions in understanding the nature of trauma and the importance of voicing it. In particular, she asks about the theme of forgiveness. And Eva Bergmann reflects on how Syrian Muslim refugee women respond to their own experience of suffering, and the possibilities offered by lament.

The last group of papers takes us into a wider canvas, as Cathy Ross looks at the different forms of violence and oppression that silence women globally. She describes various missional approaches that women have practised, as a way of responding to oppression. Nicole Ravelo-Hoerson looks to her context in South Africa to ask about women's self-imposed silence and ways of gaining their voices, and suggests that gendered spaces in society offer a step towards empowering women. Karen Shaw discusses how a theology of resistance might be theologically sound, responsive to particular contexts, and lived practically.

These chapters bring the needed voices of women to the missiological discussion around Christianity and Islam. The papers are multi-perspectival and multi-disciplinary. They are not a conclusion; rather they open up the conversation for other readers, women and men, to join in. We welcome you into it, to read, reflect, and participate in practice and discussion.

1

Veiled: Muslim Women in Modern Mission Strategies

Veiled: Muslim Women in Modern Mission Strategies

Cathy Hine

Introduction

In 1852, Mrs McKenzie, wife of an East India Company merchant, and Lady Mary Kinnaird, wife of a London banker, established the mission organisation that today is Interserve. They recognised that women, secluded in the *zenanas*[1] of India, were hidden from the gospel and from education and health care. A deliberate and intentional engagement, challenging the prevailing cultural hegemony, took education and health in the name of Jesus to women who were otherwise marginalised. This innovation in mission practice opened new doors for women missionaries that included the opportunity to train as doctors,[2] a field that had been closed to women until this time.

Today, while women still make up the largest proportion of mission workers, we are seeing their numbers[3] decline. Few international mission organisations are led by women,[4] despite women constituting the majority of workers throughout the history of mission.[5] While the emergence and growth of

---

[1] The secluded women's area of the home.

[2] At the request of one of the Indian rulers, the women of Interserve requested Queen Victoria to permit women to train as doctors. The first one who completed her training and went to India died on the way, and the second died shortly after arriving. It was this early request that opened new opportunities for women.

[3] Interserve is seeing a decline in the number of women engaging in ministry, anecdotally this has been confirmed as true in many other major mission organisations. In April 2013, Fifty-eight percent of Interserve workers were women, three-hundred and twenty eight married women and one hundred and forty-six single women. It was noted at the time that the number of women joining Interserve was declining.

[4] In response to this lack of space for women to define what mission looks like, there are an increasing number of organisations with a cross-cultural focus that are started and led by women, usually filling a niche area of ministry. For example: She is Safe; Vision Communications; Arab Women Today; EME Ministries.

[5] Dana Robert has warned 'Recent information indicates that Southern Baptist women are beginning to turn away from missions. If history is any indicator, with the women muzzled, it will only be a matter of time before the mission program in the entire denomination begins to decline'. Quoted in Ross, Cathy. More than Wives: Rediscovering the Little "m" in our Mission History, in *Putting Names with Faces*. Edited by Christine Lienemann-Perrin, Atola Longkumer, and Afrie Songco Joye. (Nashville: Abingdon Press, 2012), 290.

the leadership of non-Western women may hold the key to the future of women in mission, the marginalisation of women with respect to missiology and mission strategy is dramatically affecting women's access to the gospel.

This is particularly true in areas of the world where Islam is the dominant religion. Missiologies and mission strategies directed toward the house of Islam are shaped by particular definitions of contextualisation that have led to a priori assumptions that focus fulfilment of the great commission on reaching men first, and the community will follow. Fran Love has stated: "...Muslim women are too often left out of strategic church planting due to... a 'gender-blind missiology' This mission theory states that missionaries need first of all to influence heads of households and leaders who will in turn influence their families and those under their authority. While based on conventional wisdom... it is an incomplete perspective both for biblical and practical reasons." (Love, 1996:135) What is the impact of contextualised mission strategies on Muslim women?

In missiology and mission practice women's participation is often veiled, or 'without faces' (Ross, 2011, quoting Young Lee Hertig), which further veils women who live under Islam. Women's work is often considered secondary in mission. In Interserve, forty-five percent of country team leaders are women, but this is due, in part, to views about the 'unassigned spouse', that the man's ministry is too important for a role that is considered administrative and powerless.

Missiology and mission practice do not develop in a vacuum. In 2010, Interserve needed to produce a gender[6] inclusivity statement, and now, a booklet on gender in its 'Vision and Practice' series. This has become necessary in an organisation started by women to reach women. Why? It is due, at least in part, to resurgent voices among evangelicals framing theologies that underpin missiologies that narrowly define how women may use their gifts and engage in ministry.

However, when we understand some of the reasons why women from within Islam become followers of Jesus, and how their journey with Jesus is walked out, we open possibilities for more gender-nuanced strategies for ministry.

Contextualisation

Phil Parshall pioneered modern expressions of contextualisation for ministry to Muslims. He defines contextualisation as "...the effort to understand and take seriously the specific context of each human group and person on its own terms and in all its dimensions – cultural, religious, social, political, economic – and

---

[6] The gender inclusivity statement says: Interserve acknowledges that God has created both women and men in His image and has called them to partner together as equals in mutual submission. IS intentionally seeks to demonstrate this by having men and women at all levels of leadership so as to release all the gifts and abilities that God has invested in the Fellowship.

to discern what the Gospel says to people in that context." (Parshall, 2003:36) Contextualisation is not cultural relativism.[7] It embraces a culture's conceptual categories, forms and symbolic motifs, while at the same time critically assessing each individual aspect of the culture according to its compatibility with the scripture. Timothy Tennent says contextualisation is about Jesus being authentically experienced in the particularities of the local context. (Tennent, 2010)

Contextualisation in mission today has been developed from definitions of culture in secular anthropology.[8] Christ and culture are seen as wholly separate, leaving little or no room for the Kingdom of God to break in. But, as David Greenlee says, true contextualisation deals with values and worldview, and is more than an approach to witness. (Greenlee, 2012) The Kingdom of God breaks in bringing transformation, the future breaking into the present. Tennent rightly asserts that all parts of culture are enhanced, or destroyed or enlivened when brought under the Lordship of Christ. (2010)

We will consider two contextualised strategies:[9] family networks and the insider movement. Both of these have informed approaches to reaching people and building the Church in countries where Islam is the dominant religion. They have highlighted and wrestled with challenges at the interface of Islam and the gospel. The question is not whether we are for or against either of these, rather we want to explore the impact of pursuing these strategies for women who follow Islam.

---

[7] Lila Abu-Lughod speaks about cultural relativism in terms of saying 'it's their culture and it's not my business to judge or interfere...' *Do Muslim women really need saving? Anthropological reflections on cultural relativism.* (American Anthropologist 4:3, 2002), 786. Parshall reflects on this when he notes that one of the dangers of contextualisation, which he says is expressed in the teaching of liberal theologians, is emasculation of the gospel; deleting those passages of scripture and parts of the gospel message that are considered offensive to the other culture. *Muslim Evangelism: Contemporary Approaches to Contextualisation* (Waynesboro: Gabriel Publishing, 2003). Abu-Lughod rightly emphasises the importance of respecting difference as products of different histories, expressions of different circumstances, and as a manifestation of differently structured desires. Contextualisation acknowledges the imperative of the cultural metanarrative but is not a licence for experimentation with anything that might fit into the local culture. Parsons views it as bringing "the Biblical metanarrative into critical relationship with the narratives of other places and groups without compromising the biblical particularity of God's own narrative identity". *Unveiling God: Contextualising Christology for Islamic Culture.* (Pasadena: William Carey Library, 2005), xxxi.

[8] Richard Niebuhr's work was formative for the development of Christian thinking in this field. *Christ and Culture* (New York: Harper and Row, 1951).

[9] Further research could helpfully explore the missiological underpinnings of these strategies, and revisit those in relation to a more gender-nuanced missiology.

Family Networks

Identifying married male, literate, rural farmers or fisherman, who were well-respected members of Muslim society, as their target group for evangelism, Phil Parshall and his team were clear who was not included: "In our context, young persons, or women of any age, would not be appropriate as an initial direction for evangelism. It was hoped that they would follow in the faith of their husband/father." (Parshall, 2012:225) Parshall's work in the 1980s was considered ground-breaking,[10] and subsequent mission strategies for work among the peoples of Islam increasingly focused on male heads of families and communities.

Dudley Woodberry, scholar of Islam and mission, agrees, suggesting that for a movement to be born, family and community decision-makers must be the focus. (Woodberry, 2005) *Research in Pakistan* by Edwards Evans also seems to affirm this strategy. Evans found that of primary converts, the first to come to faith in a family, only ten percent were women, and no husband had followed. Where men were first to come to faith, at least twenty women and other family members had followed (Evans, 2012).[11]

The evidence seems irrefutable. Or is it? The work of women practitioners in the field seems to challenge the conclusion that if you reach the man you reach the family. Yvette Wray says this about work in Bangladesh: "We knew that if Muslim women would become believers, then the entire family would follow. Gaining access to Muslim women to share the gospel had been the impossible task..." (Wray, 2006:146) In Kazakhstan, women are coming to faith and being followed by their husband and family members. (Lindhal, 2006). Another worker noted: "Our organisation... has focused on mass evangelism and reaching men, believing that women would follow men. But in West Africa, Muslim-background believer (MBB) churches are mostly made up of men. Muslim women have not automatically followed their MBB husband's faith... reaching Muslim men will not ensure that women are reached." (Thompson, 2006:110) Mary McVickers also challenges this assumption that the gospel will move along kinship lines: "often the gospel is heard by men and moves through their relationships with one another rather than across gender lines within kinship", although, she acknowledges, there are exceptions. (McVickers, 2005:128)

There is a cultural context issue that has not informed missiological and strategic thinking. Male BMBs are raised in cultures where women's identity

[10] Ramsay Harris affirms this in the foreword to Parshall's book "Muslim Evangelism'. He identified Parshall's influence in two areas: ministry and the way people do ministry.

[11] Evans also noted that three of the seven female converts who were first to come to faith were killed, whereas only one of the sixty male converts were killed. He identified four reasons why it is harder for women to come to faith: it is harder for them to think outside of the box; harder for them to physically move outside of the home to meet Christians; harder to declare change of faith in the family and community; and there were punished more severely than men in matters of honour.

and value is ambiguous. Normative cultural, political and religious discourses have relegated women to the private sphere, controlling them through a range of social, legal, economic and educational practices. Contextualised strategies have often failed to negotiate these complexities, simplifying the framing of practice to the superficial, easily recognised 'cultural norms' around male headship. This is seen, for example, in the Believer from a Muslim Background (BMB) in the Middle East, with a strong witness as a musician, who said that he did not witness to his wife because she was 'just an illiterate village woman'. (Stricker, 2006)

Rebecca Lewis has challenged conventional mission thinking on contextualisation and the family, saying: "The women of Islam could very well be the gateway of the Gospel in Islamic networks." (Lewis, 2004:76) Within most communities of followers of Islam it appears that men are the power brokers shaping beliefs and practices. In the public sphere that is true. But the public and private spheres intersect. Religious power and authority are in the hands of both the Imam and women. Whereas the Imam's power is community-based and exercised through the mosque, women engage in their rituals and practices in private, within the family context. (Mullin, 2006) The greatest keepers of tradition within Islam,[12] along with the most vocal advocates for change, are women.[13]

When Parshall's story of reaching Muslims in Bangladesh through family networks became a strategy for all countries where Islam is the dominant religion, the trajectory of mission strategies began to veil Muslim women. Assumptions were made about what would happen within family networks. The interplay between the public and private spheres was ignored. Women's agency was denied. Their marginalisation increased.

Insider Movement

Kevin Higgins defines insider movements[14] as: "A growing number of families, individuals, clans and/or friendship-webs becoming faithful disciples of Jesus

---

[12] In a study of Muslim women's activism in Egypt, Sherine Hafez has noted that women are the "Entrusted keepers of the family… [who] often acts as the mediator between the secularising and modernising projects of the state and family.' *An Islam of Her Own: Reconsidering Religion and Secularism in Women's Islamic Movements* (New York: New York University Press, 2011), 59. She refers to women as guardians of tradition and national identity who are entrusted with raising the future generations.

[13] Women like Irshad Manji, Amina Wadud, and Asma Barlas are seeking to redefine Islam from within. Often rejected by their own community, they refuse to accept that they do fit within Islam and challenge what they describe as 'masculine interpretations' of Islamic discourse and practice.

[14] In light of the highly divisive nature of this strategy, and the framing of all responses to it as either insider or extractionist, I wish to say that I am neither advocating or opposing this strategy. The debate has been a long and heated one, and both the *International Journal of Frontier Missiology* and *St Francis Magazine* have carried a

within the culture of their people group, including their religious culture. This faithful discipleship will express itself in culturally appropriate communities of believers who will also continue to live within as much of their culture, including the religious life of the culture, as is biblically faithful. The Holy Spirit, through the Word and through His people will also begin to transform His people and their culture, religious life and worldview." (Higgins, 2004:156) The practice of mission is premised on the gospel addressing the specificities of cultural contexts. The Insider Movement has adopted a particular approach to what that looks like.

The challenge of the Insider Movement for women followers of Islam is that it reifies culture and fails to accept that not every cultural expression of Islam is good for women. Women, their needs, their challenges in hearing about and following Jesus, are subsumed under a rubric that says the socio-political and religious norms and symbols of their community are enough; that they provide appropriate symbols of faith by which women should follow Jesus. Sherine Hafez's work on women's Islamic activism challenges such assumptions. She reminds us that the normative political, social and religious discourses that women live under leave them caught in the double bind of the Islamic agenda and their gender. (Hafez, 2011) The way women are imagined in their society and the impact of that on both their identity and space to act warns mission strategists of the dangers of uncritically embracing cultural and religious forms for the gospel.

The Insider Movement strategy has been debated at a range of levels, but whether by its proponents or opponents, it is almost exclusively debated by men.[15] This absence of women's voices reflects another aspect of their veiling within this strategy.

This critique of the Insider Movement is not a validation of its opponents. Opposition is largely masculine driven and often unable to hear the other.[16] The demands for theological validity, within particular practical expressions, have blinded opponents to the religious hegemony being created. They have emphasised certain expressions of Christian faith, often with strong patriarchal

---

range of articles discussing the issues associated with this as a strategy. My concern in this section is to address the question of whether this strategy has veiled Muslim women and so impacted the ways we consider presenting the gospel to them.

[15] From Spring 2000 (edition 17:1) to October – December 2013 (edition 30:4) 121 articles on contextualisation and the insider movement were authored by men, 13 by women and 6 by couples. *The St Francis Magazine*, from 2005 to present, have published 86 articles on issues of contextualisation and the insider movement authored by men, 1 by a woman and 2 by couples. This no doubt reflects a broader issue for women in mission, but in this context, the issues of contextualisation within the Insider Movement framework are male dominated and driven.

[16] The work of 'Bridging the Divide' has enabled the two sides to come together and listen to each other. And further work by scholar-practioners such as Tim Green and David Greenlee, has identified alternate ways of addressing the essential issues of BMB identity and community.

interpretative overtones. This 'anti-insider' strategy is equally guilty of failing to recognise the cultural realities into which the gospel needs to penetrate. Women followers of Islam are veiled in their strategies, as they are in those of Insider Movement proponents.

Contextualisation is essential in articulating the coming of the Kingdom of God, the gospel bringing transformation of lives and communities. However, in the recent history of mission among Muslims we see Muslim women veiled in strategies that reify culture and build on foundations that separate Christ and culture.

Women, Missiology and Mission

In what ways might our present missiological discourses and praxis veil Muslim women? Cathy Ross, in 'Without faces: Women's Perspectives on Contextual Missiology' (Ross, 2011), explores how the language and worldview of mission strategies today comes largely from the arenas of military and management, 'managerial missiology',[17] describing its impact on mission strategies as a "cold, reductionist term turning Christian mission into a manageable enterprise using information technology and marketing techniques." (Ross, 2011) Strategic initiatives such as Finish the Task, Vision 5:9, Ethne, AD 2000 and Beyond give focus to the task by emphasising growth, numbers, targets. They are premised on a particular ecclesiology, eschatology and theology of mission. Muslim women are veiled within these missiologies. Vision 5:9, a network committed to building the Church in areas where Islam is the dominant religion, has not included women in its strategic focus until its latest strategic document.[18] It has focused on unreached people groups. The unattended danger of this focus is that the marginalised within people groups usually remain hidden and further marginalised. The research arm of Vision 5:9, committed to the research and promotion of fruitful practices in reaching Muslims, has only one chapter on women in their book, *Fruitful Practices: Global trends, Fruitful Practices and Emerging Issues among Muslims*. This is not representative of the number or place of women in Islam today. Ross's description of a women's missiology "based on a real resistance to a male dominated mission practice that can emphasise power, domination, control as well as endless activity and programmes" (Ross, 2011) exhorts us to seek for a missiology that does not veil women under Islam from the gospel.

---

[17] "the belief that missions can be approached like a business problem. With the right inputs, the thinking goes, the right outcomes can be assured. Any number of approaches have been hailed as the 'key' to world evangelization or to reaching particular groups – everything from contextualization to saturation evangelization. Most while successful up to a point, also have been shown to have limits".
http://www.missiology.org/?p=24 (accessed 10 October 2014)

[18] It is interesting to note that Vision 5:9's engagement with women is led by a man. It is unclear if this is because women are included under a broader 'family' ministry area.

Women in Mission

For 100 years, Interserve was an all women's mission. In 1900, forty-one of the ninety-four registered mission boards in America were Women's Boards. (Ross, 2011) But then, "by the early decades of the twentieth century they had merged and integrated with the General Boards, almost certainly to the detriment of the involvement of American women in mission. The women succumbed to a variety of pressures: appeals to denominational loyalty, criticisms about duplication of resources and inefficiency, assurances that they would be represented in decision making structures and that their concerns would be acknowledged and served in the new 'integrated' structures. Unfortunately, the reality was very different. This has sadly resulted in a silencing of women and what women have to offer in the sphere of missiology." (Ross, 2011) In 1959, men were accepted as workers within Interserve, and while its history as a mission started by women to reach women is celebrated, in a recent activity to select stories that celebrated its work over the last twentyfive years, more than three-quarters of those first selected were stories of men. It was only with deliberate intentionality and advocacy that more women's stories were included.[19]

The increased articulation of women's subordination and gender delineated ministry roles in evangelicalism is formative. During Interserve's International Orientation it was noticed that an increasing number of new workers' theological framework makes it difficult for them to embrace women in leadership and ministry in the organisation. Influential Bible teachers like John Piper, Tim Keller, Don Carson and Mark Driscoll, debates in the global Anglican fraternity about the ordination of women, the influential paper by the Sydney Anglican Diocese,[20] have all given voice to a strongly complementarian theology and definition of ministry practice. Mission is being influenced, and there is a need to ensure that Muslim women are not veiled in mission strategies derived from particularised interpretations of scripture.

No public strategy of any international mission organisation mentions women. The key words of strategies are church planting, church planting movements, the unreached, and evangelism.[21] Interserve's International Priorities, 2010 – 2014, included women under Priority Area 3, Growing in Fruitfulness: 3.2 "Recapture our distinctive heritage by strategically engaging in ministry to women who are marginalised in their community" (Interserve, 2009). SIM, Serving in Mission, do not have a women-specific strategy, but seven of six hundred and thirty-five projects have women in the title and a further one hundred mention women in the project description. (Marshall,

[19] See Naomi Reed 'A Plum Tree in the Desert': London, Authentic, 2015.

[20] See The 1999 Sydney Anglican Diocesan Doctrine Commission Report: The Doctrine of the Trinity and Its Bearing on the Relationship of Men and Women

[21] An internet search of mission agencies' web-sites showed that no agency has women in their public strategy.

2014) Parshall in his book, Muslim Evangelism, says single women should be restricted to institutional ministries. (Parshall, 2003)

Muslim Women's Faith Journey

There is a growing body of research on women journeys to relationship with Jesus from within Islam. It acknowledges that issues for men and women are different.[22] We conclude by examining some of the significant issues and how they might inform mission strategies that are more inclusive of women.

The 'inaccessibility' of Muslim women and their apparent lack of interest in the gospel is considered a challenge by some. (Love, 1996, Reisacher, 2005, Adeney, 2000) What that inaccessibility looks like is contingent on strategy, and the way it defines accessibility. As a practitioner I have lived in both Pakistan and Egypt. Many hours were spent sitting drinking chai in staff rooms, the girls' rooms, my room at the college where I worked. I learned about life, the practical challenges and emotional pressures. I attended life events, laughed, cried and prayed through the everyday and the catastrophes. I learned to do life with the girls, staff, and families of both. How accessible were they? If I was willing to do life with them they were absolutely accessible, open, inviting. Maybe it is strategy that makes Muslim women inaccessible.

The physical veil can make women appear inaccessible. Returning to live in Egypt in 2008, each time I walked on the street I sensed I was withdrawing. I had lived there before, and in many ways it was home. I realised I was reacting to the fully veiled women whose numbers had grown over the years. It was hard to connect with women who seemed invisible to me. Only as I recognised my reaction and challenged my assumptions and fears could I feel compassion and a desire to reach out to these women. With more women choosing to veil, we need love and compassion that ensures these women do not become doubly veiled.

---

[22] Evelyne Reisacher, in research among North African converts, identified the following significant areas that are different from men who convert: fear of being rejected by the family, some of which is because girls do not have the same freedom as males; women are more resilient than men because it is harder to convert. Because men have more freedom they do not have the same cost when they choose to follow Jesus; women are attracted to Jesus because of the way he treated women, they find their real identity in Jesus; women find it more difficult to define their identity as women who follow Jesus in a Muslim context, because they are seen as the representatives of Islam, embodying family, and symbolising the private sphere; shame, and the way women's decisions bring 'shame' on the family; the male guardian who protects/prevents women from independence in life and its choices; married women's role as guardians of Islam and those who pass it on to their children; women's emotional sensitivity helps them connect with Jesus; limited mobility which means women cannot freely go out or access the public square. North African Women and Conversion: Specifics of Female Faith and Experience in *From the Straight Path to the Narrow Way: Journeys of Faith* edited by David Greenlee (Waynesboro, Authentic, 2005), 50.

Fran Love has described the conversion of Muslim women as a "process of discipleship in which their real life questions are answered, not in a systematic way, but as they arise from the woman herself". (Love, 2006:5) Women need encounter with Jesus, and truth that transforms the reality of today, giving security for tomorrow. They respond to Jesus when their felt needs are met as they experience truth. Reisacher's research in North Africa shows women are attracted to Jesus because of the way he treated women. (Reisacher, 2005) Mary McVickers says that women often start the journey of faith from a place of desperation, and manifestation of Jesus. (McVickers, 2005)

There are also the questions of identity. Women find it more difficult to define their identity as women who follow Jesus in a Muslim context because they carry within their self all that it means to be a good Muslim wife, daughter, mother, woman. (Reisacher, 2005) Women's identity is tied to their familial and social relationships. Diana Colby says that the system of honour and shame inscribed on Muslim women's bodies is the single most important reason why more men than women are coming to faith and visible in BMB fellowships. (Colby, 2000) The construction of alternative communities, places of belonging, and identity in Christ are important in the journey of Muslim women with Jesus.

Muslim women are embracing the journey with Jesus from places of need, brokenness, marginalisation, encounter, and revelation. Strategies that define ministry from a place of power, strength, knowledge, and rightness, will continue to veil Muslim women because they do not reflect their journeys of faith. Mission and missiology needs a more nuanced and gender-sensitive approach[23] that reflects the journey of these women to faith. Greater reflection on the beatitudes and the coming of the Kingdom of God that turns power on its head, embracing weakness, sacrifice and powerlessness, can be a new starting point for a journey with women who live under Islam.

Final Word

Strategies inform, challenge, provide tools, push the boundaries of experience in making Jesus known among the peoples who follow Islam. However, we have yet to learn that there is no single strategy that will see the Kingdom of God breakthrough across nations under Islam. In our passion to see Jesus made known, we have been guilty of veiling Muslim women to the gospel by embracing strategies and methods that separate Christ and culture, blindly binding women to systems of power and injustice within their socio-religious

[23] Cathy Ross speaks of a missiology of emptiness and hiddenness which is informed by Jesus' model of incarnation; a missiology of comforting, consolation and healing reflecting the power of the Holy Spirit to comfort and heal; a missiology of hospitality and relationship that is listening, learning and seeing the other; a musicology of sight, embracing and flourishing that sees the other and welcomes and embraces them. "Without Faces": Women's Perspectives on Contextual Missiology.

and political culture. Our own cultural backgrounds have marginalised women in mission, drawing a veil on women who live under Islam.

This is a new invitation for women to begin to reflect and imagine new ways of ministry with Muslim women. Anthropologists would be horrified at the use of imagery around lifting the veil. We can redeem that imagery by reminding ourselves that the veil that separated us from God was torn when Jesus died, and in Christ that veil for women followers of Islam is also torn. Our missiologies and strategies should not separate them from encounter with the One God.

References

Adeney, M. 'Why Muslim Women Come to Christ'. pp. 101 – 122 in *Ministry to Muslim Women: Longing to Call them Sisters.* Edited by F, Love and J Ekheart (Pasadena: William Carey Library, 2000).

Colby, D. 'Islamic Reformation and Fundamentalism's Impact on Muslim Women'. pp. 64 - 78 in *Ministry to Muslim Women: Longing to Call them Sisters.* Edited by F Love and J Ekheart (Pasadena: William Carey Library, 2000).

Evans, E. 'Coming to Faith' in Pakistan'. pp. 167 – 185 in *From the Straight Path to the Narrow Way: Journeys of Faith.* Edited by David Greenlee (Milton Keynes: Authentic, 2006).

Greenlee, D. 'How is the Gospel Good news for Muslims'. pp. 205-220 in *Toward Respectful Understanding and Witness among Muslims.* Edited by E.A. Reisacher (Pasadena: William Carey Library, 2012).

Hafez, S. *An Islam of Her Own: Reconsidering Religion and secularism in Women's Islamic Movements,* New York and London: New York University Press, 2011.

Higgins, K. 'The Key to Insider Movements: The 'Devoteds' of Acts', *International Journal of Frontier Mission,* 21:4 (2004): 155 – 163.

Interserve. International (Fellowship) Priorities: 2010 – 2014. *In:* INTERSERVE (ed.) *Internal Document.* Kuala Lumpur: Interserve, 2009.

Lewis, R. 'Strategizing for Church Planting Movements in the Muslim World', *International Journal of Frontier Missiology,* 21, (2004): 73 – 77.

Lindhal, V. 'Stories Along the Silk Road: Reaching Muslim Women in Central Asia, Russia and China'. pp. 129 – 137 in *A Worldview Approach to Ministry Among Muslim Women.* Edited by Cyntian Strong and Meg Page (Pasadena: William Carey Library, 2006).

Love, F. 1996. 'Church Planting that Includes Muslim Women'. *International Journal of Frontier Mission,* 13:3 (1996): 135 – 138.

Love, F. 'Christ, the Hope of Muslim Women'. pp. 3 – 22 in *A Worldview Approach to Ministry Among Muslim Women.* Edited by Cyntian Strong and Meg Page (Pasadena: William Carey Library, 2006).

Marshall, D. July 1, Personal Correspondence, 2014.

McVickers, M. 'Experiencing Jesus: Reflections of South Asian Women'. pp 125 – 136 in *From the Straight Path to the Narrow Way: Journeys of Faith.* Edited by David Greenlee (Waynesboro: Authentic, 2005).

Mullin, S. 'Faith on Camelback: reaching non Arabic-speaking Urban, Less-educated Muslim Women'. pp 75 - 91 in *A Worldview Approach to Ministry Among Muslim Women.* Edited by Cynthia Strong and Meg Page (Pasadena: William Carey Library,

2006).

Parshall, P. *Muslim Evangelism: Contemporary Approaches to Contextualisation,* Waynesboro: Gabriel Publishing, 2003.

Parshall P. 'Contextualisation'.pp. 221-232 in *Toward Respectful Understanding and Witness among Muslims.* Edited by E.A. Reisacher (Pasadena: William Carey Library, 2012).

Reisacher, E. 'A. North African Women and Conversion: Specifics of Female Faith and Experience'. pp. 109 - 124 in *From the Straight Path to the Narrow Way: Journeys of Faith.* Edited by David Greenlee (Waynesboro: Authentic, 2005).

Ross, C. Without Faces: Women's Perspectives on Contextual Missiology. *The Twelfth Annual Louis J. Luzbetak, S.V.D. Lecture on Mission and Culture.* http://www.youtube.com/watch?v=DmHgP8C1RbA. Accessed July 2012.

Stricker, B. 'Communicating Christ in Contexts of Persecution'. pp 205 - 216 in *A Worldview Approach to Ministry among Muslim Women.* Edited by Cynthia Strong and Meg Page (Pasadena: William Carey Library, 2006).

Tennent, T. C. *Invitation to World Missions: A Trinitarian Missiology for the Twenty-first Century,* Grand Rapids: Kregel Publications, 2010.

Thompson, L. W. 'How Will They Hear? Reaching the Muslim Women of Sub-Saharan Africa'. pp. 109 - 127 in *A Worldview Approach to Ministry Among Muslim Women.* Edited by Cynthia Strong and Meg Page (Pasadena: William Carey Library, 2006).

Woodberry, J. D. 2005. 'A Global Perspective on Muslims Coming to Faith in Christ'. pp 11 – 22 in *From the Straight Path to the Narrow Way: Journeys in Faith.* Edited by David Greenlee (Waynesboro: Authentic, 2005).

Wray, Y. 'A Life of Ironies: Reaching South Asian Educated Urban Muslim Women'. Pages 139 - 149 in *A Worldview Approach to Ministry Among Muslim Women.* Edited by Cynthia Strong and Meg Page (Pasadena: William Carey Library, 2006).

Veiled: Muslim Women in Modern Mission Strategies: Response 1

Dwi Handayani

Introduction

Cathy Hine's paper, "Veiled: Muslim Women in Modern Mission Strategies" offers an extensive look at the crucial place of Muslim women in mission. She presents the realities that women are usually neglected in mission strategies. She challenges the assumption that women are not the important key for evangelism. Moreover, she also provides some provoking facts that show the important roles of women with Muslim-background believers.

I found this paper really interesting and inspiring. Although I live in a country with the biggest Muslim population in the world, I had never really learned about the Muslim women and their significance in evangelism.

Cathy uses imagery that in missiology and mission practice women's participation is often veiled, a very interesting imagery that shows how the Islamic view of women influences Christian mission.

She also mentions that the number of women workers in mission is declining. Although I do not have any data that shows the number of women missionaries in Indonesia that are trained to reach the Muslim women, the number is not many, at least in my city Bandung.

Contextualization

Cathy challenges Phil Parshall's strategy of contextualization and reminds us that there is a danger of "uncritically embracing cultural and religious forms for the gospel". She offers a critical view on contextualization within a family network in the Muslim society and on the insider movement. In this response, I would like to offer an Indonesian perspective on the issues and some contributions that strengthen the argument that women do play a crucial role in mission.

Muslim Wife and Mother

As Cathy mentions in the article, strategies to reach to the Muslim communities in Indonesia also generally focus in reaching men as the head of the family with the assumption that he will bring the whole family to Christ.[1]

She also says, “the marginalization of women with respect to missiology and mission strategy is dramatically affecting women’s access to the gospel”, a very strong statement that I totally agree with.

I did a simple survey of 14 people who have parents of different religions, one Muslim and the other Christian:

No	Name	Mother	Father	Children	
				M	C
1	Helen	M	C	7	1
2	Anto	M	C	4	
3	Moses	M	C	2	3
4	Anton	M	C	2	
6	Rudi	M	C	1	
7	Yadi	M	C	3	
8	Iman	M	C		4
9	Leni	M	C	2	
10	Lili	M	C	3	
11	Heri	C	M (MBB[2])		3
12	Jono	C	M		2
13	Ica	C	M	5	4
14	Edi	C	M		2

The result of that simple research shows that mothers/wives have a very strong influence on their family’s faith. It confirms Cathy’s argument that Muslim women do not automatically follow their MBB husband’s faith. In fact, many children followed their mother’s faith.

My student, Helen is a MBB, her father is a Christian but never shared his faith with his wife. Out of 8 children, only 2 sons were chosen to follow their father’s faith, and the rest were educated as Muslims by their mother. At age 10, one of her Christian brothers, who lived with his Christian grandmother and remains a Christian and now has become a pastor, brought Helen to Christ, while the other brother became a Muslim because of his mother’s influence.

---

[1] An interview with a leader of evangelistic works among the Sunda people in Bandung.

[2] Follower of Jesus from a Muslim Background.

Muslim Single Women

Cathy does not specifically talk about Muslim single women in the article. However, Phil Parshall in his book *Muslim Evangelism: Contemporary Approaches to Contextualization* writes:

> "The family is a great asset to an evangelistic ministry among Muslims. It is the norm of Muslim society. All Muslim girls are married, most of them by age 16. The male is usually married no later than 30 years of age. Muslims really cannot understand the single lady missionary. They have no category or role for her in society. This makes life, in a practical sense, very difficult for single ladies in the Muslim land. It is my opinion that they can best find fulfillment in institutional outreaches rather than seeking to engage in traditional evangelistic roles. I have never witnessed directly to a Muslim lady." (2003:134)

This statement is not all true in Indonesia. There are many Muslim single women who are open for friendship with Christian single women.[3] The role of the single woman missionary is very much needed in Indonesia.

It is true that in rural areas many women are married at a very young age, but in a city like Bandung, we can find many single Muslim women, college age and above who choose to remain single for a certain period of time while pursuing their career.[4] These single women are well-educated and relatively open-minded and longing for friendships.[5]

From 2010 to 2012, I taught Christian Ethics in a Christian university, Maranatha. I was very surprised to find that one third of my students were Muslims, including four young Muslim women wearing hijab. However, they were very open and attentive to the topics discussed in the class.

From Women to Men

Parshall also says that evangelism must be done within the same gender: "I have never witnessed directly to a Muslim lady. My wife has never shared

---

[3] See Azimah Rahayu, *Catatan Wanita Lajang (A Diary of Single Women)* (Jakarta: Syaamil Cipta Media, 2005), this book is a compilation of stories (perhaps some are true) about being single Muslim women in Indonesia.

[4] The Muslim communities in Indonesia, fully aware of the growing number of single Muslim women, has therefore produced numbers of articles, sermons and magazine that talk about the life of single Muslim women. See Berbahagia Menjadi Lajang (Happy to be A Single Women), *EraMuslim,* 2 Februari 2014. Bolehkah Melajang? (Is it Okay to be Single?), http://www.konsultasisyariah.com/bolehkah-wanita-melajang/. *sy-Syaikh Muhammad bin Shâlih Al-'Utsaimîn rahimahullâh,* Nasehat Bagi Wanita Lajang (An Advice for Single Women), http://akhwat.web.id/muslimah-salafiyah/fatwa-ulama/nasehat-bagi-para-wanita-lajang/

[5] For number of years in Indonesia, the number of young women enrolling in the university is increasing. For example, the number of female students and gradutes from media and communications degrees at university is much higher than male students and graduates. Michele Ford and Lyn Parker, *Women and Work in Indonesia* (Abingdon, UK: Routledge, 2008), 136.

Christ with a Muslim man. Our honouring the dictates of Muslim culture, which say that one must communicate only with members of the same sex has been much appreciated." (2003:134)

Parshall's statement does not apply in Indonesia, where the Muslim communities are very open to the outside world and the women are relatively free. Even in their communities, there are wide opportunities for female preachers who also preach to both men and women.[6]

One of the most strategic positions is being a teacher or lecturer in a university. As a female lecturer in a university, I have a huge opportunity to share the Gospel to my students.

In February 2015, I had the opportunity to lead a discussion on "religious freedom" in the biggest Islamic university in Bandung. More than 100 students and lecturers attended the discussion, male and female, and they were very attentive and active in the discussion.

Muslim Women to Their Wider Community

Cathy reminds us that our missions "have been guilty of veiling Muslim women to the gospel" and by removing that veil I believe we will not only remove the boundaries that separate the Muslim women and Christ, boundaries that are "blindly binding women to systems of power and injustice within their socio-religious and political culture" but we will also open "the gateway of the Gospel in Islamic networks" not only from women to women but also from women to men, from women to their wider communities.

One characteristic of Muslim women in Indonesia that is different from some other Islamic countries is that women have a very wide door in society. Muslim women in Indonesia actively put themselves on the front lines of many social issues such as justice, corruption, human rights, gender and equality. The feminist movement in Indonesia is endeavouring to empower women whilst remaining Islamic. (Love and Eckheart, 2000:12)

Julian Millie describes the lives of older Muslim women in Bandung who usually join religious study groups, travelling all over town in their spiritual pilgrimages. One reason he proposes for the piety of these women is the concern they feel about social issues like corruption and rising crime: they believe that acquiring religious knowledge will help strengthen society against such perils. (Inside Indonesia 103: Jan-Mar 2011)

---

[6] See Eka Srimulyani, *Women from Traditional Islamic Educational Institutions in Indonesia: Negotiating Public Spaces* (Amsterdam: Amsterdam University Press, 2012). Pieternella van Doorn-Harder, *Women Shaping Islam: Indonesian Women Reading the Qur'an* (Urbana: University of Illinois Press, 2006). Masooda Bano and Hilary Kalmbach, *Women, Leadership, and Mosques: Changes in Contemporary Islamic Authority* (Leiden: BRILL, 2011). Bianca J. Smith and Mark Woodward, *Gender and Power in Indonesian Islam: Leaders, Feminists, Sufis and Pesantren Selves* (Abingdon, UK: Routledge, 2013).

With this important characteristic of Muslim women and their role in society, it is essential to focus on reaching the Muslim women in Indonesia.

The Identity of Muslim Women

The way we perceive Muslim women definitely impacts the way we do mission. By seeing them as poor victims, powerless and uneducated, we are putting an invisible veil that can be a serious hindrance for evangelism.

My Muslim cousin recently complained to me, "the real oppression that I feel is the Western perception of Indonesian Muslim women who are wearing hijab." A similar protest is expressed by Afia, a Muslim woman journalist who writes many articles about Indonesian Muslim women:

> "The image on the bottom left struck me as a familiar stereotype of Indonesian women, ... the lowly-educated housemaids.... It also struck me that when I read the news about my country in English, the reports about Indonesian Muslim women-related issues tend to portray us as unfortunate creatures repressed by unfair, misogynist – and of course, Islamic-based – laws." (August, 23: 2013)

Muslim women are frequently perceived by Christian missionaries as victims and our mission is influenced by the urge of freeing them from the oppression of their culture. (Love and Eckheart, 2000:12)

Deep inside the outward appearance as a women with hijab or even a veil, Indonesian Muslim women are longing to establish their identity as confident, intelligent and elegant Muslim women. (Hooker, 2011)

Conclusion

The traditional approach of Muslim evangelism has been guilty of veiling women in many ways. The stereotyping of Muslim women all over the world strongly put boundaries that separate them from the Gospel and the love of Christ.

As Cathy suggests in her final word, we need "to begin to reflect and imagine new ways of ministry with Muslim women."

References

Afia, On Portrayals of Indonesian Muslim Women: In Search of the Missing Pictures, *Muslimah Media Watch*, August, 23: 2013

Hooker, Virginia. Shaping Modern Muslim, *Inside Indonesia* 103: Jan-Mar 2011.

Love, F and Eckheart, J. *Ministry to Muslim Women: Longing to Call Them Sisters*. Pasadena: William Carey Library, 2000.

Parshall, P. *Muslim Evangelism: Contemporary Approaches to Contextualisation*, Waynesboro: Gabriel Publishing, 2003.

Veiled: Muslim Women in Modern Mission Strategies: Response 2

Karen Scott

Introduction

I am excited and grateful to see the issues Cathy Hine raises in her article being addressed. They are of the utmost importance in seeing the Kingdom of God established among women from a Muslim background and strategic to the overall missiological task – and strategic to the heart of God.

The two main areas of focus in my response to Cathy's paper will; (1) discuss the benefit for women, both from the West and those living in Islamic countries, to be involved in innovative mission strategies which includes holistic community development and; (2) provide practical engagement opportunities that will directly influence how attitudes and behavior can be changed. Resulting worldview change offers women opportunity to follow Jesus while engaging in vibrant, contextual, missiological witness as they network across gender, ethnic and socio-economic boundaries.

I contend that, in large measure, the problem of the double-veiling of Muslim women in missiology, as Cathy describes, begins in the structured, traditional church in the West, a church which is largely rooted in conservative evangelical Christian theology and hermeneutics. I was disturbed by her statement regarding the resurgence of conservative views on women and their roles among evangelicals. The subtleness of this can be deceiving and it needs to be considered seriously as women's roles in the church are discussed and determined.

Response

One of the joys of writing this paper is the opportunity it gives me to respond through the lens of holistic transformational development, the lens of *shalom*.[1] I

[1] A biblical world view offers a total salvation that includes salvation and fellowship with God, forgiveness and reconciliation between humans, victory over sin, deliverance from demonic oppression and from structural evils, justice, peace, health and meaningful lives. In other words, it offers *shalom* (Bryant L. Myers, At the End of the Day, in *Serving with the Poor in Asia: Cases in Holistic Ministry.* Edited by Yamamori, Meyers, Conner, editors 1995),134. Meaning more than peace, Bruce Bradshaw remarks, "*Shalom* is a concept that communicates the sense of 'human welfare, health and well-being', in both spiritual and material aspects" *Bridging the Gap: Evangelism,*

am gratified to see a resurgence of a more holistic theology, well described by the term *shalom*, as seen in the blending of word and deed as a seamless whole within the church. It is through this lens that I can concur with Cathy when she states, "…there is a strong need to ensure that women are not veiled in mission strategies derived from particularised interpretations of scripture."

Rather than substantiate her well-stated claims further, I turn to biblical transformational development,[2] where I have gained some insight that could be helpful in discipleship of Muslim Background Believing (MBB) women and be a lens through which the biblical story will offer fresh interpretation for the Western church. I have witnessed, first hand, women becoming more confident in themselves as well as becoming more visible and valuable to their male guardians through community development programs – and therefore, I contend, positioned to be able to participate more fully in the faith walk of the *jamaat* (congregation).

My PhD research conducted in Bangladesh affirms that contextualized church planting (CP) strategies do not always have the intended results. The research points out that contextualized church planting in this country did not result in Muslim women being more visible, in either religious or social matters, than before they were brought into the Christian faith (Shepherd 2007, a pseudonym). Without careful consideration of the context of women, these strategies appear to be continuing the age-old cultural hegemony mentioned by Cathy. Per my research, this subservient sense seems to be carried over into the newly formed MBB *jamaats* (congregations), illustrated by the lack of discipleship programs for women MBBs. It was also revealed by the lack of special meetings for women and the little knowledge they and their children have of the Christian faith (Shepherd, 2007). As evidenced by Cathy's' paper and my research, the ground-breaking strategy of focusing on heads of families, as used in Bangladesh must take into consideration the cultural context of women. In Bangladesh, they do not attend the mosque and are not considered able to understand spiritual things; they are regarded much like the example of the BMB musician in Cathy's article, "just an illiterate woman," and therefore not considered important to the religious life of the family or community.

Development and Shalom. (Monravia, CA: MARC,1993), 17.

[2] Holistic development as described by Bruce Bradshaw, PhD, development practitioner and lecturer: Do we advocate justice and minister to the poor, naked, sick, hungry, and oppressed because it gives us the opportunity to preach the Good News to them? Or is advocating justice and ministering to the poor, sick, naked, hungry, and oppressed, in itself, good news? Holism affirms that ministering to the poor, sick, naked, hungry, and oppressed and preaching the message of eternal salvation is Good News (Bradshaw, 1993).

Biblical Transformational Development

About the time that non-governmental organizations (NGOs) were gaining a foothold in Bangladesh, tools such as Participatory Rural Assessment (PRA[3]), Theater for Development (TFD[4]), and Appreciative Inquiry (AI[5]), began to emerge that helped in the process of discovering a people's core values (worldview level). These tools introduced a more participant and capacity building partnership with the community. They are now being used with amazing results in many agencies in the country. I posit that my research makes a valid claim for the use of progressive techniques such as these, to be incorporated into discipleship strategies for women. *These activities allow women to become more mobile and visible to their male care-givers.*[6] I contend that a seamless integration of physical and spiritual capacity building, which biblical development programs involving community engagement can provide, is paramount to appropriate holistic church planting and discipleship programs and will positively affect women's access to the gospel.

Significant behavior changes in traditional roles appear to be taking place in rural communities in Bangladesh as development projects and micro-credit activities unleash the amazing potential of rural village women. Although local to Bangladesh, these changes take place in a larger global development community.

At the present time, it is politically correct to be working toward the "up-lift" of women. This appears to be a window of opportunity for Christian development practitioners and may very well be important in bringing a heightened awareness of women to those involved in CP programs. Biblical

---

[3] Participatory Rural Assessment (PRA) is a growing family of approaches and methods to enable local people to share, enhance and analyze their knowledge of life and conditions, and to plan, act, monitor and evaluate.

[4] Theater for Development has been created as an effective tool for social development and is being used in various places around the world. Simply put, TFD is drama aimed at educating its audience in using creative ways to solve pertinent social issues to boost community growth. TFD has been used in research, evaluation, monitoring and in advocacy.

[5] Appreciative Inquiry (AI) is an organizational development process that engages individuals within an organizational system in its renewal, change and focused performance. It is a capacity-building process that selectively seeks to locate, highlight, and illuminate the life-giving forces (values) within an organization, group or community. Appreciative Inquiry is both a way of being in the world and a process for working with change in any human system: families, groups, organizations, communities and the Church.

[6] I have a wonderful memory of a rural Bangladeshi woman in a green sari standing in front of several men from the US. With her head covered, she was looking directly at them and telling about the ponds that the women had stocked with fish. Her concluding remark was classic, "We're even thinking of starting a sawmill!" (Shepherd:1). What affected me most profoundly was the proud look on her husband's face – not a look I often saw.

transformational development and discipleship, using tools described above, must go hand in hand. *Discipleship practices incorporated with biblical transformational development activities negates much of the paternalistic and hierarchal tendencies of more traditional discipleship and Christian teaching* – strategic in preventing a gender-blind missiology.

Search for Solutions

Overall, I believe that the importance of women will become understood in the Muslim world among both women and indigenous leaders as it becomes more understood in the West.[7] On the other hand, it would be exciting to see the growing church among Muslims, through their own hermeneutic, speak into this topic with biblical sensitivity and new vision for the inclusive role of women in spiritual matters.

Cathy mentions that the numbers of women going into mission work is declining. I am not familiar with the current statistics of mission workers, but I was greatly concerned with the picture I saw when attending Vision 5:9 meetings, a network committed to CP among Muslims, of which I attended two area, and one regional meeting between 2007 and 2011. By attending these events, I became aware of what were to me 'missing women'.[8] From personal experience, I knew that women did not attend mission meetings in the numbers of men, but this glaring absence of women disturbed my heart. Most of the men were older and had adult children. Their wives would not have had the same responsibilities in the home at this time in their lives. Why were they not in attendance? By not being present, in circles where decisions are made, women are not able to be part of the debate over mission strategy, which directly relates to the effectiveness of the strategy's implementation. I contend that because they were seen as complementary to their husbands in the missionary endeavor, rather than integral to the task, they did not recognize (nor did their husbands or mission agencies) that they were also strategic to the success of mission efforts.[9] When I attended Vison 5:9 events, I belabored the point that few women were in attendance and that Vison 5:9 documents did not specifically mention women or children (which I hoped would alert the Network to the root

[7] Encouragement could be found in the 'Emerging Church' phenomenon. By not 'throwing out the baby with the bath water', there are several core values to this movement which are helpful in gender issues within the church. A helpful resource is Phyllis Tickle's *The Great Emergence: How Christianity is Changing and Why*. (Grand Rapids, MI: Baker Books, 2008.)

[8] Listed in the June issue of *Network News* (#21, June 2015), a journal of Vision 5:9, two women, Evelyne Reisacher and Farida Sa'idi, now co-facilitate the Family Taskforce.

[9] I had a completely different experience when attending a Micah Network regional meeting in 2007 (Micah Network is a network of Christian development practitioners/agencies described in another footnote). Women were in almost equal numbers to men – what an exciting and refreshing picture.

of the issue). I like to think I was instrumental in the formation of Strategic Initiative 5 – Family. I would have preferred women and children mentioned intentionally in each initiative. However, I was encouraged to see an initiative that did include them.[10] Thankfully, I discovered, through my education at Fuller Theological Seminary and my involvement in transformational development, that women are as necessary to the task as their male counterparts. It was in visiting with rural Bangladeshi women, that I discovered women are NOT impossible to reach with discipleship programs.[11] One focus group of MBB women wanted to continue meeting which meant they would have to leave their home, at least a two-hour trip. When I asked if this would be possible they responded, "Of course, why not? We will say we are going to visit relatives." Conventional assumptions that the gospel must flow across gender lines, from men to women, as articulated in Cathy's paper, were dispelled, not by ignoring the women's context and culture,[12] but by speaking to the women themselves, something not possible for male workers. I strongly urge female mission workers, who have access to women, to participate in organizations that are doing holistic witness; development activities provide legitimate access to women along with the other benefits to the women's families and community.

---

[10] I am usually against using terms such as "women's issues" after reading anthropologist Sarah White. She first brought to my attention the concept of using gender as a more inclusive point of reference when discussing issues related to women. She argues that it is power and power relations that are central to gender relations. Contemporary discussions of women's work and power within the family, arising out of her fieldwork, bring together male-orientated analyses of class and female-orientated debates on gender that demonstrate their interdependence in both practical and analytical terms (*Arguing with the Crocodile: Gender and Class in Bangladesh.* Dhaka, University Press, 1992). Therefore, placing men and women in a gender reference, prevents addressing "women's issues" as separate problems, which, in fact, acts to marginalize women rather than empower them.

[11] While it may be true that decision-makers must be a focus, as missiologists surmise, Cathy illuminates the complexity of this assumption and offers pertinent examples that challenge current missiology. It is true that decision-makers are and should be a focus, but should never be the only focus – again, anthropology and community development practices can guard against this narrow picture of a community.

[12] This is an example of the kingdom of God breaking in as it reveals that contextualization strategies do not have to be responsible for marginalizing women. Disciplines such as anthropology and sociology can offer techniques to discover a people's worldview and cultural practices from the people themselves (women in this instance) and which offers a gender-nuanced missiology as mentioned by Cathy Hine. As Donald B. Kraybill reminds us, "Here was a man with the wisdom of a prophet who readily violated social custom when it oppressed people" (*The Upside-Down Kingdom.* Scottsdale, PA: Herald Press, 1990), 251. We must be free to "experiment" with contextual ways to reach women and to also challenge unbiblical practices in all cultures.

Conclusion

Resources to assist in the missiological task can be found in many areas: books; articles; Christian development agencies; church planting networks; and specific networks of women. In our digital age the web offers many opportunities for linking us together. The organization, Christians for Biblical Equality has many resources including a short curriculum for middle and high school youth that affirms gender roles (Armstrong, 2013). Resources such as these can shape young minds that are not yet steeped in a conservative, traditional hierarchal and patriarchal mindset.

Through women becoming more active in the public sphere, e.g., in community development and community engagement activities, participating in business opportunities, and so on, women, from East and West, will overcome their reticence in attending meetings predominantly attended by men. Thus, women will be in the center of missiological debate and their voices heard. As Western women become more visible, these networks will enhance communication among mission agencies and churches regarding gender issues. They will be sources of encouragement by providing links to men and women advocates in the areas of academic and story writing for publication; there will be greater involvement in speaking and teaching. Advocates that support individual women as they venture into uncharted waters will likewise be identified through these networks. We will see an exponential increase in the number of women that follow *Isa* (Jesus) and who contribute in innovative ways to a more balanced missiological engagement with Islam.

We have learned from Cathy's article that strategies must be challenged and debated; the cultural context of women must be understood as never before. I am excited by her invitation to, "...begin to reflect and imagine new ways of ministry with Muslim women." I also invite you, the reader, to the task.

References

Armstrong, Jenny Rai and Aaron. *Called Out: Godly Living for Missional Teens*. Minneapolis, MN: Christians for Biblical Equality, 2013.

Bradshaw, Bruce. *Bridging the Gap: Evangelism, Development and* Shalom. Monrovia, CA: MARC, 1993.

Kraybill, Donald B. *The Upside-Down Kingdom*. Scottsdale, PA: Herald Press, 1990.

Myers, Bryant L. 'At the End of the Day'. pp. 195-204.in *Serving with the Poor in Asia: Cases in Holistic Ministry*. Edited by Tetsunao Yamamori, Bryant L. Myers and David Conner..Monrovia, CA: MARC Publishers, 1995.

Shepherd, Christina (Pseudonym). *The Influence of Savings-Based Micro-Credit on the Status and Role of Rural Bangladeshi Muslim Women*. PhD Dissertation, 2007.

Tickle, Phyllis. *The Great Emergence: How Christianity Is Changing and Why*. Grand Rapids, MI: Baker Books, 2008.

White, Sarah C. *Arguing with the Crocodile: Gender and Class in Bangladesh*. Dhaka, Bangladesh: University Press Limited, 1992.

2

A Feminine Reading of Christian Missions or A Question of Belonging

A Feminine Reading of Christian Missions in the Middle Eastern Context

Kathryn Kraft

Within Christian missiological studies, there is a growing interest in understanding how missionary pursuits can help promote not just conversion, but also belonging amongst converts to Christianity. The search for belonging among faith changers is influenced by how they and the people around them understand the nature of their beliefs and of conversion.[1] A person's spiritual journey and self-perception influence the extent to which a convert may or may not find belonging, and where. Religious deviants, as converts are often described in sociological studies, live with a sense of social stigma (Downes and Rock, 2003, Stark and Finke, 2000). They may therefore search for belonging among others who have similarly deviated from their community norms, and they also are likely to embark on a process of developing a coherent narrative that explains their beliefs and their new sense of self (Sremac, 2010). Furthermore, there are important gender distinctions, as feminist theory suggests that women define themselves more in terms of relationships and significant affective ties than do men (Ebaugh, 1998:108, Stark and Finke, 2000), which can mean that social connections are particularly important for women converts as they develop their stories and sense of belonging, indeed often more important than any doctrinal narrative.

In considering the journey of a convert in relation to missiological pursuits, it is telling to consider how converts, the supposed recipients of said pursuits, perceive the endeavours and values of Christian missionary groups. This is difficult to do, as different streams of Christian missions are built upon very different underlying ideas about conversion. Mainstream missiology, conscious of historical memories regarding colonialist enterprises, forced conversions and efforts to "civilise" new converts, tends to shy away from research about faith-changing. Meanwhile, evangelical missiology, while often avoiding use of the actual term "conversion", sees "mission first and foremost as related to making worshippers for the Creator [and] is derived from a conversionistic theology" (Payne and Terry, 2013). Nonetheless, there is some common ground. All missionary endeavours have, by definition, historically entailed sending people

---

[1] Recognising that "convert" is a contentious term for many, I will use it in this article to refer broadly to people who have changed, or turned, in their faith identity, that is, "faith changers". "Conversion", therefore, is the act of turning from one identity, or set of beliefs, to another.

from one place to another in order to enact a change or somehow influence others.

In order to take a broader view of how missionary efforts relate to the lived reality of converts, in particular those from a Muslim background, this paper will present a case study of one woman whose conversion narrative is somewhat unique in comparison to the image of conversion typically portrayed in missiological studies or other academic literature. Indeed, her journey as a Muslim woman who came to claim a relationship with Christ may not be understood by all Christian missionaries as constituting Christian conversion. The purpose of this case study is not to assess her conversion experience; rather it is to understand how missiological priorities relate to her sense of self and her spiritual journey.

Framing the discussion around an ecumenical missiological declaration, this paper explores how the woman portrayed in the case study might understand and respond to the various priorities and values of Christian missionary communities. By so doing, I seek to explore the space around one possible feminine view of missions and belonging in the Middle Eastern context.

This analysis is intended to provide a feminine view, rather than a feminist view; in other words, the perspective discussed in this article is not intended to identify a woman-centric missiological framework, rather it is to understand how the missions community engages with the values and priorities of a woman. In recognition that the voices of women have not been as predominant in missiological discourse,[2] a feminine view is intended to help amplify and highlight insights into missiological priorities. While this paper is built around a case study of one woman, additional insight is gleaned from my research among converts in the Arab Middle East.[3] It is important to note that the analysis of missiological arguments was not conducted by this woman; rather I, a Western woman and academic, sought to put myself in her shoes and build a

---

[2] To understand better the breadth of women's voices in missiological discourse, I conducted a brief review of two leading journals, one ecumenical and one evangelical. In the *International Journal of Frontier Missions*, a premier evangelical missiological journal, there were only two articles authored by women during 2012-2014. One of those was co-authored with her husband, and the other article was published alongside an article by her husband. Many of the articles in the journal about missiology in Muslim contexts begin with short stories and anecdotes; all of these were stories about men. Another leading journal, the *International Bulletin of Missions Research*, focuses more on ecumenicalism and missions history, and has had at least one woman contributor to each of its editions since 2012, adding up to not quite one-fifth of its contributors being women, though many editions had only one woman out of 9 or more authors.

[3] Data presented in this paper is taken from my doctoral research conducted in Egypt and Lebanon during 2004-2005. This research was published in my book *Searching for Heaven in the Real World* (Oxford: Regnum Books, 2012), and all references to previous research and interviews with converts refers to the research presented in that book.

sensitivity for her views, values and experiences. Thus, what may be seen here is my feminine view, shaped by the views of other women, in particular those of a woman called Um Muhammed, according to her story as she told it at the time that I met her.

The framework for this analysis is "Together towards Life: Mission and Evangelism in Changing Landscapes", a statement presented at the World Council of Churches assembly of 2013. This ecumenical statement about missions and evangelism is built around the concept of *missio dei*, that is, the mission call of the Triune God. It focuses on four key developments seen as significant during the past decade of churches' endeavours to understand and engage in the mission of the Holy Spirit: Spirit of Mission, Breath of Life, which looks at the role of the Holy Spirit in individuals and communities; Spirit of Liberation, Mission from the Margins, which addresses God's call to justice and mercy; Spirit of Community, Church on the Move, which explores unity in the Church and in Christian community; and Spirit of Pentecost, or Good News for All, about evangelisation.

Introducing Um Muhammed

Um Muhammed[4] was in her fifties when I met her, a healthy middle-aged woman dressed in the typical garb of a Muslim woman in her neighbourhood: dark-coloured *abaya* and a large headscarf tied neatly under her chin. We met in the home of a Christian family who lived in the same building as her. Um Muhammed had lived in the building since she was married, more than twenty years previously, but the Christian family had only recently moved in.

She told me she was a village girl who had attended but a few years of school. In her late teens, she married a distant relative who took her to live with him in the capital city of their country. She told me that they married for love and that her husband really did love her, which turned out to be a blessing when she could not get pregnant. Both her family and his had expected her to bear them a grandchild within a year of marriage, and she herself wanted very much to be a mother, but years passed and she remained alone, with her husband, in their small flat in the city. She feared that her husband would divorce her, but more importantly, she felt lonely, living far from her family without any children to keep her company.

The neighbourhood where they lived was somewhat unique in that Muslims and Christians lived side by side. Most Middle Eastern capitals are religiously diverse, but few neighbourhoods host significant numbers of people from different religious traditions. Um Muhammad's neighbourhood, though, was one of these. She was a bit suspicious of the Christians, but also a bit in awe of

[4] Identifying descriptors and minor details have been removed or changed out of respect for maintaining her anonymity while still seeking to preserve the integrity of her narrative

them. As a child, she had been taught that Christians were the holders of supernatural power, and that churches were deeply spiritual places.

So, she was friendly with her Christian neighbours, occasionally visiting them for tea or receiving them in her home. They knew about her trouble conceiving, and it was a Christian friend who suggested she visit the local Orthodox church and pray there. Um Muhammad initially hesitated, but as her desperation increased, she decided that she was willing to try. She described her decision to visit the church as full of fear and hope: fear that it would not work but also fear of the spiritual power she might encounter in the church; hope that, as all else had failed, this might finally be what would defeat her infertility.

Um Muhammed walked into the church, unsure of what to do. She did not share the details of her visit with me, but she told me that, while praying in the church, Jesus entered her heart. He entered her heart, and she also knew that she would conceive.

Indeed, her son Muhammed was born shortly thereafter. Finally, she had a child to keep her company, a boy to name in the family's tradition of naming the firstborn after the Prophet of Islam, and assurance that her husband would not divorce her to try for a family with another woman. But more importantly, she said, Jesus had entered her heart. Throughout Muhammed's life, his mother told me, she lived with Jesus in her heart, something of which she was confident, but otherwise her life continued as might be expected of a Muslim housewife in the big city, far from her family, raising a young boy. Her Christian neighbours were happy for her, and remained friends, but they knew little about their own religion, so could offer little by way of explanation about how this miracle had happened.

When Muhammed was a teenager, an evangelical Christian family moved in to her building. They invited her over for a visit, and as Um Muhammed sat in their lounge, a book on the shelf caught her eye. She asked her hostess what that book was, and the Christian woman told her it was a Bible, the book of the Christians. Um Muhammed's eyes widened, and our hostess narrated to me that her guest ran out of the house without any explanation. A few minutes later, though, she returned, carrying another Bible in her hands.

Um Muhammed explained that she had owned this Bible since she was young. An uncle had received it as a gift from a Latin American man whom he met many years previously, and she had for some reason inherited it. The book had sat on her shelves as a decoration, a family heirloom of sorts, during the decades she had lived in the big city. She never knew what it was and had not thought to investigate. To learn that it was the Scripture of the faith that had somehow become her own during that visit to the church, the Scripture of the God who had opened her womb, was confirmation of the truth that she had known in her heart. It was also saddening, though, to accept that she had lived as a secret Christian believer for so many years without any teaching, while the Book had been within arms' reach all along.

The Christian woman asked Um Muhammed if she would like to start studying the Bible with her, and she readily agreed. As they read through the books of the Gospels, the teachings of Jesus and other Christian Scriptures, Um Muhammed often commented that she was glad to be finally learning the details of what she had already known to be true.

Um Muhamed's story may be exceptional; it is difficult to tell because it is characterised by the fact that engagement with Christians, with missionaries, or with any other Christ-following community was not a central component of her faith narrative, though she did celebrate that engagement when it happened. There is no way of knowing how many women such as Um Muhammed live with Jesus in their hearts. But even if we do consider her story as exceptional, it might be seen as a story that epitomises some of the attitudes with which women approach faith, Christianity and the message of the Gospel, but a story the likes of which is not often explored in missiological discourse.

In the following sections, I will narrate an attempt to explore how the four themes of the mission of the Holy Spirit within *missio dei*, as outlined in Together Toward Life (TTL), help understand Um Muhammed's story, how Um Muhammed might perceive these themes, and in so doing to suggest what priorities and values in missionary enterprises may be most meaningful to her on her spiritual journey.

Spirit of Mission: Breath of Life

The "Spirit of God, which 'swept over the face of the waters' in creation, descended on Mary and brought forth Jesus" (TTL, 13). TTL emphasises the role of the Holy Spirit in the world, in Creation and in individuals, observing that the Spirit works in "mysterious and unknown ways beyond our imagination" (TTL, 15). At the core of Um Muhammed's story is an act of the Holy Spirit in her life that is difficult to explain empirically or even logically. Her story echoes those of mothers in the Bible, including Mary, but perhaps more notably, the stories of Mary's cousin Elizabeth or Hannah, the mother of Samuel. Social science empiricists may dismiss the miracle of her conception, while mission strategists are unlikely to develop any replicable model based on a story so firmly rooted in the miraculous.

This emphasis on the Spirit of God calls Christians to a human humility inspired by awe of a God who is seen as sovereign over all of Creation. A sense of God's power emerges clearly in Um Muhammed's story. It was an aspect of Christianity of which she was aware before she visited the church, and it was the means by which her personal transformation took place. Indeed, I have found in my research exploring narratives of people born into Muslim families who embrace a Christian faith, that the supernatural act of God is central to many people's stories. Visions, dreams, or miraculous healings are an important part of many converts' narratives and help provide a sense of coherence to their understanding of their faith journey.

This emotive aspect of faith has been highlighted in sociology of religion as important for many converts. Intellectual change, or the process of rejecting a previous doctrine and/or embracing a new doctrine, actually often follows from an emotional or relational change (Stark and Bainbridge, 1985, Yang, 1999, Roald, 2006). Gaudeul (1999) found that many converts out of Islam in his network spoke of love in the new community as the thing that drew them most profoundly to Christianity. They were seeking a deep connection and, when they found it, they were ready to commit to the doctrines taught to them by the Christian community. It bears noting that, while doctrine follows the emotive for many, this is not always the case; for many other converts, intellectual argument is in fact the precursor to the emotive change (van Nieuwkerk, 2006:102).

Emotions and spiritual wonder continue to be important to converts as they build their sense of self and belonging within a new faith identity. For Um Muhammed, it was the central, in fact the sole, expression of her faith for years. Even scripture engagement can take on a more emotive than instructional role in spiritual development (Farah, 2013). Some converts told me that listening to the stories of the Bible and to Bible readings was a meaningful spiritual exercise for them, more for the experience of listening than for the meaning of the texts. This may be reminiscent of their Muslim upbringing, as Qur'anic recitation is an important ritual in Islam, regardless of whether the listeners or reciters understand the words in Arabic which they are reciting, but this type of engagement is also found in Christian traditions such as those of monastic liturgy (Norris, 1997).

Another aspect of the Spirit of Mission highlighted in the document is that of transformative discipleship: "Authentic Christian witness is not only in *what* we do in mission but *how* we live out our mission.... Mission spirituality resists and seeks to transform all life-destroying values and systems wherever these are at work in our economies, our politics, and even our churches" (TTL, 29, 30). This transformation is on both a personal level and a societal level. Um Muhammed's story does not include an account of such transformation. When I met her, she came across as a joyful person, but this may or may not have been an outcome of the transformative work of the Holy Spirit in her life; it may be that she always had a cheery personality. At the same time, she said that when she finally opened a Bible and began studying its teachings, it was giving words to what she already believed: this may suggest that there was some Spiritual sense of engagement with God's teaching in her heart. I met another convert who also spent years believing before attending any Christian instruction or reading a Bible; he told me that in the absence of a physical Bible, God had taught him. Both he and Um Muhammed, and other converts whom I have met, were excited and proved eager pupils when finally presented with an opportunity to study the Bible.

Nonetheless, Um Muhammed did not see it as her role to demonstrate her faith and values visibly in society, and she did not seek to challenge cultural norms. She continued to wear *hijab*, gave her son a Muslim name, and continued to play the role expected of a dutiful Muslim wife. This could be indicative of her understanding that these lifestyle choices were not sinful in nature, or they may alternately suggest that she saw no connection between her heart faith and God's wider transformation of lives and society.

Largely in response to such diverse outward expressions, or non-expressions, of faith, the theme of "identity" has garnered extensive attention among evangelical missiologists with a conversionist theology. Missiological studies have unpacked a variety of different aspects of identity, and it is widely understood now that identity for Muslim-background converts is much more complex than merely whether one identifies as Muslim or Christian. LD Waterman's (2014) "LIFE Scale" seeks to capture this complexity by specifying eight dimensions of "life in Christ". These include: heart, beliefs, spiritual activities, core (ego) identity, social identity, collective identity, and cultural embeddedness. On this scale, Um Muhammed's "life in Christ" may be rated as high on the heart scale, and possibly high on core identity, but low on all the other dimensions. While Waterman does not argue that a believer who ranks low on many dimensions is less of a believer, and in fact suggests the opposite, there may still be some implicit sense of legitimacy that comes from a life in Christ that takes on more of the dimensions, unlike Um Muhammed.

Though living lonely and isolated in her adopted faith, Um Muhammed seemed to be comfortable with any duality between her beliefs and her heritage. Her story, therefore, may not evoke any sense of identity crisis, but many other female converts do wrestle with issues of identity. Many women struggle to know how to describe themselves, and are unsure in which community they belong. Many female converts from a Muslim background, in particular, struggle when they decide to engage actively in a church community, as many of them wear a visible symbol of their Muslim-ness in the form of *hijab*. The headscarf traditionally excludes them from Christian community, and this feeling of exclusion can also spark identity conflicts. Similarly, women are more likely than men to experience limitations on their movements by their fathers, brothers or husbands, which may also create a sense of exclusion or be a barrier to belonging. In comparison, Um Muhammed did not express these feelings of exclusion because she did not expect to be welcomed into a Christian community. For Um Muhammed, the TTL's statements about the Spirit of God in her heart are likely to resonate more strongly than a consideration of her new identity in Christ.

Spirit of Liberation: Mission from the Margins

"Jesus relates to and embraces those who are most marginalized in society, in order to confront and transform all that denies life" (TTL, 37). For Um Muhammed, this happened on a highly personal and individual level. The crux of her faith journey lies in a physical act of mercy upon her, a woman with low literacy, from a village and living in a poor neighbourhood in a big city, fearful of social disenfranchisement due to her infertility. When Jesus "entered her heart", he also restored her social position.

Warrick Farah, in his analysis of "emerging missiological themes in MBB conversion factors" reviews various studies of conversion written by evangelical missionaries and notes that, while there are some gender-specific barriers to conversion that challenge women more than men, there are other ways in which the message of the Christian Gospel is particularly meaningful to women. "Female conversions are strongly influenced by an awareness of Jesus' treatment of women in the gospels [and] include greater degrees of practical and experiential factors" (Farah, 2013:17).

It is therefore, perhaps, not surprising that many women missionaries have historically been involved in ministries addressing physical or emotional needs, such as education, childcare or health. In fact, historically, care for society has been enshrined in many Christian traditions. For example, the Roman Catholic Church has a series of papal encyclicals outlining the importance of charity in truth, and churches of all denominations across the Middle East and Africa have historically been responsible for leading educational and medical establishments. William Cohen (2003:387) outlines how, historically, European Christianity up until the 14th century stressed the importance of helping the poor: the poor were seen as incarnating Christ, and since it was more difficult for a rich man to go to heaven than a camel to go through the eye of a needle, then helping the poor was seen as essential for salvation.

Missionary efforts until the late 20th century originated primarily in Europe or North America and were directed to countries with higher poverty, and so the efforts of missionaries included various ministries to support body and mind, as well as spirit. The Christian Missionary Society's 1920 manual on medical mission, for example, stated that, "The true medical missionary... regards his medical work as the Gospel translated into action; it is a testimony to a God of love, and a proclamation of the fact that He cares for man; it is an object lesson in Christianity, and thus not only opens the way for the preaching of the Gospel, but itself delivers the message" (in Jennings, 2008:42). This understanding that the physical body is an integral part of the spiritual being, that physical healing is integral to spiritual healing, was an important element of Um Muhammed's spiritual journey.

However, with population growth and urbanisation, secular authorities stepped in, so to speak, to meet people's physical and educational needs in Europe and, later, North America. Consequently, there has been a growing gap between those churches that continue to focus on such ministries and those which see their priorities as evangelistic. Debates in the 1970s, which accompanied geo-political and academic trends separating the religious from the secular, raged between churches that prioritised social justice which were primarily mainline Protestant and Roman Catholic, and those that prioritised evangelism which were primarily Evangelical. To some degree, conversionist ministry was subsequently sidelined in mainline Protestant and Roman Catholic churches, while spiritual care for the whole person was sidelined in Evangelical missions (Robert, 2014).

In my research among converts, one of the most common critiques against missionaries cited by believers from a Muslim background was that they thought it disingenuous to attempt to separate the message from their lifestyles, which many evangelical missionaries were perceived as doing. Those who lived in nice homes and who sent their children to expensive schools, but who did not show generosity to their Muslim neighbours who were less well-off, were seen as hypocrites, as were those who made an effort to avoid providing material support to converts claiming they wanted to avoid accusations that they were bribing people to convert. In contrast, many converts were interested in setting up community development projects, building their skills to provide counselling to victims of abuse, and providing food packages to the poorest in their midst. Though Um Muhammed's story of transformation was more individual, it was similarly transformative on the physical and material levels.

Justice, human dignity, liberation, inclusivity, healing and wholeness are emphasised in Together Towards Life as part of mission from the margins, and are valued by women such as Um Muhammed who saw her life as affected as much by her social status, the opportunities available in her neighbourhood, and her extended family, as it was by her creed or personal relationship with Christ. It is worth noting that evangelical missions originating in other parts of the world are more likely than Western evangelicals to include the physical and the emotional elements of the spiritual experience in their approaches (Smither, 2011:6).

Spirit of Community: Church on the Move

TTL describes the church as an expression of the love of the Triune God. "This communion (*koinonia*) opens our hearts and lives to our brothers and sisters in the same movement of sharing God's love. Living in that love of God, the church is called to become good news for all" (TTL, 55). Such a vision of community can be powerful among converts and people considering adopting a Christian faith. As mentioned above, conversion theorists have argued that faith-changing is more often about relationships, or lines of affinity, than it is about embracing an ideology. Faith decisions are often highly influenced by loved ones, social pressure, or how one believes s/he is seen in the eyes of others. Sociologists Starke and Finke wrote (2000:117), "Conversion is seldom about seeking or embracing an ideology; it is about bringing one's religious behavior into alignment with that of one's friends and family members." Even when conversion is a personal decision, it is deeply influenced by reactions and input from other people (Ebaugh, 1998). Monika Wohlrab-Sahr (2006:76) in her research found that women converts to Islam in Germany were rarely dealing with theological doubts or questions; they had already rejected their Christian heritage. Meeting other converts, on the other hand, was significant in their decision. Women converts whom I met very often converted for relational reasons; these included relationships with Christian men, the example of close family members, or persuasion of friends. This important role of relationships was much more predominant for women than it was for men.

Church played an important role in Um Muhammed's life. A church building, as home to the religious establishment of Christianity, was how she first discovered her new faith. Her story is unique to most conversion literature, though, because from her account it seems that she entered the church alone.

She entered at the encouragement of others, and out of a desire to preserve and create family relationships, but she went on her own. In this sense, she challenges ideas about the role of relationships as described by conversion theorists, but her story does provide a powerful illustration of the TTL statement about the deeply communal nature of God. No one taught Um Muhammed about the Trinity, but her entire conversion experience was summarised as a spiritual relationship: Jesus entered her heart.

TTL goes on to explain the importance of human community within a church context. It observes that sometimes there is a competitive, even antagonistic, tension between different churches and appeals against this saying that "Jesus became our Christ not through power or money but through his self-emptying (*kenosis*) and death on the cross.... The church is a servant in God's mission and not the master. The missionary church glorifies God in self-emptying love" (TTL, 62). Indeed, Um Mohammad's story is a powerful demonstration of how churches, as a part of the worldwide Christian communion, point to a greater image of Christ. Raised in an all-Muslim village, she knew of Christians but knew little about them. When she moved to the city, she became friends with women who were Orthodox Christians, who themselves knew little about their church, much less about differences between their denomination and others. They suggested she go to an Orthodox church to pray, not because it was Orthodox, but because it was the local church. Um Muhammed's spiritual transformation took place in this church building. She did not indicate that she asked the priest at the church for instruction; it seems that she simply went home and continued with her life until an evangelical woman moved into her building. This evangelical woman had a Bible translation developed by a mainline Protestant missionary nearly two centuries ago, published in an edition which Um Muhammed herself also had. It was through this relationship that she began to study her new religion.

There is no sense of division in Christianity in her story. "The Holy Spirit, the Spirit of unity, unites people and churches too, to celebrate unity in diversity both proactively and constructively" (TTL, 66). Other converts who I have met also see Christianity as one whole; when they encounter division they are deeply disappointed and in some cases look for ways to fight it. Unfortunately, this struggle against Christian division has not often succeeded, and in fact has sometimes spawned new divisions. It is important, though, to recognise the high value that people who chose a Christian faith place on Christian unity, as a reflection of God's love.

There is another important relational aspect of church, which is the role of local congregations. "While cherishing the unity of the Spirit in the one Church, it is also important to honour the ways in which each local congregation is led by the Spirit to respond to their own contextual realities" (TTL, 72). Jindra (2011) writes, in the context of social science studies of conversion, that social relationships are essential as converts develop their identity and their role in their new faith community, and that this process happens both passively, by learning through the example of friends, and actively in conversations with co-religionists. Studies into deviance, particularly secret deviance, emphasise the importance of how one is perceived in the eyes of others: a convert from a Muslim background to a Christian faith can only fully be herself in the company of a few people, so the input of those few is important. Being a part of a church or, perhaps more importantly, being welcomed into church community, is therefore very meaningful. This may be particularly important for women, as to some extent women develop their understanding of themselves based on how they see themselves in the eyes of others. Feminist identity theory generally agrees that women tend to define themselves in terms of relationships, and according to the expectations of the important people in their lives (Josselson, 1990:3; Hoover, 1997:25).

Um Muhammed did not, for many years, have the opportunity to engage with other Christians as members of a shared community of faith. Her Orthodox Christian neighbours, themselves not strongly indoctrinated into Christianity or active members of their church, did not see Um Muhammed as a convert to their religion, and indeed, it did not occur to Um Muhammed that her experience of Jesus might lead her to join a church. It was not until a Christian woman began studying the Bible with her, away from the trappings of institutional religion, that Um Muhammed found church community. Indeed, it is unclear from Um Muhammed's narrative whether she would even describe herself as a faith-changer. On one hand, she believed that Jesus dwelled in her heart and found her convictions affirmed in the teachings of the Bible. On the other hand, she did not turn away from Islam in any clear act of rejection, something generally considered important in conversion studies (Iannacone, 1995:291), nor did she make efforts to find a community of people who believed as she did.

The lack of external indicators of conversion, however, may be more a function of living without a community reinforcing her new beliefs. Without relationships to pull her into Christian community, Um Muhammed stayed close to her family. Without the reinforcement of the types of stories that are shared in a church context, she did not develop a testimony that fits a typical Christian narrative. Conversion research has found that growing into a new religious identity involves interacting with others who have both shared and different perspectives of their chosen faith (Bourque, 2006:237-239). As converts engage with others in the new faith community, they start to use the group's rhetoric and language of transformation (Rambo and Farhadian, 1999:30). This process is called biographical reconstruction, and is important for converts as they develop their new sense of identity and belonging in a faith community.

Um Muhammed's story is not unusual in lacking social support for biographical reconstruction. Many Muslim women who have an experience of Christ, or who are attracted to a Christian faith, lack the opportunity to engage socially with Christians or to participate in church community, even with other converts. Sometimes protective fathers, brothers, husbands, or even mothers or sisters, restrict their movements. As holders of honour for their families (Bourdieu, 1965:223; deSilva, 2000:34), families are often cautious and protective of the movements and activities of their women, particularly young single women. Other women may simply have too many household obligations to think of leaving home to participate in church activities. In particular, once a woman becomes a mother, engagement with co-religionists often feels like a luxury compared to her duty to her family. Furthermore, her husband may want to ensure that she raises his children as good Muslims. So, for a variety of reasons, women who have actively tried to engage in Christian community when they were single pull away from church after married.

The experiences of these women tend to sadden Christians, who would like converts to continue growing visibly in their new faith. Some Christians may even see women such as Um Muhammed as reverts, that is, people who have returned to Islam. In some ways, they are. In other ways, they are living as secret believers. Either way, living without relational reinforcement of their beliefs is costly to them, though it seems unlikely that the cost is a loss of faith, rather it is loss of a coherent Christian narrative. It is noteworthy that Um Muhammed met her Christian neighbour when her son was 18 years old. He had only just become an adult, old enough to make his own decisions and live life independently. This freed Um Muhammed to pursue her own passions. She did not tell me exactly how long the Christian family was living in her building before they met, but it is possible it was some years until Um Muhammed had the opportunity to engage socially with them and find the Bible on their shelf.

Spirit of Pentecost: Good News for All

In this final section, we come to the call to evangelise. The Lausanne Movement's Cape Town Commitment (2011) states, "Evangelism is the outflow of hearts that are filled with the love of God for those who do not yet know him." TTL further clarifies by stating that evangelism "focuses on explicit and intentional articulation of the gospel" (TTL, 85). This includes, but is not necessarily limited to, invitations to, or encouragement of, personal conversion. Different churches articulate evangelism in different ways, and indeed this is a contentious topic within Christianity, but most leaders from all denominations now agree to avoid proselytism, that is, use of any type of coercive means to recruit converts. Additionally, most leaders from all denominations now agree that some form of witness or outward-focused ministry is an important role of God's church.

As stated above, though, there are varying views about the importance of seeking to bring in new converts. Evangelical missiological studies tend to approach their scholarly pursuit with the implicit understanding that conversion is a primary goal of Christian ministry. In contrast, other denominations may seek to be welcoming and inclusive to new converts, but they see this as something quite separate from their evangelistic acts, which are more in keeping with St. Francis of Assisi's famed call to "Evangelise always; if necessary use words." TTL specifies that evangelism through "presence" must still contain a message, and be bold and inviting: "Evangelism is sharing one's faith and conviction with other people, inviting them to discipleship, whether or not they adhere to other religious traditions. Such sharing is to take place with both confidence and humility, and as an expression of our professed love for our world" (TTL, 83).

Um Muhammed was, in fact, not evangelised at all. She was not invited to personal conversion, nor did she witness any outward expression of God's love by Christians or representatives of churches. Her Christian neighbours showed her some care and concern, but Um Muhammed did not describe that attention as any unique or noteworthy demonstration of God's love, just the goodwill of kind neighbours. Her story is not unusual in this sense. Many converts in the Middle East seem to have reached a new faith decision as a result of a supernatural experience, reading a Bible or other Christian text out of curiosity, or otherwise becoming interested in learning about Jesus without any active involvement of Christians. The challenge of these stories, though, is that missiologists cannot calculate how many such people exist. Is Um Muhammed an anomaly because of her journey to faith, or is she an anomaly because she actually became friends with a Christian at a later time?

Additionally, when considering the nature of evangelisation, it is noteworthy that many women converts prefer not to actively evangelise their family members, in the sense of inviting them to personal conversion. For some, there is a fear that they will be persecuted by their family, and for many, there is a lack of confidence in their ability to articulate doctrinally complicated ideas. But for other women, it simply is not their priority. Um Muhammed did not think that what happened in her heart needed explanation or promotion among others: it was a highly personal experience, one that God could replicate for them if he so chose but not one she could bring about in their lives. It was a gift. While it seems from her story that she would be very happy if others were to have that experience of Christ, she is convinced that "it is only God's spirit who creates new life and brings about rebirth" (TTL, 82).

Women whose journey did involve more study and engagement with Scripture, as well as more theological doubt, may value their family members too much to alienate them, at least for a season. Some converts I met in my research shared that they avoided speaking of their new faith with their loved ones for a long time, years even. When they did so, they were able to point out that they had been "changed" for years already during which time they had been good daughters. Their ability to live as Christian presence and to choose the time and the way in which they shared about their new faith became a powerful witness to the message of what they believed.

The emphasis placed on evangelisation by some missionary groups has spurred extensive discussion about contextualisation. Making the message of the Gospel culturally relevant has, since the 1970s, been a bedrock principle of evangelical missions. In 1972, after a meeting of the World Council of Churches, a report was published which stated, "'Contextualization should be the focal concern because through it alone will come reform and renewal. Contextualization of the Gospel is a missiological necessity'" (in Thomas, 1995:175). The Catholic Church, in fact, did this actively until the 18th century (Morrison, 1992; Jenkins, 2002:30-32), but more recently there is a tradition among Protestant missionaries of seeking to encourage local expressions of Christianity (Hiebert, 2005:31). "The gospel takes root in different contexts through engagement with specific cultural, political and religious realities. Respect for people and their cultural and symbolic life-worlds are necessary if the gospel is to take root in those different realities" (TTL, 97).

Before this, particularly in contexts where Western countries colonised areas with large Muslim populations, there often seemed to be only two options for a convert from Islam to Christianity: publicly declare a new faith and be baptised, which often came with a high social price, or flee to an American or European country. Alternately, converts could choose to live as secret Christians (Goldsmith, 1982:135). The idea of converts preserving Islamic cultural form, however, has grown in popularity among Evangelical missionaries, and Muslim converts have been encouraged to consider continuing to call themselves Muslim, maintain some degree of Muslim ritual in their lives, and avoid frequently associating with cultural Christians (Woodberry, 2005:20). In more recent years, this has led to a rising popularity of something called "Insider Movements", which are characterised, among other things, by converts seeking to remain within their communities in order to exert a spiritual influence on their family members or neighbours.

It is hard to place Um Muhammed's story within the framework of contextualisation. As suggested above, some might see her as a highly contextualised believer, indeed so contextualised that her faith may be seen as syncretistic: neither purely belief in Christ and nor purely Islamic. Evangelical Christians may question the authenticity of her faith if seen in this way. Others might see her as a secret believer, someone who is Christian in her heart but who for social reasons, perhaps cultural preferences or family pressure, chooses to keep her Christianity a secret. Alternately, though, I would suggest that the concept of contextualisation does not apply to her. Though I did not ask her this directly, she said nothing to suggest that she hid from her husband or her Muslim friends the fact that her womb was "opened" in a church, and that something deeply spiritual happened in her heart. In fact, Jesus "entered her heart" in an Orthodox Church, and she was fully cognizant – even proud – that that her new faith was in some way Christian, and so she does not fit typical descriptions of being highly contextualised.

She did continue to practise Muslim rituals, but not because of social sensitivity or because of a theological justification for why they were a culturally-relevant adaptation of Christian practices, rather because, according to what she shared with me, she did not see any contradiction between her lifestyle and Jesus dwelling in her heart. She did not "understand" the Gospel before her conversion took place, and she did not recite a creed or pray for forgiveness. Her story is much simpler than that: Jesus entered her heart. So current debates about contextualisation do little to help understand the nature of this event in her life: when Um Muhammed began to study the Bible and learn about the message of salvation in the Gospels, she affirmed that this was what she already believed, but not that she had already studied and learned it. Her story is, therefore, less about contextualisation than it is about her understanding of the nature of the Gospel and a move in her heart which is difficult to capture in words.

I felt very privileged to meet Um Muhammed. She told me her story with such cheer and enthusiasm, and the friendship she shared with her neighbour was a poignant combination of inter-religious friendship and Christian unity. Her story gives hope in a spiritual reality, that there is indeed more to what humanity can see or accomplish by our own means to achieve a sense of belonging within both hearts and communities. Christian Missiology is a discipline which seeks to understand the history and the present of Christian efforts to bless the world, and this feminine reading of the World Council of Churches statement on Missions and Evangelism has revealed a number of ways in which women like Um Muhammed can engage with, benefit from, or even contribute to missionary endeavours. It also, however, has provided a strong reminder that one of the greatest gifts of faith is mystery and belief in a sovereign God.

References

Bourdieu, Pierre. 'The Sentiments of Honour in Kabyle Society'. pp. 191 – 241 in *Honour and Shame*. Edited by J.G. Peristiany. London: Weidenfeld and Nicolson, 1965.

Bourque, Nicole. 'How Deborah Became Aisha: The Conversion Process and the Creation of Female Muslim Identity'. pp. 233 – 249 in *Women Embracing Islam*, edited by Karin van Nieuwkerk. Austin: University of Texas Press, 2006.

Carroll, Janet C. 'My Pilgrimage in Mission'. *International Bulletin of Missionary Research* 38:1 (2014): 30 – 34.

Cohen, William B. 'The European Comparison'. pp. 385 - 410 in *Charity, Philanthropy, and Civility in American History*, edited by Lawrence J. Friedman, Mark D. McGarvie. Cambridge: Cambridge University Press, 2003.

deSilva, David A. *Honor, Patronage, Kinship and Purity*. Downers Grove, IL: InterVarsity Press, 2000.

Downes, David, and Paul Rock. 2003. *Understanding Deviance*. Oxford: Oxford University Press, 2003.

Ebaugh, Helen Rose Fuchs. 'Leaving Catholic Convents: Toward a Theory of Disengagement'. pp. 110 – 121 in *Falling From the Faith: Causes and Consequences of Religious Apostasy*, edited by David G. Bromley. London: Sage Publications, 1988.

Farah, Warrick. 'Emerging Missiological Themes in MBB Conversion Factors'. *International Journal of Frontier Missiology* 30:1 (2013): 13 – 20.

Gaudeul, Jean-Marie. *Called from Islam to Christ*. London: Monarch Books, 1982.

Goldsmith, Martin. *Islam and Christian Witness*. London: Hodder and Stoughton, 1982.

Hiebert, Paul G. 2005. 'Worldview Transformation'. pp. 23 – 34 in *From the Straight Path to the Narrow Way*, edited by David H. Greenlee. Milton Keynes, Bucks: Authentic, 2005.

Jenkins, Philip. *The Next Christendom*. Oxford: Oxford University Press, 2002.

Jennings, Michael. "'Healing of Bodies, Salvation of Souls': Missionary Medicine in Colonial Tanganyika, 1870s-1939." *Journal of Religion in Africa* 38 (2008): 27 – 56.

Jindra, Ines W. "How Religious Content Matters in Conversion Narratives to Various Religious Groups." *Sociology of Religion* 72:3 (2011): 271 – 302.

Josselson, Ruthellen. *Finding Herself.* Oxford: Jossey-Bass Publications, 1990.

Hoover, Kenneth. *The P.ower of Identity: Politics in a New Key*. Chatham, NJ: Chatham House Publishers, 1997.

Iannaccone, Laurence R. “Risk, Rationality, and Religious Portfolios.” *Economic Inquiry* XXXIII (1995): 285 – 297.

Khalidi, Tarif. *The Muslim Jesus*. London: Harvard University Press, 2001.

Lausanne Movement. “Cape Town Commitment: A Confession of Faith and a Call to Action.”, 2011.

Mallouhi, Christine. *Miniskirts, Mothers and Muslims.* Grand Rapids, MI: Monarch Books, 2015.

Morrison, Karl F. *Understanding Conversion.* London: University Press of Virginia, 1992.

Motte, Mary. ‘My Pilgrimage in Mission’. *International Bulletin of Missionary Research* 38:3, 2014): 140 – 144.

Norris, Kathleen. *The Cloister Walk.* New York: Riverhead Books, 1997.

Payne, J.D. and John Mark Terry. *Developing a Strategy for Missions (Encountering Missions)*. Grand Rapids, MI: Baker Academic, 2013.

Rambo, Lewis R., and Charles A. Farhadian. ‘Converting: stages of religious change’ pp. 23 – 34 in *Religious Conversion: Contemporary Practices and Controversies*, edited by Christopher Lamb and M. Darrol Bryant. London: Cassell, 1999.

Roald, Anne Sofie. ‘The Shaping of a Scandinavian Islam’. pp. 48 - 70 in *Women Embracing Islam*, edited by Karin van Nieuwkerk. Austin: University of Texas Press, 2006.

Robert, Dana L. ‘Forty Years of North American Missiology: A Brief Review’. *International Bulletin of Missionary Research* 38:1 (2014): 3-8

Smither, E.L. ‘Missão Integral [holistic mission or the “whole Gospel”] applied: Brazilian evangelical models of holistic mission in the Arab-Muslim world’. *Verbum et Ecclesia* 32:1 (2011): 11 pages

Stark, Rodney, and William Sims Bainbridge. *The Future of Religion.* London: University of California Press, 1985.

Sremac, Srdan. ‘Converting into a New Reality: Social Constructionism, Practical Theology and Conversion’. *Nova Prisutnost* 8 (2010): 7 – 27.

Stark, Rodney, and Roger Finke. *Acts of Faith.* London: University of California Press, 2000.

Thomas, Norman F. *Classic Texts in Mission and World Christianity.* Maryknoll, NY: Orbis Books, 1995.

Tottoli, Roberto. *Biblical Prophets in the Qu'ran and Muslim Literature*. Richmond, Surrey: Curzon Press, 2002.

Vahiduddin, Syed. “Islam and Diversity of Religions.” *Islam and Christian- Muslim Relations* 1 (1990): 3 – 11.

Waterman, L.D. ‘LIFE Scale: Exploring Eight Dimensions of Life in Christ’. *International Journal of Frontier Missiology* 31:3 (2014): 149 – 157.

Wohlrab-Sahr, Monika. 2006. ‘Symbolizing Distance, Conversion to Islam and Germany in the United States’. pp. 71 - 92 in *Women Embracing Islam*, edited by Karin van Nieuwkerk. Austin: University of Texas Press, 2006.

Woodberry, J. Dudley. ‘A Global Perspective on Muslims Coming to Faith in Christ’. pp. 11 - 22 in *From the Straight Path to the Narrow Way*, edited by David H. Greenlee. 11 – 22, Milton Keynes, Bucks: Authentic, 2005.

World Council of Churches. “Together Towards Life: Mission and Evangelism in Changing Landscapes.”, 2012.

Yang, Fenggang. *Chinese Christians in America.* University Park, PA: The

Pennsylvania State University Press, 1999.
Zebiri, Kate. *Muslims and Christians Face to Face*. Oxford: Oneworld Publications, 1997.

A Feminine Reading of Christian Missions in the Middle Eastern Context: Response 1

Views of Mission in North Africa and the Middle East as Seen by Christians from Muslim Background

Bassma Dabbour Jaballah

Introduction

The last decade or so has witnessed a rapid growth within the conservative evangelical world in particular of intelligent, devoted women in roles of leadership such as Beth Moore, Joyce Meyer, Ann Graham Lotz and others. Women preachers and Bible teachers are of great impact in our evangelical circles worldwide today, and this wave of change of women's role in our modern society has reached the Muslim world. The so-called Arab Spring brought a new era of freedom and responsibilities, with both secular and liberal movements calling for an Islamic reformation, which is more tolerant toward differences and inclusive to women on certain religious roles as well (Ben Slama & Ben Dana, 2015).

Are we ready to embrace such movement of liberation for women in the Muslim world in particular, who are eager and willing to take over more leadership roles? I do not claim to have the answer immediately but I believe we would do well to start considering a response. Before we get to that point we probably need to review and examine the tools and approaches we have been duplicating over the centuries in mission to reach Muslims for Christ, in particular women.

Mission in the 'Muslim World'

Before going further with this paper, I need to explain that my writing context is the North African and Middle Eastern (NAME) area of an Arabic and Berber-speaking Islamic culture. Why do I need to highlight such fact? First, I am more familiar with this context than others, due to my background and the nature of my work. Secondly, from my own experience Islamic ideological practices differ from one context to another. We all know Islam was born and developed in the NAME, and is strongly rooted within that culture more than anywhere else since it is the majority religion 91.2%, while in Western countries, Islam is the visible minority religion such as in Europe 5% and Americas 0.5% (Pew Research Centre, 2010). Thus, Islam had to adapt its doctrine and practices to go in accordance with its context and respond to its diverse environment (Ramadan, 2011;41).

Consequently, in this response paper I will share briefly my input and views of what I have experienced and witnessed of God's mission specifically among the Arabic-speaking Muslims from NAME background in almost two decades of my life. I will be looking at this subject from both lenses: the lenses of former Muslim and of the missiological clergy. I will try as much as possible to be objective in explaining my approach of mission to the Muslim world; nevertheless I mention that my experience as an insider may unintentionally affect my motivation. I will give a brief overview of Islamic ideology with regard to the Christian faith and women, and then I will examine Folk Islam and its social impact in an attempt to bring some light to a very complex socio-economic context strongly shaped and manipulated by religion. My goal is to extract a few practical tools that could help us frame a biblical feminine approach to mission in a Muslim context.

In order to accomplish this, I will start from a key idea from Kathryn Kraft's research. In her study, Kathryn tells us the story of an Egyptian folk Muslim woman from her Western perception, which displays a fascinating reminder of the work of the Holy Spirit in our environment. Um Muhammad, she explains, was raised in an all-Muslim village and knew of Christians but knew little about them. She moved to the city and became friends with women who were Orthodox Christians, who themselves knew little about their church, much less about differences between their denomination and others. They suggested she go to an Orthodox church to pray, not because it was Orthodox, but because it was the local church. Her spiritual transformation took place in this church building. She did not indicate that she asked the priest at the church for instruction; it seems that she simply went home and continued with her life until an Evangelical woman moved into her building.

The story is very common in our Muslim world, yet typically Middle Eastern as Kathryn explained in her paper. While I personally identify with a certain "similar experience" that I will be sharing with some details in the next pages, I acknowledge that Kathryn has demonstrated knowledge of the Islamic context as well as a crucial emphasis on the undeniable work of the Holy Spirit.

There is no doubt that God has been always at work to draw people near him all the time. The Bible reminds us often about the work of God over human history and the countless encounters between God and Bible characters (Genesis 17:5, 28: 10-16; Acts 9: 1-7). God has never stopped working even within closed Muslim societies, and even without an active work of missionaries (Qureshi, 2014). I have heard of and personally witnessed stories of conversion as result of dreams and visions where Muslims see Jesus clearly speaking or calling them to follow him. In some stories, an entire village had the same vision and came to accept Christ as their own savior through clear revelation similar to Paul's conversion (Acts 9). The Bible clearly endorses such statements.

> "And afterward, I will pour out my Spirit on all people. Your sons and daughters will prophesy, your old men will dream dreams, your young men will see visions. Even on my servants, both men and women, I will pour out my Spirit in those days. (Joel 2: 28-29 [NIV])

In Kathryn's story, the Holy Spirit is noticed as being the behind-the scenes actor orchestrating the entire event. The Holy Spirit worked in the life of this lady patiently and graciously toward helping her to experience one blessing at a time and meet with her in her brokenness, at first during an encounter with her Orthodox neighbour. Parenthetically, I would like to clarify a bit further some misconception about Orthodox and traditional Christians: the recent martyrdom of hundreds of Orthodox Christians from all different ethnic groups in Iraq, Syria and Libya has once again proven to not only the world but to our evangelical circle the authenticity of the Orthodox Christian faith by enduring persecution and facing horrific tortures and slaughter. If this says anything it speaks clearly of the strong roots of the Christian liturgical teaching of the scripture within the Orthodox church. Their strong faith stands as a reminder of Romans 14:8.

The Holy Spirit embraced this woman a second time as related by Kathryn, when her barrenness was removed and she was able to bear a child. Thirdly, when she met the evangelical missionary family. If this story demonstrates anything it proves once again that God has never stopped working in the very dark and isolated places.

While Kathryn used the story of Um Muhammed's encounter with Christians as a narrative of salvation work, I am cautious when it comes to the use of certain theological concepts such as conversion and spiritual formation, particularly within the Muslim context. My experience in mission work taught me I should not take anything for granted. Thus, using cases such as Um Muhammed to extrapolate theological constructs of conversion brings out my scepticism. Since the Bible is my ultimate reference book, I would like to use it here to examine Um Muhammed's's "claimed" conversion in the light of 1 John 5:1: 'Everyone who believes that Jesus is the Christ is born of God.' Would this verse endorse Um Muhammed's declaration and be used as an evidence for this precious woman's conversion? Before answering such a question let me again clarify the Muslim understanding of Jesus. In order to understand and develop a biblical approach to mission within the Islamic context, we should refresh our minds about the Islamic faith, Jesus' image in it and how a Muslim perceives it.

The 'Muslim' Jesus

I will discuss this concept only briefly as many are already familiar with Islamic concepts and have done some study of Islam: and this material is easily available elsewhere. As a former Muslim myself, I always found the Qur'anic narrative about Jesus controversial and deceptive to its Muslim readers. Jesus is described in the Qur'an as a great prophet and healer. Islam also claims to hold high respect for Jesus as a prophet and messenger sent from God. It is important to remember that prophets in Islam are venerated because they are considered without sin, although there is not a clear Qur'anic or Hadith statement except in Sura 3:51-52. Thus the concept is open to interpretation and confusion. However, prophets in Islam are all monotheists and some *Ulama* (Muslim scholars) such as Bukari, Muslim and Abu Hanifa...consider them to be Muslims even before the rise of Islam: the word used in Arabic in the Qur'an (Sura 2:126-138) is "*Hunafa*" – those who were born originally Muslim. Their entire mission was to claim that there is only one god and consequently Muhammed is his messenger. According to the Qur'an and Hadith, Muslims have understood Jesus as a prophet who is able to heal, even raise from the dead with the power of Allah (Sura 3:49). The Hadith (Muhammed's sayings) and Sirah (Muhammed's biography) tell stories about the supernatural power Jesus had, and thus most Muslims have grown in such an environment where they have been taught all these things. These common stories shared over generations are powerful in Folk Islam, as well as the traditions passed on by the *Ulama*, since few Muslims take the time to seriously study the Quran. Muslims in hopeless situations will desperately seek one who will deliver them from the pit of despair, and thus we have a common response of the seeking Muslims who trust implicitly in the power of the prophets and saints for intervention in daily life.

To understand Kathryn's interpretation of Um Muhammed's claim that Jesus entered her heart we may need to examine both the Western concept of salvation as well as her context and background. I don't personally know what she said in her mother tongue, nor what was meant, but in my scepticism I question what Um Muhammed believed about Jesus, and if this belief led to saving faith. I might suggest that Um Muhammed meant: I highly revere and believe in *Issa* (the Qur'anic name for Jesus). This then raises the question: who is this Issa?

Today in Cairo a well-known Orthodox priest named Abuna Makari carries on a vital ministry among Muslims in healing and exorcism, in particular among women. His ministry is so popular that many Muslims do not see any trouble in going to his church in order for them to be healed. Can we consider this a conversion? Theologically and biblically, we have to be very careful on how to use the concept of salvation. A verse to consider is I Timothy 2:5-6: "For there is one God, and there is one mediator between God and men, the man Christ Jesus, who gave himself as a ransom for all..." and others John 14:6, Acts 4:12, Hebrews 9:15, 12:24. Does the Muslim see Jesus as one mediator among many, including Muhammed, when Jesus must necessarily be the only mediator for salvation? I often use the Biblical explanation as given by Paul in Romans 10:9: "If you declare with your mouth, 'Jesus is Lord,' and believe in your heart that God raised him from the dead, you will be saved." Here we understand two defining actions that must be taken in order for the person to be considered Christian: first the person must confess with his/her mouth, and secondly, the person must believe in his/her heart; neither goes without the other. The Bible goes further to explain why that is so important in verse 10: 'For it is with your heart that you believe and are justified, and it is with your mouth that you profess your faith and are saved.'

The Biblical Jesus in Missions to Muslims

One should be aware of the fact that Islam has deceived its followers when it comes to the image of Jesus in the Quran. Muslims who know only the Quran think that Islam speaks highly of Jesus and thus revere Him. It is hard for such Muslims to understand the differences between the Islamic narrative about Jesus and the original biblical narrative. Furthermore, Islam, and in particular the Qur'an, revokes Jesus' deity explicitly in several passages (Sura 4 "An-nissa" 156-158 and Sura 19 "Maryam"), and thus according to the Bible in 2 John 7, the *Issa* of the Qur'an is not the Jesus of the Bible. Therefore, we need a better explanatory approach of whom Jesus truly is in order to obey the Biblical mandate to make disciples of all nations.

I personally do not at all recommend the use of the Qur'an as a tool to reach out to Muslims . I believe that our starting point sets the foundation for the rest of our proclamation. I believe that boldness of claiming the biblical truth with prayer and the power of the Holy Spirit is required. I encourage presenting conversion as stated in Romans 10 and an exegetical discipleship program as the way to lead a seeker to a deeper understanding of the Christian faith. I concur that the best place to start a conversation about the Bible and help Muslims "understand the Bible's story from beginning to end is actually to start in the middle, with the death and the resurrection of Jesus." (Deyoung & Gilbert, 2011:68)

In our days, social media has caused significant shifts in our approaches in mission. Field missionaries no longer need to hide or pretend or work undercover except for security reasons in certain places with security risks. Muslims do know that we Christians are there to evangelize them. Therefore, we no longer need to hide and we should not in order to declare the good news of salvation in obedience to our master commandment Mathew 28:18-20. At the end, it is up to the Muslim person to accept or to refute the message. Of course this is all requires wisdom and special cultural and biblical knowledge, as well as great evangelistic effort through prayer and fasting.

If we have to define our mission statement today among Muslims I might say the following: our vision is to bring reconciliation between the true God and human kind through the ministry of love, grace and redemption. So I am not inventing anything new. I am reminding us of the core values of our existence, which is to be peacemakers of the good news, proclaiming to the lost the Gospel of salvation, and making disciples in a hostile world. Thus, we may see the true meaning of mission as Allan Hirsh once described it: 'Worship is offering ourselves back to God, Mission is offering the world back to God.' Our desire and motive must and should be always to offer the lost back to God as another sign of worship. Subsequently, our mission has two main aspects in our NAME context:

Mission of Healing

Many Muslims today, more than at any other time in history, are hurt and suffering. They are puzzled and confused with the horrific atrocities that ISIS is committing. True seekers are searching and questioning (Sultan, 2009). We do need to be ready to provide them with answers. Many Muslim thinkers and scholars today, such as Tariq Ramadan or Ayaan Hirsi Ali, have been calling for reformation within Islam. Muslim women in particular are desperately looking for another alternative. They have been always discriminated against in Islam (Richter, 2011:100 – 110) and now with the rise of a "fundamentalist" Islam calling for literal application of Sharia, many Muslim women are no longer remaining silent. Voices from those such as Dr. Nawal El Saadawi (Egypt) or Ragd Alfaisal and Sakeena Almuchaikass (Kingdom of Saudi Arabia) or Dr. Dalenda Largueche and Olfa Youssef (Tunisia) have been raised louder and louder these days in defense of a liberal position on women.

The world of Christian mission absolutely must consider such strong, intellectual women within Islam. It needs to move out of the image tailored in our minds and replicated in books depicting simple naive women marginalized and uneducated who are awaiting for a western missionary to 'liberate' them. Our mission in the Arabic-speaking Muslim world today is about healing and extending grace to hurting men and women created in the image of God and beloved by Him, many of whom are turning to atheism as an alternative to religion since they have rejected the only god they have ever known.

Another challenge for Christians who hope to bring the Gospel message to Muslims is to overcome deep wounds caused by historical events in which the Church has been implicated; for example the Crusades, colonialism and the missionary work aligned with it, and the Palestinian-Israeli conflict.

Barriers to our witness are many. Others arise from a socio-political discourse that seeks to lay blame for current problems at the feet of the 21st-century Christian Church that has not wrestled with the complex issues involved. These may be overcome by mission workers sensitive to their context and prepared to answer Muslim objections. We must first be ready to dialogue about these hurts and to accept that today's Muslims may be stuck on Western mistakes of the past and failures, real or imagined. For the minister of the Gospel, this is a step, which cannot be overlooked. Westerners involved in mission must correctly understand history and the socio-political context of the Arab Muslim world. Unfortunately, many mission workers, in attempting to contextualize their message, have gathered their information from sources that are biased against Christianity and antithetical to the Bible and the Gospel message. In seeking to be accepted by the secular academic community, we have blindly accepted their false presuppositions regarding historical, social, anthropological or political realities. To love my Muslim neighbor and to understand his/her context does not mean that I surrender a balanced perspective of historical cause and effect, for example. Nor am I the one who abused their country a century ago. A discussion of personal and corporate responsibility may be beneficial. However, after listening to Muslim interpretations, and after acknowledging their wounds, I can move the dialogue along to present-day realities and personal decisions to encounter their Savior and Lord.

We do not negate that those whom we love and to whom we witness of the Gospel may have wounds inflicted upon them from (so-called) Christians of the past or the present. Yet we must ultimately point people to Jesus, and encourage them not to fixate on fallible humans. Ann Graham Lotz states clearly in her book the impact of the hurts caused by Christians in the life of those to whom we minister: 'I refuse to let religious phonies destroy my heart for the one who loves me and draws close to me when I am wounded. I refuse to be robbed of life's greatest treasure- a personal, permanent, passionate relationship with God through faith in Jesus.' (Lotz, 2014:18).

Mission of Reconciliation

Christians are called to reconcile Muslims with the true God. Our mission as Christians begins with fixing the wrong image they have had of God. I grew up with a 'god who punishes and hates' as stated by Wafa Sultan in her book that has a similar title. I use a lower case g for god when I refer to the god of Islam as I do not believe that the Muslim god is the same God of the Bible. The God of the Bible is triune God: God the Father, God the Son and God the Holy Spirit, while Islam refutes Jesus' deity and totally refuses the concept of the Trinity (Sura 5:73). As Christians in missions, we need to bring boldly back the correct image of God as described in the Bible: God is love (1 John 4:8) and 'God so loved the world that He has given his begotten son Jesus to save the World' also (John 3:16).

I do not claim that it is an easy mission, it has never been nor will it be today. The Bible warns us that we will face persecution. But, our determination to seek His will and face first will win (Romans 8:37). As Christians learn to walk their talk the world will stand amazed as many did when they saw the twelve Coptic Christians martyrs being slaughtered at the hands of ISIS on the beach of Libya crying out loud the name of Jesus in Arabic: "Yasou3", witnessing to the entire world that: 'For to me, to live is Christ and to die is gain' (Philippians 1:21).

The bottom line is that we need to focus more on serving God in mission by evangelizing, baptizing and making disciples, changing lives one at time each and everyday.

References

Abuna Makari https://www.youtube.com/watch?v=LxA1BhAGV3k

Ben Slama, Raja & Ben Dana, Rym. 12 Août. *Rapport General, Congrés des intellectuels Tunisiens contre le terrorisme*, 2015.

Deyoung, Kevin, and Gilbert, Greg. *What is the mission of the church*? Wheaton, Illinois: Crossway, 2011.

Hirsi Ali, Ayaan. *Heretic: Why Islam Needs a Reformation Now*. New York: Harper

Collins. 2015.

Lotz Graham, Anne. *Wounded by God's People*. Grand Rapids, Michigan: Zondervan, 2013

Pew Research Centre http://www.pewforum.org/files/2009/10/Muslimpopulation.pdf , accessed Aug, 14, 2015.

Qureshi, Nabeel. *Seeking Allah Finding Jesus*. Grand Rapids, Michigan: Zondervan, 2014.

Ramadan, Tariq. *Islam la réforme radicale*. Paris: Presses du Chatelet,2008.

Richter, Rick. *Comparing the Qur'an and the Bible: What they really say about Jesus, Jihad, and More.* Grand Rapids, Michigan: Baker Books, 2011.

Sultan, Wafa. *A God Who Hates*. New York: St Martin's Press, 2009.

Woodberry, J. Dudley. (ed) *From Seed to Fruit: Global Trends, Fruitful Practices, and Emerging Issues among Muslims*. Pasadena: William Carrey Library, 2008.

A Feminine Reading of Christian Missions in the Middle Eastern Context: Response 2

Jenny Taylor

Let me thank you also for giving me the chance to respond to Kathryn Kraft's paper – a paper that puts the case study of one woman's experience of blessing in the context of missiological theory about the work of the Holy Spirit. I will not go so far as to say this 'feminises' the discourse for me, as Kathryn might wish, because I have met supposed feminine qualities – intuition, empathy, compassion, nurture – most supremely in the manliest of mission statesmen, and vice versa – courage, stamina, resoluteness, physical endurance and so forth, in the most womanly of women.

That women are absent from the discourse however does not surprise me. They do perhaps tend to be more polymath, dipping in and out of the academy as a way of servicing their practice. Perhaps men are more mono-focal! But as a producer of discourse, as Interserve's editor for six years and later publisher of a number of books by Interservers on Islam by women – Sally Moreton, Margaret Wardell, to name two, it does not surprise me that Interserve is a major contributor to this excellent conference.

Missionary women are still pioneering change throughout the world, often I suppose from what Kathryn says, without writing about it. Perhaps they are too busy. Or, as Michel Foucault says, there are many discourses at war with each other, and some are present by their silence, which is not the same as absence. I am inclined to take that view. There is, of course, the élite discourse of the *International Journal of Frontier Missions* and the *International Bulletin of Missions Research*. And certainly women seem to be absent from *there*. But women throughout their history have made a huge contribution and continue to do so. Evangelical PhDs, even comparative PhDs, on women in Islam are there aplenty. I think of All Nations' tutor Carol Walker – she was recognized with an invitation to give a paper on her work on women in the Qur'an to a gathering of Islamicists at Lambeth Palace a couple of years ago. Dr Ida Glaser's extraordinarily rich study of women in an inner-city parish of Newcastle with reference to the post-fall chapter 3 in Genesis and in the Qur'an qualified her to found her own Institute in Oxford, the Centre for Muslim Christian Studies. I later published this PhD as *Partners or Prisoners? Thinking about Women in Christianity and Islam*..

But the pioneer par excellence of work on folk Islam – because this is the subject of this paper – was BMMF and later Interserve missionary, Vivienne Stacey, whom you are proposing to honour this week and whose name is absent from much discourse. Vivienne was a scientist at Imperial College, London at the time of her conversion, who served for 39 years mostly in Bannu in northern Pakistan. Of 11 books registered under her name in the catalogue of the British Library, three deal specifically with the work of the Holy Spirit among Muslim women. *Christ Supreme over Satan: Spiritual Warfare; Folk Religion and the Occult; Practical Lessons for Evangelism among Muslims* and *Women in Islam* are her three most famous. Yet only *one* of these eleven was published by a mainstream publisher, Hodder & Stoughton; the rest were produced either by the mission, or even more obscure Pakistani or German study centres. Where pioneering women are concerned we perhaps need to search in the margins for what has been rendered invisible, just as a missionary of my acquaintance began to search under the beds and in the cupboards of Tanzania for the deaf and disabled whom she could not find in the streets and sitting rooms. They had been removed, rendered invisible. As David Smith, the theologian who wrote *Crying in the Wilderness* has often said, the centre is renewed from the margins – and the margins are bound therefore to be alive and febrile with ideas and contributions. We must go there and find out. There are countless examples of this from Celtic Columba's mission to Scotland, through St Boniface's mission to Germany, the former arriving by coracle from a small remote island off the British mainland to an even smaller island Iona by coracle, and proceeding to evangelise Europe. Diaspora African inheritors of the slave legacy have had immense impact on worship and mission through the Pentecostal churches they founded in America, one of whose offspring is Holy Trinity Brompton – the HTB made famous by the Alpha Course. Slave schools of Africa like St Paul's Limuru produced several Presidents. This is to name but three outstanding examples where the marginalised have moved mountains and changed our perception.

And that's why I commend this exceptional and bold conference for seeking to reinstate a category in mission that is so easily overlooked or suppressed: women pioneers. Even the missions historian Jocelyn Murray denied, in my hearing, the ground-breaking work in education and zenana welfare of ZBMM's women in India in the 19th century. She reckoned they were mere ciphers for men, and that the famous book *Shadows Fall Apart* was a hagiography. But a quick check of the minutes of the very first meeting in Pall Mall of the Female Normal School Committee – which became Interserve – shows that under the chairmanship of Lady Kinnaird, the only man present was a vicar – taking the minutes.

From Cathy Hine's ground-breaking work on women's activism against violence in Pakistan, to Ida Glaser's work encouraging the Muslim reading of Christian texts in Oxford, women are still showing the way, against apparently overwhelming odds.

Often – and this has been my experience – existing models do not by definition prove hospitable to what shifts the paradigms. Pioneers *have* to do it anew. And commend it when we see it.

I will never forget some vocal Anglican women berating Lesslie Newbigin's Gospel and our Culture Programme – on the management committee of which I was the sole woman – berating them I say for their sexism. They were all nearly-dead white males, they howled. I was rendered invisible – tokenised – and ignored completely. Whereas in fact I was plugging away valiantly producing the first video resource for churches on mission to western culture which subsequently made it into the core curriculum of two theology degree courses. Working also with the mainstream media to get exposure for the whole project – including from Mike Wooldridge of BBC News, Melanie Phillips then of the Observer, and Melvyn Bragg of BBC Radio 4's flagship Start the Week programme: publicity that Newbigin was later to say had 'converted' him to the role of journalists, from which my own organization, Lapido Media, Centre for Religious Literacy in World Affairs and a prolific producer of discourse on our own, emphatically new terms, has emerged.

So, having got that off my chest... what we have in Kathryn's paper is a vital and sensitive *listening* to the subject of all our missiological endeavour. Here is a feisty compassionate portrait of a lonely housewife, unable to bear the child she must have to satisfy the legal, social and emotional burden laid upon a married Muslim woman; the Orthodox friends who told her to visit the church for the help she had not received elsewhere and what happened then. 'Jesus came into my heart.' And at the point that He did so, she also, it would appear, conceived and later gave birth to her son. This event did not however lead her to a church, and neither she nor her neighbours regarded her henceforth as a Christian. She neither shed the hijab, nor did her life change in other observable fashion.

But this cameo nonetheless is intriguingly suggestive, leading perhaps to the conclusion that the World Council of Churches is too remote from ordinary people to encompass them in its schemas and pointing to new possibilities of thought. Some fascinating conundrums are thrown up. Here is a woman who named the name of Jesus but whose conversion remained an ambiguous matter; a seemingly natural process of help sought, grace received and, had it not been for her spotting a book 18 or so years later in the home of an evangelical Christian neighbour that looked exactly like her unexplored Bible at home, that might have been the end of the story: a mere anecdote of the workings of grace in a context of djinns, magic and supplication: folk religion in other words. This is a conversion that possibly wasn't, according to the rubric. An example of evangelism that did not specifically evangelise. A model of church unity and interfaith relations that ducks all those rationalisations completely. So here in the document "Together towards Life: Mission and Evangelism in Changing Landscapes", a statement presented at the World Council of Churches assembly of 2013 we have a highly differentiated frame from which to hang rationalisations that actually evade the facts on the ground.

Um Muhammed remains in a sense *unreached*. Her story as told here theoretically turns the tables on the great missionary enterprise itself, and finds it not so much wanting as irrelevant! This proves oddly reassuring on the one hand: God seems to be at work without agency. It also encapsulates the lived reality of the vast majority of Muslim people in the world who are far better versed in the categories of the spiritual realm than we are in the West. As Bill Musk says in the Introduction to his *The Unseen Face of Islam*: 'In our strong separation of the sacred from the secular, in our materialism, humanism and scientism, Westerners, compared with many of our contemporaries, live in a dull, one-dimensional universe.' We Christians collude to the detriment of our mission in a denial of the Old and New Testaments' spiritual liveliness, with their references to spiritual phenomena that evade the scientific method.

The Holy Spirit and his work cannot be constrained by categories currently fashionable; that Spirit that is at work in us, prevenient, blows where it will. Is it forcing the story to claim for Um Muhammad an experience of the Holy Spirit? The World Council of Churches document appears not to mention the kind of religiosity countenanced by Sufism, the majority religion of the Muslim world; a reality thought to have been itself influenced in the Middle Ages by contemplative Christianity. One of the most extraordinary lacunae in the coverage of the Arab Spring in Egypt and the controversial subsequent ouster of Muhammed Morsi was the negative Sufi experience of it: tens of thousands of ordinary Egyptians whose shrines were destroyed by the Muslim Brotherhood (MB), forced to abandon their saint worship under the pressure of the Wahhabi strain of Islam espoused by the MB, and who refused to vote for their oppressors. The West's media entirely missed not just the Coptic suffering, but much of the Muslim suffering too.

Are mission priorities actually consonant with the reality of common grace? Part of the work of the Holy Spirit according to the WCC is the building of a sense of 'self-in-community'. Whether what Um Muhammed experienced was in fact the Holy Spirit or not, the effect was the same as if it had been. That whether she was converted or not, as a woman she received physical and social healing. Are any of us defining and situating the Holy Spirit too narrowly? Do we really believe He is at work without us having anything to do with it?

Certainly Protestant, Catholic and Evangelical missions have had *different* emphases in their view of work that corresponds with the Holy Spirit's priorities.[1] What has always been less emphasised by all of them has been care for the emotional person. Certainly, with 50 per cent of congregants in our UK churches, according to one estimate,[2] being somewhere along a spectrum of

---

[1] Missions in America rather more than the UK had divided their approaches into sacred and secular and Kathryn points us to work on this in the US. But Anglicanism, by definition a mix of Puritan and Anglo-Catholic covenants, and then Evangelical para-churches containing both Anglican and non-conformist elements, regarded mission from the outset as being the work of the Holy Spirit – the missio dei – as manifest in works of physical and material compassion. Certainly, the emphasis of the Lausanne Movement inspired by Billy Graham and John Stott in 1974 was an attempt to correct a bias towards evangelism in some societies. But care for the whole person was axiomatic with the two missions I know best, one of which was Anglican and English – the Church Mission Society – and the other, Interserve, a para-church multi-national organization which was founded precisely to provide a Christian-based education for girls and medical care for women.

[2] Estimate by the Schema Institute, Fulham Palace, London. Conversation between author and founder Agnes Sullivan.

mental illness, and clergy still preaching about depression as a sin, missions need to be leading the way into the unreached hinterland of women's emotional deprivation.

But the biggest question of all remains: is what we have here a conversion narrative? Did it, or could it, have had wider agency? The answer is a guarded 'No but...'. Conversion, in my own experience, was a long and quite complex process.

'This understanding that the physical body is an integral part of the spiritual being, that physical healing is integral to spiritual healing, was an important element of Um Muhammed's spiritual journey.' And indeed of my own. An intuition of anticipated grace, an expectation of the receipt of tangible, physical blessing or *Baraka* was at work. She intuited that she simply had to *receive*. She did not 'understand' it, but *anticipated* it, and in that sense Kathryn makes very powerfully the case that the missiological mandate is often merely a *report* of what is true, of what is going on *already* and that a faithful keeping pace with it, rather than a plan for action, is what is required. This is very important in defence of the Gospel in hostile secular environments, where mission has the appearance of cultural imperialism, or the depositing of something alien by force, whereas in fact it is merely a *following after* the already active *missio Dei.*

Um Muhammed had a divine encounter of some kind and called it 'Jesus' because she was in a church and the name of *Isa* is well-known in folk Islam for its power: second only in fact to that of Muhammed and at whose birth djinns were shut out of three of the seven heavens (Musk, 1989:69). According to Stacey, this is normal. 'God's names can be used in an automatic way in order to try and secure blessing, protection, healing or revenge,' she says (1984:82). Kathryn states her subject was marginalised. Her pregnancy set her free and restored her status. The *missio dei,* framed here as 'Spirit of Liberation' by *Together Towards Life* is demonstrated but not corroborated. What happened fitted into a pre-Christian worldview whether or not it fits into the World Council of Churches' worldview. And by Kathryn's own account did nothing to change either her behaviour or her community: both equally signs of the Spirit's work according to the WCC, and therefore possibly a sign to *them* of His absence.

Murray T Titus in his book *Islam in India and Pakistan* has a chapter entitled 'Saint Worship' (1959:137-152) which also seems to situate Um Muhammed's experience outside the conversion threshold. He writes: '...to the masses the belief in saints, and their ability to grant requests, fulfil desires, and perform miracles is still a real, positive and practical belief.... The belief in the miraculous powers of saints to help and to heal covers almost the whole category of human need.... The graves of saints are visited by litigants seeking victory in law cases; by the farmer who has lost a horse; by the woman who desires a child...' Stacey quotes this and other testimonies, and agrees with them from 'wide travelling in the Middle East and North Africa that '[f]olk Islam is widespread and it affects those of other communities as well as its own. Many Muslims agree that the power to perform miracles (*karamat*) is a sign of the blessing of God.'

She specifically cites experience at a Christian hospital in the north of Pakistan where 'If healing is not given elsewhere, the religious practitioner (*pir*) will give permission to the patients to go to the Christian hospital.' Even if healing happens, says Stacey, there are two problems and this is the nub of our discussion here: one is where nominal Christians get involved in the folk practices of other communities which is the sin of conforming to this world of which the apostle Paul writes and forbids in Romans 12:2. The other is that the 'wonderful power of God' is not seen by all as much as it could be. If Christians obeyed Paul's second plea that believers go on being renewed by the Holy Spirit and transformed in their lives, "instead of fear there [would be] praise"'(Stacey 1986:87). Did Um Muhammad go on being renewed in some way?

Folk religion is therefore perhaps a sign of God's immanence, his common grace, his presence in a world he created and enlivened, his compassion for the poor. However, when Christians are tempted to be squeezed into the mould of those around them especially if they are nominally Christian and not born again and renewed by the Holy Spirit (Romans 12:1,2), says Stacey, everyone is short-changed. None of this appears to figure in *Together Towards Life*.

Seen through a prism of *calling* as opposed to choice, something profound *does* happen to those Muslims who experience the power and love of Jesus, even if their circumstances militate against going further. And I believe Jean-Marie Gaudeul helps us finally to interpret Um Muhammed's encounter. He says right at the outset of his book *Called from Islam to Christ,* 'Muslims who convert to Christianity have been *called* to do so by God.... We have no right to tell God his business' (1990:1) This sets a radically different frame in which converts are to live – one which affords far greater protection for them than the freewheeling (and threatening to many Muslims) Western idea of personal choice. As Kathryn clearly states: something *happened.* God can be said to have taken the initiative.

There is clearly a spirit world, however categorised. And there is the work of the Holy Spirit within it, entering and converting, healing and restoring. I would refer you to Bill Musk and Vivienne Stacey who explored these phenomena over the course of 40 years of praxis. It may be that the World Council of Churches needs to be pointed to their work, so they and we might discern more clearly the practical possibilities of a visitation by *the* Spirit to a poor woman in an otherwise intolerable and socially paralysing space – and be better prepared to harness it.

References

Gaudeul, Jean-Marie. *Called from Islam to Christ: Why Muslims become Christians.* Crowborough: Monarch, 1999.

Musk, Bill. *The Unseen Face of Islam: Sharing the Gospel with Ordinary Muslims* Eastbourne: MARC, 1989.

Stacey, Vivienne. *Christ Supreme over Satan: Spiritual Warfare.* Lahore: Masihi Isha at Khana, 1986.
---- *Practical Lessons for Evangelism among Muslims* Wiesbaden: Orientdienst, 1984.
---- *Women in Islam* London: Interserve, 1995.
Titus, Murray T. Islam in India and Pakistan: A Religious History of Islam in India and Pakistan (Rev. ed.). Calcutta: YMCA Publishing House, 1959..

3

(Re)forming Identities and Allegiances

(Re)forming Identities and Allegiances

Moyra Dale

Prelude

This paper is undergirded by five assumptions, described in anthropology, sociology, and philosophy.

1. Lovers

At our core, we are lovers: we are made to love. Augustine understood this, centuries ago: "Thou hast made us for thyself, and our heart is restless until it finds its rest in thee."

Or, as some sociologists and philosophers describe it, we are animated by desire, we are desiring beings, "embodied agents of desire or love" (Smith, 2009:47); and we are formed by what we desire. It is our wants and needs that shape how we respond to the world around us each day. At the same time, teleologically it is the object of our love, our desire, that shapes what we seek to become, and thus makes or forms us as people. Going back to Augustine, when our heart, our desire, is not focused on God, then our desires take us in other directions, and we can become even de-formed by what we desire, what we love.

Being made to love, or created as lovers, means that we are relational beings, made to relate to the world around us, as our love or desire (ideally fulfilled in God) is mediated by the people or objects around us. Our desires, then, are shaped by the cultural context in which we find ourselves. This cultural context both gives form to the particular material and relational world, but also the way in which we are involved in it, the available roles or models of what we can become.

Joseph, citing recent literature on desire and the desiring female subject, suggests that in the Middle East, "the desires of female and male subjects both become animated by culturally specific notions of subjectivity that embed desire within relational matrices." (2005) Hafez describes "desire as a productive force that makes possible who we are. Desire both creates and, in turn, is created by cultural and social experiences, by historical traditions, by state agendas, and by individual negotiations." (2011:3) 'Desire' is defined as "the multifarious wants and needs that underlie subject formation. …an ongoing process rather than an ultimate objective." (2011:5)

2. Ways of Being

We live out our desires in particular ways of being – of walking, talking, dressing, being in space and interacting with others. These practiced ways of being both express and at the same time also form our desires, our love. The way we walk or stand, the clothes we wear, the way we speak, mark us as belonging to a particular tribe, a group to which we (consciously or unconsciously) give allegiance. Mauss, observing how different nationalities swam, walked, dug or marched in identifiably different ways, took the term *habitus* from Aristotle, to describe these "techniques of the body," or learned ways of using the body. He suggested that these patterns of movement, whether climbing, running, punching, sleeping or dancing, are acquired through imitation of significant social figures. Bourdieu developed the idea of *habitus* to explain socially-transmitted patterns of (inter)action and power, social tendencies to behave and talk in particular ways. Asad and Mahmood (drawing on Foucault) prefer to focus on how these 'techniques of the self' may be intentionally used towards the desired *telos*, or mode of being. They cite Aristotle's use of *habitus* to refer to disciplined practice in cultivating a particular virtue or ability (the pianist's practised fingers).

Whether purposeful or involuntary, our repeated/practised ways of being in daily life are indicators of what we love, of the community to which we give allegiance and of the person or imagined *telos* into which we are being conformed. "Ritual is the way we (learn to) believe with our bodies." (Smith, 2013:92) How we know things is determined by how we live in the world. "So a social order or a social body recruits me by conscripting / my body through the most mundane means: through bodily postures, repeated words, ritualised cadences." (Smith, 2013:94-5) Another way of describing these ways of inhabiting particular historical and cultural contexts of place and time is 'performative practices', where 'practices' refers to their habitual and reiterative nature, and 'performative' suggests both their enacted and formative character.

3. Liturgies

Ways of being, of walking and dressing, eating and talking, and every other action of daily life, come together to form bigger enacted narratives, stories of who we are and how we function. Gee used the term 'Discourse' to describe this '"identity kit" which comes complete with the appropriate costume and instructions on how to act and talk so as to take on a particular role that others will recognize.'[1] These narratives are associated with particular places and times and actions. They are enacted narratives, lived-out stories of what we believe about who we are and how we relate to the world around us (Bruner,

[1] https://www.ed.psu.edu/englishpds/Articles/CriticalLiteracy/What%20is%20Literacy.htm, Accessed 2/4/2015.

1988): and also of what we believe in, what we desire or love or long for. Our loving, our forming, is shaped or taught by the communities and places and practices which we inhabit. In describing how worship works, Smith writes that: "Pedagogies of desire form our habits, affections, and imaginations, thus shaping and priming our very orientation to the world. ... It is in such practices that our love is trained, disciplined, shaped, and formed. And it is, to some extent, only in such practices that this can happen." (Smith, 2013:13) Smith is writing about Christian worship, but he begins his earlier book in the same trilogy by a rich description of entering a temple which turns out to be a shopping mall, inviting the worship or allegiance of the patron in sound, space, smell and visual enticement, and also through repeated phrases and patterns of interaction.

A liturgy can be defined as *prescribed words and responses, ways of relating to a given space and the people in it, in the context of worship.* Liturgies are then ways of being (including around clothing, food and posture), according to particular narratives or beliefs that invite our allegiance, associated with specific places and times and actions. As lovers, desiring beings, we are made to adore, or to worship the object of our desire. Hence, in order to hold together worship and desire, allegiance and formation, I am following Smith (2013) in naming these enacted narratives, combinations of phrase, place and practice, as 'liturgies.' Individuals live out communal liturgies, embodying group fealty, whether to peer group or family, sect or street gang; and that community shapes and is identified by how we live and move.

4. Multiple Identities and Allegiances

For any person-in-the-world, identity is not singular, but multiple: and our identities and allegiances may compete with one another. Someone may have narratives or liturgies that connect them with their extended family, other liturgies that characterise their daily interaction with colleagues in the workplace, others that may come into play around the sporting field, and still others in overtly religious contexts. Identities and allegiances exist at personal, communal, socio-cultural and global levels: and each level includes specific stories which are communicated through particular liturgies, patterns of ritual words and actions in the spaces and times to which they belong. Narratives of family and workplace may be in conflict: or of national, ethnic and religious loyalties. Barnett (2013:30) describes a friend who has found his sister is secretly dating someone, and is torn between the conflicting demands of family honour (leading towards honour killing), and what he perceives as Christian individual freedom (leading to immorality and family shame). While there may be some hierarchy or order among the conflicting identities or allegiances, entailing different liturgies or ways of being and behaving, that order is not immutable and can change (Maalouf, 2000).

5. *Re-stor(y)ing*

Sharon Hafez is visiting a 'gama'iyah', an Islamic private voluntary organization in a suburb in Cairo, wanting to learn about women's Islamic activism there. She is taken to meet Doctora Zeinab, director of the PVO, who asks her "Why do you do what you do?" Hafez pauses to reflect and then explains that it is 'the thrill of unlearning,' and 'the possibilities of other ways of knowing' that have brought her. Doctora Zeinab nods, and then tells everyone in the room, "*Kol wahid fina 'ando hadaf* [Each of us has a goal]. *Wi kol wahid fina biyhaqaq alhadaf dah bi tariqtoh* [And each one of us pursues this goal in his or her own way.'" (Hafez, 2011:3)

Doctora Zeinab knows that each one of us is shaped by the goal, the *telos* that determines how we pursue it. Hafez's interest in this group of Islamic women is in the possibilities of unlearning known narratives or liturgies, and of pursuing other ways of knowing and being.

Through their lifetime, people live out the stories, the liturgies around desired goals that shape them. People continue to tell and retell the narratives of different and sometimes-competing identities and allegiances, and in retelling, recollecting, they may thereby sometimes re-story their lives. Points of conflict or tension may open the space for a restor(y)ing, or re-membering of their story and their identity. Barnett's friend finds another narrative, combining honour and mercy: he finds a suitable friend to introduce his sister to and helps them get married. An alternative liturgy, another *telos* is found for their story. A narrative of *da'wa*, Islamic mission, may open up hitherto unavailable options for women's education. Different desires are signalled by other liturgies and ways of being.

* * *

We are lovers (1), and we live out our loving in our bodies, in particular ways of being in space and time (2). These ways of being are parts of larger narratives or liturgies, involving specific patterns of speech and action, place and period (3). We all have multiple identities or allegiances, signalled by particular liturgies and loves: and these identities and allegiances are different and sometimes conflicting (4). Points of conflict and difference, and opportunities to retell the narratives by which we live, open up possibilities to restor(y) our lives, in terms of a different love, with its associated liturgies and allegiance (5).

Building on these five assumptions, this paper will explore four areas that emerged as significant in forming identity and allegiance, in personal, social and socio-cultural global dimensions: Community, Models, Texts, and Music. The primary context of discussion will be a women's mosque programme in the Middle East, which I attended between 2005 and 2007. Women's stories will give shape to the desires and practices, loyalties and liturgies over the various dimensions. As we look at the different areas, their liturgies and ways of being, and the divergent identities and allegiances that they evoke, we will be asking, where is the reforming, happening, and where could it take place? How does this re-storying affect their liturgies, their ways of being and of loving.

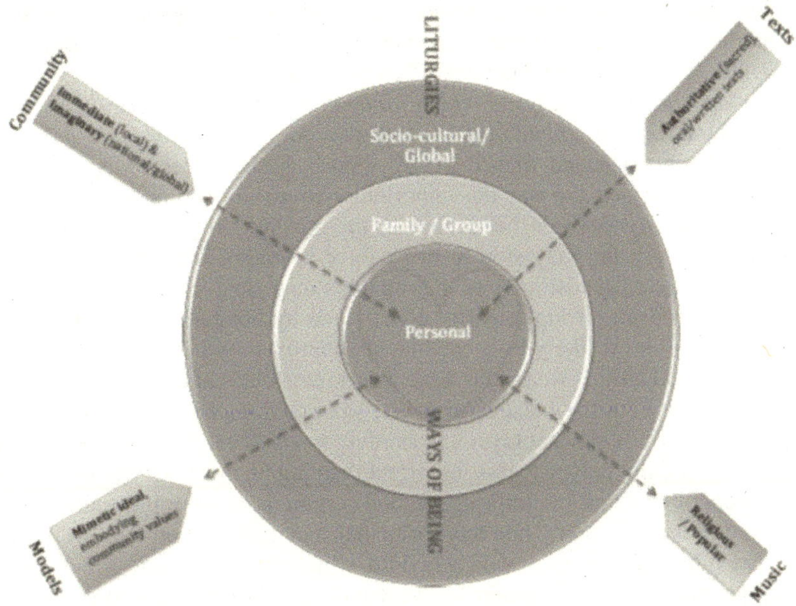

Community

Fadiyah sits in the small circle of girls on the upper balcony of the mosque, where a young woman is teaching about the practice of Islam. Fadiyah's attention is divided between listening to the young woman teaching, and thinking about going to the shopping centre of town after class with her friends to look at clothes.

Fadiyah is a teenager, born into a middle-class family in a suburb near the mosque. In secondary school, she attends some of the mosque classes for girls about Islam, and their summer programme. She would like to go onto university and study engineering when she finishes school. However, her family expects that she will be engaged soon and married when she is about eighteen.

Communal Allegiance

We are born into communities, who form how we perceive ourselves, others and the world. The first community to which we belong and which shapes our identity is our family.

Joseph defines the self in Arab societies as characterised by relationship, or connectivity. She describes "persons in Arab societies as embedded in relational matrices that shape their sense of self but do not deny them their distinctive initiative and agency." Family interactions are based around patterns of roles, authority and expected behaviour. Middle Eastern society is animated by patriarchy, which allocates power along lines of gender and age (1999:11,12), with women and men differentially affected.

What are the communities to which Fadiyah belongs? What are the ways of being that characterise them? And the liturgies that shape them?

For Fadiyah, extended *family* is the primary basis of her social network. However, sometimes she has the opportunity to go on excursions with other young women friends from her school or the mosque programme. They walk around the shops, and may stop to drink juice in one of the popular cafes. In western societies, friendship or peer groupings may rival kin loyalty: however Fadiyah's friendship group is partly constrained by her family; and long-term friendships will most likely be those that are approved by her parents, and then by her in-laws. Fadiyah wears the *hijab* over modish but modest clothing. With encouragement from the mosque teachers, she practices a number of the daily prayers – she finds dawn prayer the hardest to observe. For her family, her observance of daily prayer is less important than public modesty, defined by the *hijab*, proper behaviour in public space, and coming home at appropriate hours.

Women have commonly had their principal social interaction with women in their extended family, or the family into which they married. Abudi notes "Marriage marks a girl's transfer from the authority of her father to that of her husband." (2011:43) The leader of the mosque programme, Anisah Huda, commented in a lecture, "There have been times when women haven't been educated, only left the house three times in their lives: 'from her mother's womb to her parent's house, from her parents' house to her husband's house, from her husband's house to the grave.'" Meltzer & Nix (2012) record teenage girls from the mosque classes quoting that saying: and on another occasion talking wistfully of their desire for a husband from whom they didn't have to ask permission every time they wanted to leave the house. Fadiyah has freedom to go to school, to go out shopping or for a social outing with her (female) friends. But she will probably be required to leave her studies to get married: and she will negotiate her freedom of movement after marriage with her husband (and probably her mother-in-law). Anisah Huda's husband talks approvingly of her religious involvement, because 'she doesn't neglect her duties as a wife and mother': these have precedence.

However, as Joseph notes, not just gender but also seniority confers authority. In adult literacy classes in Egypt, the influence of mothers- and sisters-in law was a more significant determiner of whether a woman was able to attend literacy classes, than her husband's expectations or her own motivation. Kraus describes the major role played by some mothers or grandmothers of the ruling sheikhs, in running tribal affairs in the Emirates (2008:30). Family identity, gender and age together fashion daily liturgies of domestic life, and relationships with family and those outside. Family allegiances constrain a person's choices and practices, whether in clothes, behaviour or friendships.

Fadiyah's behaviour, her daily ways of being at home and in public, is shaped according to a liturgy of modesty and family honour (Joseph, 1988,:37).

Her immediate family is middle-class conservative Sunni. While she now lives with her parents and siblings in a newer suburb apartment building, the extended family (some scattered around the world in the Gulf states or Western countries), has links back to land and the older suburb from which the family came. The liturgy of family honour and female modesty tells a story of women who marry in their upper teens, a liturgy at odds with Fadiyah's own dreams of studying at university and becoming an engineer.

Within traditional kinship patriarchies, liturgies around the community value of family honour dominates patterns of behaviour, with particular application to the body of the woman (Ahmad, 2009:L.2130), in biological and also "bodily and social virginity," safeguarded through "physical threats," together with "the segregation of gender spaces and the active mobilization of the institution of social gossip and reputation. 'Because you are a girl, and people will talk if you do this,' is rhetorically how Arab women come to acquire their gendered subjectivity." (Abu-Odeh, 2010: 923-4; Kressel, 1992) Allegiance to extended kin then becomes a performance of modest modes of walking, talking, encompassing what women wear and what spaces they enter, which secures the reputation of female and family. Personal desires or ambitions may conflict with family pressure and maintaining public reputation. Family members are accountable to enforce appropriate behaviour: Joseph discusses the role of brothers as responsible for their sisters (1999b:134).

In kinship patriarchy, the honourable family is the desired *telos,* which is accorded priority over individual desires. Ways of being are defined in terms of behaviour that brings honour to the family: and it is gendered. Women learn the liturgies of how to sit, walk, dress, respond to others, through imitation and family constraint, according to the norms of their kinship community.

Where religious identity is more central, particular pious liturgies can also find their place within the home, whether sufi *dhikrs,* formal *salah* prayer by the individual or with others in the household, or Qur'anic recitation with extended family, female-only or mixed.

The women's programme at the *mosque* offers an alternate community through the mosque, although attendance may often go along family lines. Religious feasts and Mother's Day, traditionally celebrated by women in homes among extended family, are observed with special programmes at the mosque. For Fadiyah and girls of her age in the Middle East, there is less freedom to engage in friendships outside the family group than there is for young men: the religious sphere is one of the few possible places where it is permissible for her to attend, and to go on trips with her peers.

Mosque dress is within narrowly defined styles, particularly after the mid-teens: full-length manteau coat (usually dark blue, or black for the older women) and hijab (often white for younger women, darker blue or black for elder women). However, the common mode includes details of material, cut, design and buttons, which show individual attention to fashion and style. The public garb modelled by the women attending the mosque programme, in dark sober colours, contrasted with their attractive colourful dress and appearance in their homes, in female-only company. This reflected the popular religio-cultural teaching that the woman is like a precious jewel, to be protected and not displayed publicly: a liturgy of appearance and presence in contrast to pervasive advertising in the streets and media.

Beyond home and allowable excursions, religious space offers alternative activities, of memorising and reciting the Qur'an, of prayer (*salah* and *dhikr*) at the mosque, classes of religious teaching, and twice-weekly lectures. Young women are encouraged to teach younger girls at this mosque or others. As in other mosque programmes, women are involved in social welfare activities to help the poor, both expressing and focused around piety (Hafez, 2011; Kraus, 2008).

This is a liturgy of the devout person, whose piety is expressed in more modest ways of dressing, but which encourages an involvement for women beyond the home: in mosque, religious learning and teaching, and social welfare.

Socio-cultural global shifts in women's education and public presence, made possible by more secular activism in the last century, have created a space that religious women now occupy. The call to personal piety finds expression in movements that impact on the political landscape. The Qubaysi movement, begun in Damascus, spreads intentionally among wealthy educated women, including a focus on teachers in schools, as well as religious programmes.

Fadiyah's extended family is from the Damascene Sunni merchant class, who continue their trade under the ruling (Alawite) president. In sociocultural / global dimensions, Fadiyah finds identity in allegiance to the nation. As a Syrian, Fadiyah is a citizen of a state based on secular socialist principles. Education is available for all, girls as well as boys. The nation as family is a common political discourse, which comes under great pressure when the nation is led by a perceived non-Muslim. Communal/national identity in the Middle East is by family allegiance, through the patriarch: and loyalty flows more thickly along extended family and sectarian lines.

If family allegiance finds its focus through the mother (*umm*), the mosque itself teaches primary loyalty to the imagined community (Anderson, 1991) of the *ummah,* the worldwide Muslim community. This challenges the state's call for primary allegiance on the basis of nationality, across confessional lines of Muslim and Christian, with sectarian and ethnic borderlines within these groups (Sunni, Shi'a, Alawi, Ismaili: Orthodox, Catholic, Protestant: urban and rural: Kurdish, Arab, Turkaman, Circassian) cutting deep divides of primary loyalty running along family and clan lines. Each of these groups has different liturgies of behaviour that are evident in the multiplicity of dress on the streets any day, and the appropriate behaviour for women. The imaginary community of the *ummah* for women in the mosque programme included little awareness of non-Arabic groups (who make up 80% of the Muslim world, in an Islam defined by the language and geography of Arabia).

In contexts where opposition is proscribed in the political realm, it may find a home in the mosque. Hence, at various times, while I was attending the mosque programme, the government restricted the opening hours of the mosque; or confined attendance only to local residents. At such times, allegiance to the mosque and the wider *ummah* conflicts with loyalty to the nation, when viewed through obedience to government edicts.

Fadiyah's allegiances are to immediate, extended and imagined national and religious communities. Beginning in family (with limited influence from friendship groups), mosque allegiance co-exists with loyalty to extended family. Her family belongs to wider social-sectarian groups, and goes beyond national to regional belongings. Less visibly, lines of religious connection also extend across provincial and national boundaries. The women's programme in the mosque is part of a wider women's mosque movement, located within a conservative (and Arab-biased) consciousness of the Muslim *ummah.* In socio-cultural/global dimensions, the imagined communities of state and *ummah* call for her allegiance.

In the current conflict in Syria, even within the Sunni community, there are multiple positions of allegiance: loyalty to the state (and its alliance with urban Sunni mercantile families) or support for the opposition. And the opposition spans a spectrum of different groups, where some are seeking to reinvent another secular (less oligarchic) state, while others are returning the Caliphate, with a range of positions (and militias) in between. The position of the Islamic State on women is seen in their paper (Winter, 2015), which returns women to a position akin to the three-fold movement above.

Model

Layla grew up in a rural area. She dropped out of school when she was fifteen: so she went to work in the fields (rural labour is traditionally disparaged by urban/educated communities). Now nearly forty, she is not married (also deprecated in her society). Some years ago she started attending mosque classes for women and memorising the Qur'an. She then began to teach other young women in classes in her local village mosque. With encouragement from Anisah Huda, she returned to study, and now is doing a university course. People in the village now call her 'Abla' (Teacher), a title of respect.

Models give tangible form to community values. Living out the approved ways of being, they are the embodied *telos* of a communal liturgy. (So the beautiful woman expensively dressed and coiffured, impeccably made-up, thinner than normal body-build, is a prominent model, a *telos* of the shopping mall temple.) Models make possibilities real, give them flesh. We discover who we want to be by finding models, people who embody what we value in how they live or dress or walk or talk. Girard proposes that all our desires are mimetic, borrowed through other people. Our desire for a given object (or *telos*) is always provoked by the desire of another desiring the same end. Through our desire, we are drawn to the model who is the mediator, and becomes the focus, of our desires (Alison, 1996; Girard, 1996; McDonald, 2003).

Mimesis is then fundamental to desire and to learning. When a given community finds its characteristics and values embodied in a particular individual, that person becomes the model, mediating the desires of community members. This suggests an understanding of leadership and influence based on the mimetic ideal and the desiring subject, where a person's influence is determined by the extent to which they embody and shape the desired community values and way of being, through their personal characteristics or abilities, and access to power and resources.

Who are Layla's models? What community values do they embody in their ways of being? What liturgies do they live out or challenge? What possibilities do they open up for those who seek to imitate them?

As *family* is the first and most immediate community, so for women, their mother is the first and often most powerful model. When I asked women in Syria about their ideal woman, most of them mentioned their mother. This is amplified by the significance of mothers within Islam. Hence Mother's Day is celebrated in the mosque, and actively commemorated by the community. The 'mother' narrative is used to valorise the domestic role and to honour women of influence in an individual's life.

Other women in the extended family can also provide models. Layla's family offered few examples of women going beyond basic education in that rural community, or positive unmarried models.

As we grow up and meet other people, the imitative options widen beyond our own family; perhaps at school, in teachers, or in other contexts. Anisah Huda presented an alternative mimetic ideal, as the teacher who exemplified the pious person. She had social credibility and influence in encouraging Layla to return to education and pursue it to tertiary level. In the mosque programme Layla met other young women teaching mosque classes, doing tertiary study, and working in professional careers such as teaching.

By her example as a religious teacher, Anisah Huda challenged the derogatory *hadith* that women are lacking in intelligence and religion. She provided Layla with another model as a religious teacher, which offered an honoured position independent of marital status.

Huda's family also demonstrates how family models can offer a trajectory beyond themselves. Huda's mother was publically celebrated as one of only two women in her village who could read. Huda herself recalls being among only four or five girls in her *shariah* school who had memorised the whole Qur'an. Huda's daughter Enas was permitted by her family to go abroad to the Gulf for tertiary study – a radical departure for girls in that socio-religious group.

Theoretical possibilities are given substance by real examples. Anisah Huda exhorted the girls in the mosque summer programme that they could take up roles of communal and national authority. They could teach, judge; a woman could be a president. (Here the mosque programme teaching challenges the common *hadith* that a country with a female leader will never prosper.) But there were few prominent female MP's of conservative Sunni background: more were from the ruling Alawite sect, modelling a different liturgy and piety. Teachers and doctors remained some of the more approved occupations for women in public space.

History may provide exemplars. Zaynab al-Ghazali (Egypt 1917-2005),[2] initially working with Egyptian feminist Huda al-Sharawi, was persuaded as a young woman to begin her own more reformist group for Muslim women by the example of one of Muhammad's (female) companions, Nusayba bin Ka'b. Zaynab's father challenged her in terms of competing models, asking the young woman, "Do you choose Huda al-Sharawi, or will you become Nusayba?" and she responded, "I will be Nusayba."[3] Anisah Huda mentioned historical women leaders such as Umm al-Darda[4] to the group of expatriate women she was teaching.

However in the mosque lectures I heard little mention of ideal women in Muslim history. On Mother's Day, Pharaoh's wife (Asya) and Mariam (Mary) were invoked,[5] but I heard far more about the *'ulama*, the male scholars, than about the *Sahibaat*, female companions of Muhammad, or his wives. And more recent examples, such as Nazira Zayn al-Din and Zaynab al-Ghazali were not talked of.

Nevertheless, Anisah Huda had a high view of the *da'iya* (religious teacher), describing her role as 'between people and God'; and in a lesson handout: "For the *da'iya* is God's mediator to people and successor of the Messengers." (*li'annah al-da'iya safir Allah ila al-nas wa khalifat al-rusul*)" Here the role of the (female) religious teacher is remarkably described in terms of prophetic (and communal) authority, as *khalifat* (follower) of Muhammad!

The ultimate cosmic ideal (and idealised) model for Muslims is Muhammad, Prophet of Islam. In lectures at the mosque, he was constantly mentioned as the perfect paradigm, particularly during *Rabia' al-Awal*, the month of Muhammad's birthday, when mosque lectures focused on his virtues. For Layla, as for all Muslims, to be a good Muslim is to do what Muhammad did: hence the *hadith* which reproduce the minutiae of his actions and words. Viewed as the final prophet and seal of all who came before, his is an unattainable example: but to the extent that Muslims are able to copy every detail of his life, they can access something of the power and blessing which he mediated (Taussig, 1993), for this life and the next.

Our learning is primarily social and imitative. Our communal allegiance finds focus in people who embody community values. For many women in the Middle East, their mother is their strongest model. Layla was able to find an alternate model in Anisah Huda and the women in the mosque programme, which offered another liturgy for her life. Potential female models in the wider socio-cultural and regional context were not drawn upon, perhaps because they received little prominence in the mosque or elsewhere: or because they came from another religious-ethnic group, a different liturgy of allegiance. Nor did historical religious women gain much attention. The daily detail of proper

---

[2] Prominent writer and founder of the Muslim Women's Association (1936-64).

[3] Shehadeh 2003:122.

[4] Famous 7th century Damascan Muslim jurist and scholar.

[5] *al-Tahrim* 66:11-12.

behaviour is established through reference to Muhammad, the cosmic model of ideal Muslim. Anisah Huda's teaching in the mosque programme ascribed remarkable significance to the *da'iya*'s role, as successor to the Apostles. However, where the perfect model is defined in the meticulous details of a male life, Layla and other women will always be less than the mimetic ideal.

Texts

Ebtisam is a serious, hard-working young woman, whose face is illuminated by warmth when she smiles. She has a couple of brothers, and helps her mother with home duties. Ebtisam is an English teacher in a secondary school. After leaving university, she took further classes in English and teacher-training in a foreign institute in the city, to develop her expertise. Ebtisam has been attending classes at this mosque for a number of years. Following Anisah Huda's example, she has memorised the whole Qur'an, and how to recite it. When not at school, she teaches girls at the mosque, helps women memorising the Qur'an, attends some of Anisah Huda's twice-weekly lectures to women, and also acts as a translator when Anisah Huda meets with foreigners.

What are the different texts around Ebtisam, and how do they shape her days? How does she use them? What are the available communities of interpretation to which she could belong?

> If one says, 'A Muslim woman ought to wear the hijab (cover her whole body except her face and hands),' or if one says it is immodest for a woman to reveal her hair, this assertion... relies on a reference to a set of Qur'anic verses, Prophetic traditions, reports about the Companions and most importantly, the cumulative juristic efforts in selecting, preserving and giving meaning to these textual sources (El Fadl, 2001:98).

We are both shaped by and shapers of texts. It is the written and often more significantly, the unwritten texts that define a community. Islam is delineated by the Qur'an and by the voluminous Traditions that interpret the Qur'an and Muslim life through the life of Muhammad. Particular traditions of *tafsir* (interpretation) and schools of law guide how the Qur'an and *Hadith* are used. While both the Qur'an and *Hadith* were first transmitted orally, and the written tradition is validated by the oral, other local oral cultural traditions also powerfully shape the lives of local Muslims, and especially Muslim women.

In the Muslim world, the text of the Qur'an is encountered first of all in its physical form. It appears in written shape: in books placed carefully on stands in places of household honour, or wound, labyrinth-like around the circumference of mosque walls and minarets, or embossed in intricate calligraphic swirls in picture frames. In aural form, it can be heard wafting sinuously over the air from minarets five times a day, or broadcast from radios, TV sets and cassette players in shop fronts, or murmured by people at prayer or as they pace, pulsing prayer beads through their fingers. The physical expression of the Qur'an, whether aural, visual or encoded in a book, was desired as the medium of God's *barakah*: blessing, or power, was intrinsic to the Qur'anic text. Padwick's description, discussing the use of the Qur'an in Muslim devotions, evokes the associated sense of the sacred:

> So the book lives on among its people, stuff of their daily lives, taking for them the place of a sacrament. For to them these are not mere letters or mere words. They are the twigs of the burning bush, aflame with God. (1961:119)

As Ebtisam was growing up, the Qur'an was always there, prominently displayed, with some of its well-known *surah*s recited in the daily prayers her mother taught her. Qur'anic verses were decoratively inscribed within picture frames on the walls of their home, and written into jewellery or amulets to wear. The call to prayer and recited Qur'an on radio and TV punctuated their days.

Less visible, but just as significant, were the *hadith* texts, the traditions which directed the minute daily detail of Ebtisam's life, from how she prayed – the five daily prayers, with their specific words, actions and number of repetitions – to which foot she used to enter and leave the toilet.

Not officially authoritative, but ubiquitously influential, was the *commercial print*, with its own liturgies of desire and worship. It surrounded Ebtisam, on food packaging in the shops and home, or in the streets in which advertisements and sacred text jostled for space. *Television*, where local and international names and liturgies kept company with one another through national and satellite channels, brought its own scripts into the lives of its viewers. As computers come into homes or are accessible (more often by young men) in street *Internet* cafes, the worldwide web accelerates the global-local interchange. Ebtisam and other women in the mosque programme watched broadcasts of local Syrian preachers and regional sheikhs from Saudi and the Gulf.

At school, Ebtisam's *textbooks*, written mostly by men, offered their particular perspectives on history and current life and affairs according to the dominant national interpretation. English textbooks (and her limited interaction with expatriates at the foreign language institute) did little to modify her received view of the western world as immoral, Christian, and oppressive.

At the *mosque*, Anisah Huda told the women that the heart is less effective if it's not *bayt al-Qur'an* (home of the Qur'an), "so, sisters, God willing, we'll memorise all the verses." Ebtisam learned the whole text of the Qur'an, with the correct rules of recitation; and passed the exams qualifying her to teach other young women. After the Qur'an was committed to memory, the women were encouraged to memorise the *tafsir* (commentary) of influential Syrian scholar Ibn Kathir (1301-1373), reinforcing a conservative view of Islam, the Qur'an and history.

The mosque programme emphasised the importance of ongoing education for women. They opened the first *mosque library* for women in the city, so women could have unrestricted access to religious and other readings. Notices on the desks encouraged the women to keep learning and reading, and Anisah Huda emphasised the same message in her lectures. The computers in the mosque library, with the satellite channels in their homes, offered Ebtisam and the other women more access to an extensive range of religious materials and teachers from the Arab world and beyond, from which they could learn. Ebtisam received and also mediated texts and their interpretation – both to the girls she taught daily in English classes at school, and also to those who attended her classes on Islam at the mosque. She trained both older and younger women to memorise and recite the Qur'an.

Ebtisam was translator at some of the classes that Anisah Huda gave for foreign women. Texts became a major part of our interaction, as Ebtisam took on the task of checking my notes from the mosque programme. Though her checking, and in her role as interpreter for Anisah Huda, Ebtisam mediates *western* published texts about this mosque programme and Islam.

It is not only the texts themselves, but the way in which people talk about and use them, that determine the *telos* towards which liturgies point. Texts used decoratively in pictures, and the Qur'an prominently displayed, can indicate piety and allegiance to the local/global Muslim community. Their presence can also be an indication of the power of sacred text in its physical form for healing, protection, blessing, and power to complete one's duties and responsibilities in this life. Texts can be memorised and recited, for merit towards the next life, and to acquire authority in this life. While religious learning and textual proficiency is encouraged, for women it may be tension with their (primary) domestic duties. The Qur'anic exhortation to learn[6] can open the way for women to leave their homes to attend the mosque classes.

Increased accessibility to texts through global shifts in education and women's literacy, and in media has contributed to the growing women's mosque movement around the world. Islamism both feeds and is fed by increased availability of Islamic materials in popular pamphlets, tapes and CD's, through to satellite programmes. The con(text) determines how (common) texts are read, used, and understood: and their impact in women's and men's lives. There are different expressions of Islam worldwide, and liberal Islam has a strong voice in the west. Unsurprisingly, I saw no evidence in the mosque programme of engaging with critical/revisionist discussion of the origins of the Qur'an and Islam. The scientific-miraculous reading of the Qur'an had more currency.

Particular liturgies of faith and gender, with their patterns of interpretation and application, shape how the readers address gendered texts in the Qur'an and *hadith,* and which *hadith* out of the expansive corpus are quoted. While the women in this mosque programme follow traditional religio-cultural liturgies of behaviour, Anisah Huda encourages them to read a (conservative) range of commentaries: and is aware of less traditional readings of the place of women within Islam. Generally, in Muslim countries, it is the conservative movements in Islam that offer more potential than their secular counterparts for quietly radical re-readings of the place of women.[7] Actions like Amina Wadud's public

---

[6] *Taha* 20:114.

[7] E.g., Sisters of Islam in Malaysia.

leading of prayer, while they are distant behaviourally, may find a closer place in the hearts of the women reading their texts in this programme.

Music

The small group of young women at the front of the mosque gathering leads the chorus with animation, one of them accompanying on a frame drum. Mona gives a vocal lead in the group. She used to sing popular Syrian songs: but has stopped since she got more involved in the mosque programme. Now, as well as memorizing how to recite the Qur'an, she turns her talent to writing songs of worship for the women to sing in the mosque. She was involved in helping produce a CD of religious songs sung by the women. Sometimes she leads the sessions of dhikr prayer before a lecture, her voice guiding the group's prayer through poignant words and tune.

Music affects us deeply: "it can profoundly alter how we view the world and our place in it… by changing not only how we feel about ourselves, but also how we feel about everything outside ourselves." (Byrne, 2012:50) Neurological studies in the past decade exploring music and the brain have shown how music engages nearly every area of the brain and its neural subsystems (Levitin, 2008:8, 85; Sacks, 2011:L190). Music links with brain structures involved with motivation, reward, and emotion (Levitin, 2008:191), so that it "stirs us at our biological roots." (Lehrer, 2011) Our neural pathways are shaped by the music distinctions of the culture into which we are born; musical preferences become a mark of group identity. As well as expressing group cohesion, music also functions as a vehicle of social bonding. Sacks describes how rhythm "synchronizes the brains and minds (and since emotion is always intertwined with music, the 'hearts') of all who participate." "Rhythm binds together the individual nervous systems of human community." (Sacks, 2011: L3355,,3392)

Across personal, social and socio-cultural global boundaries, what kinds of music does Mona encounter? And into what liturgies and communities do the different forms of music invite her?

Music is part of life in Syria. The aural encounter with the Qur'an has already been noted, and finds its place amid the other daily surrounding sounds of life.

Contemporary pop singers from Syria feature amid others from Lebanon, Egypt and the Gulf, from the CD's and radios of young people, and on the TV screens in the restaurants which they frequent. The pop singers come and go, but the velvet tones of Fairuz still continue as they have for decades, singing classic songs of love and of patriotism: the radio reflects the popular dictum, "Listen to Fairuz in the morning." The voices of Fairuz in Lebanon and Syria, and Umm Kalthoum in Egypt, have defined their nations.

Mona grew up hearing contemporary Arabic music over the radio and in the streets. With her teenage peers, she enjoyed listening to and singing popular songs. Other singers and music groups in restaurants and concerts offered more traditional cultural music, returning to folk instruments such as the *oud, qanun* and *nay*. The recited Qu'ran was a constant counter-challenge to popular music, heard from mosque minarets, in houses and shopfronts, and murmured by the women at the mosque, sitting in ones or twos as they memorised it. Sacks describes how entire books can be held in memory through the power of music to embed sequences, using rhyme, meter and song (2011: L3287).

If texts are read in the context of particular communities of interpretation, the complex rules of Qur'anic oral recitation (*tajwid*) are common across the Muslim *ummah*. The women in the mosque programme spoke (Syrian) Arabic, and also read and wrote in (formal) Arabic. Everyday written Arabic has different syntactic-phonetic rules and a contrastive lexicon to spoken dialects; but Qur'anic recitation is not like reading a newspaper or textbook: it entails a distinct way of configuring speech organs. In *tajwid*, the reciters are using language in a formation that is distinctly that of the mosque and neither of the home nor of civic institutions. Correct pronunciation in recitation is seen as a pious duty. "The intent of *tajwid* is the recitation of the Qur'an, as God Most High sent it down... knowledge of it is a collective duty." (Muhaysin, cited in Nelson, 2001:14,15). Graham and Kermani warn that "Chanting the Qur'an is potentially an actualisation of the revelatory act itself, and thus how the Qur'an is vocally rendered not only matters, but matters ultimately. ...it is in its oral recitation that the Qur'an is most clearly experienced as divine." (2006:118, 119)

The power of the recited Qur'an is attested to by stories of people who became Muslims because of the beauty of the sound, even without understanding it. The aural presence of the Qur'an, while captivating in its own right, also evokes the ambivalent attitude to music: with Islam there is a sharp dispute about the admissibility of music (*sama'*), which also constrains performance of the Qur'an. Nelson comments:

> There are basically two positions on the polemic: those who reject *samā'* unconditionally and those who accept it conditionally. However sharp their apparent divergences in the debate, *these two positions share the basic premise that music is a powerful and affecting force* (Nelson, 2001:50).

Women singers and reciters encounter a double ambivalence in Islam, about women's voices as well as about music. In the Middle East, cultural tradition insists that their voices should not be publically audible, particularly if they are perceived as alluring. Folk-tales testify to the beguiling effect of a woman's voice. Within Islam, the extent to which a woman's voice is *awrah* (shameful) is vigorously debated, and the controversies shape performance of the Qur'an. While the most skilled Qur'anic reciters have studied music, recitation is sharply distinguished from music. Um Kalthoum, national singer in Egypt, used to be a Qur'an reciter in her youth: however, unlike other parts of the Muslim world such as South East Asia (Rasmussen, 2010), the public tones of female reciters of the Qur'an are no longer heard in the Middle East in mixed contexts.

Mona's enjoyment of local and regional pop-singers was mitigated by the liturgies of their lives: the clothes they wore, the way they walk, the mixing of the sexes, all push beyond the edge of comfort of cultural boundaries. Prevalent perceptions of the immoral lifestyle of pop singers, together with the words and video-clips of songs, reinforces the place of pop music as antithetical to proper piety. It was a narrative in which she felt uncomfortable. Ramadan is a time when the polarities are sharply defined: when the Qur'an is heard and recited throughout the month in mosques and homes, at the same time as TV channels feature the most popular singers and the best soap operas to help their viewers endure the rigours of fasting.

Within the mosque, Mona found a permissible place to exercise her musical gifts, in leading in the *tarniim* (hymns) in *dhikr* sessions, and writing and helping perform *anashiid* (choruses) for celebratory times of Muslim holidays and graduation parties at the mosque. *Dhikr* at the mosque was seen as part of mainstream Islam, rather than as specifically Sufi (Shannon, 2004:381). Sometimes led by Anisah Huda, sometimes by Mona or other young women, the *dhikr* session before the lecture was seen as an essential part of the women 'preparing their hearts' to listen to the teaching. Sometimes short invocations which were repeated multiple times, there were also longer songs to God, and also to Muhammad (especially in *Rabia al-awal*, the month of Muhammad's birthday).

While Mona could lead singing in the women's mosque programme at the mosque, she had to be careful that her voice was not audible beyond the women's section if men might be present in the main part of the mosque below. Anisah Huda would check the volume of the microphone to make sure her voices and those of the other women could not be heard in the men's section (although the reverse was a frequent occurrence). In such a context, where the seductive potential of women's voices is emphasised, it was a bold and controversial move of the women's programme to issue a CD of women's voices singing *anashiid.* To avoid censure, all the songs were chorused, so that no individual woman's voice was perceptible. Similarly, the photograph of the group of women on the front of the CD was slightly out of focus, so that none of the young women in long blue coats and white headscarves could be individually distinguished: thus propriety was maintained and the possibility of anyone being identifiably attractive in looks or voice was obviated.

Across ethnic, sectarian, and national boundaries, Mona joins other young people in Syria and beyond in listening to the music of Sami Yusuf, the globally-influential English-Azerbaijani singer, whose lyrics are usually in English or Arabic. She enjoys other popular singers from the Gulf, usually male, dressed in white *gallibeyah* and turban, singing religious themes, most often accompanied only by the permitted *duff* (frame-drum).

Re-storying

We have explored some of the different identities and allegiances available for women in the mosque programme, through the lenses of community, mimetic ideal, texts, and music; and their configurations in personal, social and global dimensions.

What are the liturgies in which they participate, with their associated telos, and the focusing desire or love which shapes them? And among their different identities and allegiances, what are the possibilities for restor(y)ing or re-membering their stories, the liturgies that shape them?

In Conflict

When narratives or liturgies collide, people seek a different way of being, a narrative that can subsume the conflicts. Fadiyah faced contradiction between her own ambitions to be an engineer and the extended family liturgy of early marriage and motherhood. Religio-cultural liturgies of the place of women, in conflict with the demands and expectations of secular feminism, may find another narrative in the place of acceptance and honour that Jesus gave to women. Tensions within families can impel people to look for other possibilities. Garrison (2014) describes the internal conflict 'Ahmed' encountered about the acts of killing that his Islamic teachers asked of him: and comments that where Muslims are killing Muslims, people look for another alternative outside Islam.

Retelling

As we listen to people's stories, we offer them the opportunity to reflect on their own lives. This retelling may enable people to see the pattern of God's work in their lives over time, or patterns of response, and to re-member their stories.

We hear their stories, we share our stories, we tell God's story.

I have discussed four significant factors in shaping identity and allegiance. Each of them offers possibilities for restor(y)ing.

Community

An alternate (Christian) community offers another possibility, another way of being, where it demonstrates integrity and love. Why Christian villages are generally cleaner than Muslim villages gets discussed in a mosque programme. Hospitality and family love can suggest new places of possibility for those who are welcomed in. Belonging before believing is a common experience for people coming to Christ.

Here we note the importance of a family or community for a new believer or enquirer, particularly if they are to sustain their walk of faith in Christ (Baig, 2013).

Model

Today, there are Muslims giving allegiance to Christ in every country, opening up possibilities for others. The tragic story of Sara Fatima Al-Mutairi, a Saudi girl murdered by her brother in 2008,[8] effectively brought the conceivability of a Saudi becoming a follower of Christ into public internet space and discussion. Other followers of Christ can model alternative liturgies, of different ways of being. Experiencing sacrificial love from a Christian is one of the elements that draw Muslims to Christ.

Here we note the importance of a model in how to live as a follower of Christ, in liturgies that include ways of reading and being formed by the Bible, ways of praying and fasting, and modest behaviour, that are culturally honouring. And we note that the importance of models also denotes a more limited role for outsiders.

Text

We see the power of God's Word in the local language (God speaks my language!), offering a different faith allegiance when people are questioning their own. (Contrast with the impact of the translated Qur'an.) Testimonies witness to the powerful impact of the Word of God, of an alternative narrative of grace not merit, of sacrificial love, of a liturgy of walking in personal relationship with the omnipotent Creator, through Jesus.

We note the importance of demonstrating ways of reading God's Word (for example, from seeking material power or blessing, to seeking meaning and personal transformation through the Word).

Music

Studies in neuroscience join with testimonies from believers of Muslim background, to show the power of music in drawing people. Conflicts between local habits of music, dance, and celebration, and Islam's restriction on instrumental worship, may find resolution in the psalms (*zabur*), where God exuberantly invokes singing and all the instruments in celebrating Him. Testimonies tell of how people have been drawn to Christian gatherings by their joyful singing.

And we note the power of local tunes for hymns in rapid church growth movements (God sings in my tunes!).

* * *

This study calls us to go beyond ways of being, details of dress, seating, prayer posture, to ask, what are the liturgies, and to what end /*telos,* towards what desire, are they directed? How are community, right models, text and music,

---

[8] http://www.sarafatima.info

evident in the liturgies into which we invite people? Some people point to Christian mission as a secularising force: we need to note the different liturgies that characterise our own lives, with the desires or loves that shape them. What different liturgies or narratives are we immersed in daily? How are they compatible or in conflict with a Christ-focused liturgy? What does that love look like in daily ways of being?

When identities and allegiances clash, how can we tell another story? – a story that doesn't dishonour every other allegiance, but can take them up into an alternative liturgy with a different *telos*, calling us to a different Love, so all allegiances become subsumed in allegiance to the One who gives us identity by first loving us, and calling us into the holy community of Christ.

We are lovers, made to love through being loved – a love which offers integration of our different allegiances and identities in Christ. People can (and do) live with competing identities, but the more dis-integration they live with, the more the possibility of collapse. This can lead people to Christ. Conversely, we need to consider that when believers experience too much dissonance and lack of integrity between their life as Christians and previous or competing identities and allegiances, it can lead them to a lack of integrated identity and a state of anomie. Asking about their experience of community, models, text and music, may help us in discipling believers, so that with them we may all live our lives in Christ Jesus the Lord, rooted and built up in him and established in the faith, and abounding in thanksgiving.[9]

References

Abu-Odeh, Lama. "Honor Killings and the Construction of Gender in Arab Societies." *American Journal of Comparative Law* 58, no. 4 (Fall 2010): 911–52. doi:10.5131/ajcl.2010.0007.

Abudi, Dalya. *Mothers and Daughters in Arab Women's Literature: The Family Frontier*. Women and Gender. The Middle East and the Islamic World. 10. Leiden: Brill, 2011.

Ahmad, Sadaf. *Transforming Faith: The Story of Al-Huda and Islamic Revivalism Among Urban Pakistani Women*. Gender and Globalization. New York: Syracuse University Press, 2009.

Alison, James. "Girard's Breakthrough." *James Alison. Theology*, 1996. http://www.jamesalison.co.uk/texts/eng05.html.

Anderson, Benedict. *Imagined Communities: Reflections on the Origin and Spread of Nationalism* (2nd ed.). London: Verso, 1991.

Asad, Talal. *Formations of the Secular. Christianity, Islam, Modernity*. Stanford, California: Stanford University Press, 2003.

———. *Genealogies of Religion. Discipline and Reasons of Power in Christianity and Islam*. Baltimore & London: John Hopkins University Press, 1993.

Baig, Sufyan. 'The Ummah and Christian Community'. pp. 69 - 78 in *Longing For Community*, Editd by David Greenlee. Pasadena, California: William Carey Library, 2013.

[9] Colossians 2:7-8.

Bano, Masooda. 'Conclusion: Female Leadership in Mosques: An Evolving Narrative'. pp. 507-33 in *Women, Leadership, and Mosques. Changes in Contemporary Islamic Authority*, 11.. Women and Gender. The Middle East and the Islamic World. Leiden: Brill, 2012.

Barnett, Jens. 'Living a Pun: Cultural Hybridity among Arab Followers of Christ'. pp. 29 - 40 in *Longing For Community*. Edited by David Greenlee. Pasadena, California: William Carey Library, 2013.

Bruner, Jerome. "Life as Narrative." *Language Arts* 65, no. 6 (October 1988): 574–83.

Byrne, David. *How Music Works*. Edinburgh: Canongate Books, 2012.

Cragg, Kenneth, and Marston Speight. *Islam from Within: Anthology of a Religion*. Belmont, California: Wadsworth, 1980.

Du Mez, Kristin Kobes. *A New Gospel for Women. Katharine Bushnell and the Challenge of Christian Feminism*. Oxford: Oxford University Press, 2015.

El Fadl, Khaled Abou. *Speaking in God's Name. Islamic Law, Authority and Women*. Oxford: Oneworld, 2001.

Gaffney, Patrick D. *The Prophet's Pulpit. Islamic Preaching in Contemporary Egypt*. Comparative Studies in Muslim Societies. Berkley: University of California Press, 1994.

Garrison, David. *A Wind in the House of Islam*. Monument, CO: WigTake Resources, 2014.

Girard, Rene. *The Girard Reader*. New York: Crossroad Publishing Company, 1996.

Graham, William A, and Navid Kermani. 'Recitation and Aesthetic Reception'. pp. 115 - 141 in *The Cambridge Companion to the Qur'an*. Edited by Jane Dammen McAuliffe. Cambridge: Cambridge University Press, 2006.

Guessoum, Nidhal. "The Qur'an, Science, and the (Related) Contemporary Muslim Discourse." *Zygon: Journal of Religion & Science* 43, no. 2 (June 2008): 411–31.

Hafez, Sherine. *An Islam of Her Own. Reconsidering Religion and Secularism in Women's Islamic Movements*. New York: New York University Press, 2011.

Hegland, Mary Elaine. "Shi'a Women's Rituals in Northwest Pakistan: The Shortcomings and Significance of Resistance." *Anthropological Quarterly* 76, no. 3 (Summer 2003).

Joseph, Suad. 'Brother-Sister Relationships. Connectivity, Love, and Power in the Reproduction of Patriarchy in Lebanon'. pp. 113 - 140 in *Intimate Selving in Arab Families. Gender, Self, and Identity*. Edited by Suad Joseph. Syracuse: Syracuse University Press, 1999.

Joseph, Suad. "Learning Desire: Relational Pedagogies and the Desiring Female Subject in Lebanon." *Journal of Middle East Women's Studies* 1, no. 1 (January 2005): 79–109.

Kahteran, Nevad. "Hafiz/Tahfiz/Hifz/Muhaffiz." *The Qur'an: An Encyclopaedia*. London: Routledge, 2006.

– – – . "Tajwid." *The Qur'an: An Encyclopaedia*. London: Routledge, 2006.

Khan, Muhammad Zafrulla. *The Qur'an, Arabic Text, English Translation*. London: Curzon Press, 1981.

Krause, Wanda. *Women in Civil Society. The State, Islamism, and Networks in the UAE*. New York: Palgrave Macmillan, 2008.

Kressel, G.M. "Shame and Gender." *Anthropological Quarterly* 65, no. 1 (1992).

Lehrer, Jonah. "The Neuroscience of Music." *Wired: Science*, 2011. http://www.wired.com/2011/01/the-neuroscience-of-music/

Levitin, Daniel. *This Is Your Brain On Music: Understanding a Human Obsession*. London: Atlantic Books, 2008.

Maalouf, Amin (Barbara Bray, translator). *On Identity*. London: The Harvill Press,

2000.
Maher, Bridget. *Veiled Voices*. DVD. Typecast Releasing, 2010.
Mahmood, Saba. *Politics of Piety. The Islamic Revival and the Feminist Subject*. Princeton: Princeton University Press, 2005.
Mauss, Marcel. 'Techniques of the Body'. *Economy and Society* 2, no. 1 (1973): 70–88.
McDonald, Brian. "Violence and the Lamb Slain." *Touchstone* 16, no. 10 (December 2003). http://www.touchstonemag.com/archives/issue.php?id=66.
Meltzer, Julia, and Laura Nix. *The Light In Her Eyes*. DVD. Clockshop & Felt Films, 2012.
Nelson, Kristina. *The Art of Reciting the Qur'an*. Cairo: The American University in Cairo Press, 2001.
Padwick, Constance E. *Muslim Devotions: A Study of Prayer-Manuals in Common Use*. Oxford: Oneworld, 1961.
Rasmussen, Anne. *Women, the Recited Qur'an, and Islamic Music in Indonesia*. Los Angeles: University of California Press, 2010.
Sacks, Oliver. *Musicophilia. Tales of Music and the Brain* (3rd ed.). New York: Picador, 2011.
Shannon, Jonathon H. 'The Aesthetics of Spiritual Practice and the Creation of Moral and Musical Subjectivities in Aleppo, Syria'. *Ethnology* 43, no. 4 (2004).
Shehadeh, Lamia Rustum. *The Idea of Women in Fundamentalist Islam*. Gainesville: University Press of Florida, 2003.
Smith, James K.A. *Desiring the Kingdom. Worship, Worldview, and Cultural Formation*. Vol. 1. 3 vols. Cultural Liturgies. Michigan: Baker Academic, 2009.
– – – . *Imagining the Kingdom: How Worship Works*. Vol. 2. Grand Rapids, MI: Baker Academic, 2013.
Stowasser, Barbara Freyer. 'Gender Issues and Contemporary Qu'ran Interpretation'. pp. 30 - 44 in *Islam, Gender & Social Change*. Edited by Yvonne Yazbeck Haddad & John L. Esposito. Oxford: Oxford University Press, 1998.
Taussig, Michael. *Mimesis and Alterity: A Particular History of the Senses*. London: Routledge, 1993.
Winter, Charlie. "Women of the Islamic State. A Manifesto on Women by the Al-Khanssaa Brigade," Quilliam (February 2015).

(Re)forming Identities and Allegiances: Response 1: Identity Crisis

Sarah Yoon

In her paper, Moyra Dale understands that as relational beings and lovers, human beings engage each other in particular modes in space and times. They have ways of expressing their identities or allegiances based on particular narratives and liturgies reflecting the circumstances in which they have lived. Human beings are also open to opportunities for recalling or reviewing their narratives. Moyra identifies four primary ways in which women's identities and allegiances are established by means of the stories of Muslim women she met with regularly in a women's mosque program in the Middle East. These primary ways are Community, Model, Text, and Music. Communities including extended family can exercise a huge influence on forming their identities, and Models are provided in the communities to follow, through their life styles, in visible ways. Texts such as the Qur'an are the most powerful agencies that shape Muslims' life styles, and Music can also touch women's emotions. Powerful though these influences are, when such Muslim women are confronted by disorientating events in their lives, it is possible that they can retell or confidently reconstruct their stories through becoming part of Christian community, living as followers of Christ, acknowledging of the Word of God, and joyful singing of Christian gatherings.

In my response to Moyra's paper, I would like to draw attention to what happens in the formation of Muslim women's identities when they explore new narratives to describe their past life. Though it is generally accurate to suggest that Muslim women nurtured in a fixed religious cultural setting will have certain identities and allegiances, it is also important to recognize that when these women meet Jesus, they can find out who they truly are and where they belong in Christ. This makes them able to see their narratives from new and different perspectives. However, these women would meet unexpectedness in the midst of retelling or remembering their stories. In some ways, these journeys are unavoidable, but necessary. I will introduce three stories of women, which illustrate unexpectedness in their new journey.

The Story of "Rahabs"

Rahab (Joshua 2) lived in Jericho; she was a prostitute who people hated and looked down upon. Because of her situation, she also thought lowly of herself. She heard a rumor that Israelites exiled from Egypt, would come and attack Jericho. Although she did not know a great deal about them, she was amazed how their God, Yahweh, led them and kept them safe in the desert. One day, she ran into Israelite spies in her house. When she realized that they were in peril, she decided to hide and protect them from the soldiers looking for them. This decision to hide and protect them was not easy, but it was a decision she had to make, because she had heard about their God, and was convinced that as she said to the spies "The Lord your God is God in heaven above and on the earth below" (Joshua 2:11, NIV).

When Rahab faced these circumstances, did she tell her family what she did, and about the Israelite spies' promise? Was she scared to be caught by her neighbors or soldiers? Did she regret what she did? These days there are many "Rahabs" who have special encounters in the Middle East and Islamic world. The following contemporary stories demonstrate how this new adventure leads them to new dimensions they never experienced before.

The Story of Khadija

Khadija is a married woman and is working as a teacher at an elementary school. When she was young, she dreamed of a happy family life with a career as a teacher. However, the reality of life was different from what she expected. She married her cousin, and now has to take care of her family and in-laws alone. Because her husband's family is poor, her husband went abroad to earn money; she also has to work to support the family. She is so frustrated with her situation. During the time I met her, she was sick and hospitalized at a charity hospital. In this hospital, she came to believe in Jesus as her saviour through the sharing of Christian workers. Although she has made that decision by herself, she is worried and confused about her new faith. First of all, she is afraid of being divorced when her husband finds out about her faith. If he finds out, she will have to leave her children. At the same time, she has many questions about herself several times a day: "I am a Muslim. How can I be a Christian?" She cannot share her faith with her family and friends, and nobody knows about her faith. As time goes by, she is wondering who she is, and where she belongs. She feels like she is lost in a maze.

One of the biggest challenges women face when retelling their *telos* or narratives with Jesus is that their decision to believe in the true God and follow Jesus is regarded as an act not only against their communities and families, but also even against their ideal models, text, and music (or communal feelings and senses). Muslim women have formed their identities and allegiances through their religious, cultural and social contexts. Religious texts set models for them to be modest and religious in their behaviors. Socio-cultural contexts define women as good daughters, wives and mothers and to be submissive to male authorities. They are expected to maintain honour and other virtues according to the socio-cultural norms accepted by male dominant societies.[1] For instance, when I interviewed Muslim women about identity issues, most of them

---

[1] I addressed details about interviews in Chapter 4 in *Identity Crisis: Standing Between Two Identities of Women Believers from Muslim Back grounds in Jordan* (Eugene, OR: Wipf & Stock, 2015), 96-132.

answered that their identities, based on religious teachings and social expectations, are being good daughters, wives and mothers. Through these interviews, I realized that many Muslim women know who they should be, but not who they really are.(Yoon, 2015:98)

In the process of establishing new identity and allegiance, people get to know "who they are" and "where they belong." Sometimes previous narratives or life styles in new believers' lives hold them back or become barriers when taking a further step in new faith. When we think of Jewish Christians from the first church community, they had to break their Jewish customs and prejudices about gentiles. Even the apostle Peter needed three visions from God to meet Cornelius (Acts 10:9-23) and had to confess a new perception about God through it (Acts 10:33-34 "I now realize..." NIV). Furthermore, when Peter was afraid of those who belonged to the circumcision group, he received a rebuke from the apostle Paul about his hypocrisy towards the Gentiles at the eating table. James P. Dretke describes Peter's crisis:

> Peter had grown up in a culture where even associating with Gentiles was a desecration... In Antioch, Peter was torn by the anxiety of trying to keep loyal to the traditions of his fathers and the pull of identifying with the Gentiles who were responding to the Gospel. Paul denounced this kind of inconsistency and two-facedness.... (1979:149)

Paul pointed out that Peter's behavior was not acting in line with the truth of the gospel (Galatians 2:11-14). The long existing identities and ways of beings which have formed in a religious-cultural background are not removable right away.

On the other hand, we also notice that these women are influenced by current situations. Standing in a transitional state threatens their abilities to retell their *telos* or narratives. Current political and global situations have changed and affected their perspectives on their lives. More liberal Islamic scholars, including a number of women, have explored new and more open interpretations of the Qur'an and other Islamic texts. The "Arab Spring," globalization, and the Internet have opened women's eyes to see their own and others' lives. Nowadays more women have the opportunity to be educated. They show much capability to accept new perspectives on women's lives. In particular, young and intelligent women are flexible in adapting new ideas and are able to balance between traditional expectations and their own desires to explore their lives in ways that may be viewed as secular and western to their families and communities. It seems that these women have become more transitional; they sit inbetween a conservative, rigid generation and a liberal, flexible one.

The Story of Syrian Refugee Fatima

Fatima is from Syria. She has an 11-year-old son. Her husband was a soldier of the free army, but he died in the war. With her two younger brothers and her son, she left Syria and came to Jordan three years ago. They were at the Za'atari camp only two weeks, and left because it was very hard to live inside the camp. They

> came to city "A". Her brothers left her and her son there, and went to Amman to make a living. At the moment, they are working at a restaurant in Amman. Seeking help from outside, she found that one of the local churches in the city has helped Syrians a great deal. During this time, she developed friendships with Christians and, with their support, has come to know Jesus personally. Her son goes to a school run by the church to teach Syrian children. At the moment, she does not have any difficulties in going to a church, and does not wear hijab. Her son also knows who Jesus is and about the salvation. She does not know anybody here in the city except helpers from a mosque and the church. She feels free to explore a new faith in the city. However, she also feels fear about her faith in the future. She does not know what will happen to her.

In recent times, women in Syria, Iraq, and Yemen have suffered from unstable political situations. In particular, Syrian refugee women have faced new and challenging situations. Because of the civil war, the extended family system has collapsed. They have left their home country and most of their extended families are scattered. Many married women lost their husbands and sons during the war. They lost their heads of family who provided everything they needed and became responsible for their young children. They want to get help to survive in their new lands/homes even from churches and Christians. They send their children to learn and get support from the church, which offers English lessons, education, and other things through church programs. Local neighbors understand these women's situations so they do not look down upon Syrians who contact Christians. However, this does not mean that new Syrian converts or seekers have total freedom to choose a new faith outwardly because they still live within Islamic countries and families. They also suffer from the uncertainty of their future. For them, it is not clear how long they will have this freedom in their new faith or how to maintain their faith in the future.

Therefore, new believers' previous identities, which have been built in the contexts of their whole lives and current transitional environments, have challenged their spiritual journey and the formation of their new identities as followers of Jesus. This is called an identity crisis. Roland Müller, a former worker in the Middle East, also speaks about new converts' struggles in what he calls, a "two- faced situation." He asserts that a new believer from a Muslim background can easily develop "two faces": one for relating to his family and community, and another for his new faith community. In this case, a new believer struggles inside between these two faces and eventually has to choose "one face" unless he can find a way to unite the two faces. As a result of this identity crisis, many new converts who struggle give up their new faith and go back to their old faith. Primarily, they have suffered not because of persecutions from outside, but from pressures from inside, especially at the beginning phase of their conversion process. From interviews with the new converts I conducted, they had undergone identity crises at the beginning. They had much emotional turmoil and confusion during this time, and many of them wanted to give up their new journey. It usually took four or five years for them to settle down in their new faith and to understand themselves as new creations of God.

Reasons for Struggles

There are many reasons why new converts experience this kind of identity crisis. Identity crisis among new converts is not caused by a difficult environment alone, but also by differing worldviews and self-understanding built over the years. Basically, the nature of conversion brings identity crisis to converts. Conversion is a transformation of worldviews and identity rather than just changing a religious belief. (Norris, 2003:171) Paul Hiebert emphasizes the importance of changing worldview in the conversion process. He asserts that "conversion to Christ must encompass all three levels: behaviour, beliefs, and the worldview that underlies these… [if] the worldview is not transformed, in the long run the gospel is subverted and the result is a syncretistic Christo-paganism, which has the form of Christianity but not its essence." (2008:11) Establishment of new identities and worldviews is challenged by clashes with old ones.

Secondly, the nature of Islam and patriarchal culture may cause identity crisis as well. As Moyra has shown in *(Re)forming identities and allegiances*, the identity of Muslim women is to a large extent formed through Community, extended family, religious Texts, and local culture such as Music. Müller also asserts that there is a high degree of conformity expected of members in Arab societies. (2006:225) Therefore, fundamentally, "Arabs fear isolation because in their view an individual or small group can only function effectively when he or she is identified with a group or a large body that can offer support and protection." (Muller 2006:225) For example, in the case of a strict Islamic response to apostasy the interpretation of Sharia might be that it is not acceptable for Arab women to convert from Islam to another religion in their socio-cultural circumstances. In conservative and patriarchal culture, Muslim women gain their status and have secure feelings from their families and male family members who have strong authority over women. Especially within the marriage, husbands are expected to control their home and wives. Sawsan el-Messiri, an Egyptian woman scholar, explains that a husband's taking control of his home and wife means that he is aware of what is going on in his house and "being aware of all her activities, knowing when she goes out and comes back, where she goes, and whom she meets." (1978:39) Hence, when women become interested in the new faith, they already have started to challenge the patriarchal system.

Lastly, in the Muslim mind, there are some fixed images of Christianity and the relationship between Christians and the West, as well as some political understandings. Muslims believe that Westerners are too materialistic, immoral (drinking, abortion, sexual liberty etc.), and accept injustice in society. (McDowell and Zaka, 1999:62) They simply recognize Christianity as a foreign religion and Christians as immoral and pro-Israel. These fixed and negative images make new converts hesitant to become Christians because they think Christians are immoral, and they do not want to adhere to Western forms of religion. Even after becoming Christians, they have confusion in discerning the truth concerning the image of Christians and Christianity. At the same time, the converts are afraid of being seen negatively by other Muslims and their communities.

Formatting of a New Identity as a New Creation

When new converts call Jesus their saviour, they are reborn as children of God and belong to a new spiritual community. The true identity of all believers is in Christ. Only God can reveal and explain who we truly are. The converts should learn that in the Christian life there are sufferings, struggles and spiritual warfare from outside and within. If, however, they are well prepared with good practical knowledge and theological understanding about their lives and sufferings, they will not be shaken easily at the beginning of conversion.

In a practical way, as Moyra suggested, an alternative community with hospitality and love is helpful. If they continue to have somebody come along as a friend or mentor, and know other reliable converts, it gives them a sense of belonging. Through interactions, these new fellowships can help them follow Jesus and develop new identities. Members of the new fellowship can also be role-models for new converts. In these fellowships, members can share their stories and develop new perspectives on their lives. Relationship and the sense of belonging to a community are crucial for convert's faith. This community should be comprised of individuals, but also of local churches. Although the situation of local churches is varied depending on where they are, churches cannot make excuses about not helping new converts because of the societal and political situation. Local churches are responsible for them, and in any form, churches should be involved in helping them as the body of Christ.

When considering the Arab's strong oral culture, using bible stories and memorizing verses will help them understand the Bible better. Lessons should emphasize the importance of having a personal relationship with Jesus and should include how to apply character and the heart of Jesus to their daily lives. Jesus' incarnation is the ideal model to be followed. For example, new converts have to know that they should try to be good family members in their homes. Jesus had a real life and family on earth. The converts have to transform existing relationships in Christ and have to re-build their identities with new perspectives.

The identity crisis that occurs in the process of conversion seems like a barricade for new converts that threatens their new faith, but it is necessary. Our spiritual journey is about finding our identity originally given to us by God.. Although these new converts go through struggles in finding and building their identity, after finding a way to integrate, they can understand who they are and be aware of their lives as women. Some of the cultural and religious aspects of their previous identities as Muslims should be challenged, but at the same time these previous identities could be the stepping stones that help integrate the new identity given by God. Finding new identity does not mean denying their whole identity.. Through these conflicts, they are moulded into a new identity and so are able to retell their stories as new creations of God. That, of course, was the experience of Rahab.

The End of Stories

Rahab (Joshua 2) was not sure how her decision would affect her family members and her future. The one important things was that she had a conviction Yahweh was really the God. Her conviction about God made her confront her own culture and community. Finally, her decision led her to save herself, her family and all who belonged to her (Joshua 6:25). Later, she became an ancestress in the genealogy of Jesus (Matt1:5) and was called a woman of faith (Hebrews 11:31). Many "Rahabs" have made decisions to follow Jesus, but are not sure of what will happen to them as a result of their decisions. However, as the Israelite spies kept their promise to save her and her family, God will keep his promise "Believe in the Lord Jesus, and you will be saved-you and your household."(Acts 16:31)

References

Dretke, James P. *A Christian approach to Muslims: Reflections from West Africa*. Pasadena: William Carey Library, 1979.

Hiebert. Paul G. *Transforming Worldviews: An Anthropological Understanding of How People Change*. Ada, MI: Baker Academic, 2008.

McDowell, Bruce A. and Anees Zaka, *Muslims and Christians at the Table*. Philipsburg, NJ: Presbyterian and Reformed, 1999.

el_Messiri, Sawson. *Ibn al-balad: A concept of Egyptian identity*. Leiden: Brill, 1978.

Müller, Roland. *The Messenger, The Message, The Community: Three Critical issues for the Cross-cultural Church-planter*. Surrey, British Columbia: CanBooks, 2006.

Norris, Rebecca Sachs. 'Converting to What? Embodied Culture and the Adoption of New Beliefs'. pp. 171-182 in *The Anthropology of Religious Conversion*. Edited by Andrew Bucker and Stephan D. Glazier. London: Rowman & Littlefield, 2003.

Yoon, Sarah. *Identity Crisis: Standing Between Two Identities of Women Believers from Muslim Back grounds in Jordan*. Eugene, OR: Wipf & Stock, 2015.

(Re)forming Identities and Allegiances: Response 2

Iris Sechter Funk

In "(Re)forming identities and allegiances" Moyra Dale has enlightened us about how identities of ordinary Arab women are formed through their everyday relationships, especially in family interactions, and how these identities constructed in local, ethnic and global levels, can be in conflict. Moyra's paper explores four areas that contribute significantly in this process: Community, Models, Texts, and Music. She questions how these areas are relevant when Christ calls people to another allegiance. I will make some reflections in order to respond to those questions in a contextual frame of North African societies of Tunisia and Morocco where I have lived with my family over seventeen years.

First, it is important to remember the major sociopolitical reconfiguration currently happening in the MENA[1] region. Thus all 'frontiers' are wavering and women's issues, like all aspects of social life, are continually shifting in response to dynamic transformations in culture and society, locally and globally (Joseph & Slyomovics, 2001:8). Speaking of how people in the Arab world are feeling, Fatema Mernissi, Moroccan sociologist, said "That we are offered to move backwards does not change the ardent desire for change. Going to another elsewhere, immigrating collectively to another present is exceedingly strong in this corner of the world." (2010:255). Arab women scholars agree that the so-called 'Arab Spring' has, after all, changed the way people speak out, and women's voices rise up. For instance, an event in the Kingdom of Morocco shows how old paradigms are confronted: On March 10' 2012, in Larache, Amina El Filali, a 16 yearold girl, committed suicide. Her family had married her to her rapist to avoid dishonour. This event raised waves of protests from the 'civil society': women of all ages and different status took the issue to the streets to push the government to change constraining laws on women. With the support of the media and social networks, in 2014 the Parliament voted to eliminate a clause of Article 475 of the Penal Code, which gave a rapist the possibility to marry the victim in order to avoid conviction. Such legislation is a key element for the fostering or inhibiting of social change (Charrad, 2001:63).

[1] MENA: Middle East and North Africa. Also known as NAME: North Africa and Middle East, as in an earlier paper.

Secondly, these *buzzing societies*[2] show that people, women and men, are searching for the new things. Today, in Tunisia and Morocco identities are been constructed through adaptations and confrontation between, on the one hand, a more conservative fundamentalist style of life and, on the other, globalization and individualization of values and social behaviors, creating new paradoxes. In this context of cultural fluidity, Moyra's paper "(Re)forming identities and allegiances" helps us to (re)think the way the Gospel takes root in a specific context. Under subheadings that are reworked from Moyra's paper, this response explores how a Christian community, modeling Christian values and developing contextually aware liturgy can and should lead to real Gospel advancement in changing societies. The approach used is to recount some real life experiences and to reflect on the lessons that they illustrate.

Community, Enriched Identities and Significances

"*I did not give birth to my daughter, for her to become an infidel.*" "*I will never forgive you. You are not my daughter.*" These are the mother's reactions to Asma, as she hears the news of her daughter's conversion to Christianity. Asma, a 23 year old student, explained "*The reaction of my family was very hard and they forced me to make a choice between them and Christ…*"

Indeed, family relationships can be difficult for many new believers, who are put under pressure by their kin, at least for a while. It was Faten's case also. Her father knew she was going to church; he himself was invited for dinner by the foreign pastor and his family several times. One day Faten told him. "*I became a Christian.*" Faten's father was not surprised, but he could not bear his daughter telling him this openly, challenging his authority, and being disrespectful to the traditions of her family and her country. Then Faten's father thought that expelling her from home would make her retreat from her decision. Faten entered in conflict with her family, and, forced to leave her home, she found refuge in the pastor's family. For many years, Faten's family refused to have any contact with her. Today, however, Faten and her family have restored relationships. She is an autonomous professional and leader in the church.

Asma and Faten confronted the authority of their parents by making public their new faith. By this act, they were undoing their assigned status and were treated as transgressors to the social order and to the moral codes of honor and loyalty.[3]

The greatest criticisms toward Christian conversions in Muslim societies are related to the notion of betrayal to the family, to the nation, and to the imagined

---

[2] Hafidha Chekir, Tunisian scholar and feminist, Conference « Les droits des femmes et les spécificités culturelles: l'attitude des Etats arabes » in the seminary « Gender, politics and sexualities. Orient/Western », In Fondation Maison des Sciences de l'Homme, Paris, March 31 2011.

[3] This reaction is not only because of Islam, but about patriarchy. It is observed in numerous societies where written or unwritten norms are trespassed by women.

community of the *Ummah*. Religious conversions force a breach in this fantasized homogeneity (Boissevain 2014:5) and show the difficulty of separating the identity of the individual from the religious belonging and nationality, substantialized in the person. This highlights the complex relationships between individuals, collectives, and Islamic states.

In the Arab world, the person is nested in a complex network of relationships where roles and status define rights and duties. Social identity is relational, plural and relative (Augé, 1994:31), and according Stahl (1977:303) classificatory. Therefore, it is fragile, because it depends on how the individual perceives himself/herself, and what people think about him/her. This fragility may produce a kind of social vulnerability for those who don't respect commonly accepted religious norms and are labelled as *outsiders* (Becker, 1966). According Moyra, the centrality of family to social, economic, political and religious life has profound implications for individual decisions and gender relationships. The distinctive socialization between of boys and girls, based on a code of honor and shame, produces different moral standards that made the woman's status fragile and has a great impact on decision making. To cross the established "*hudud*" (limits) endangers women in their protected status. According to Joseph and Slyomovics (2001:8) "family both supports and suppresses women. This paradox of support and suppression, love and power, and generosity and competition compels both attachment to, and struggle within families". In consequence, familial rejection triggers a process of social vulnerability which Robert Castel calls *disaffiliation* (1995:224) that combines deficits of filiation (primary social ties) with forms of collective protection (work, collectives). The decision to follow Christcan trigger this process of disaffiliation.

The encounter with Al-Messiah confers an identity that is not based on gender status, merits or classifications. The person is enriched by their "new" identity as God's child and becomes part of God's family: *"I thank God for blessing me with an alternative family, broader and loving, inside and outside the Church (building)!"* says Asma. The new identity in Christ leads to rearrangement of the hierarchy of allegiances that in turn can enrich other identities, and doesn't always need to compete with the loyalty to the family. In the beginning, family ties could be dislocated, but later be reestablished when believers care about their beloved ones and respect them is demonstrated.

Church as Resilient Community

As pointed by Moyra, "An alternate (Christian) community offers another possibility, another way of being, where it demonstrates integrity and love." The Church community is ontologically a mirror of God's grace and love to individuals and communities. When rejection happens, the Church should become an *extended caring* family. Through a welcoming fellowship and supportive service, the church demonstrates the real mean of *agape*, the unconditional love and grace of our Lord to restore people to their worth and dignity, and to help them to endure adversities. This resilient ministry should include both emotional and social support to fight disintegration and enable people to develop their own strengths by mitigating adverse effects. As an example, the church in Tunisia has started a ministry amongst women who suffer spiritual or moral wounds and sexual violence. A feminine Tunisian team visits Church groups across the country to help women to overcome traumas.

Almost all countries in the region are going through social and political conflicts, with high levels of unemployment, pauperization and youth frustration, along with imposed limits on freedom of conscience. Apart from the traumatic events than can be experienced by many women (and men and children), Christians are facing discrimination and persecution because of their faith. In this situation, the Church as Community needs to develop a *contextual theology and practice that responds to suffering, persecution and martyrdom.*[4] Sometimes, our teaching and worship convey values such as "well-being", pleasure and comfort and, like a medical treatment, we try to suppress suffering. Without trivializing the suffering, because our Saviour came as a Suffering Servant, walking with Jesus means to live a servant life, with the security that God is with us, helping us to overcome hardships, rather than expecting a successful life without troubles. The Lausanne Covenant (1974) notes: "A Church which preaches the cross must itself be marked by the cross". In order to avoid this dichotomy, the Christian Community in MENA, should work in holistic way, where theory and practice, evangelization and social engagement, physical and spiritual needs are integrated in the same Gospel.

Models and Sociological Shifts

In North African societies, the models are multiple and coexistent:

> Meriem is a 23 year old student of English at Tunis University. She is always connected to Facebook, chatting with friends around the world, wearing jeans, and loose hair. She is a 'typical' modern young woman that goes out to cafeterias with friends. Meanwhile Hind, 21 years old, dresses in hijab, and is part of the Salafist movement that is growing among students at the University of Manouba.

These two girls incarnate the social models constructed, not only in local, but in global levels. The globalization and individualization of values have an impact on ways of being, which produces a polarization between 'modern Western' and 'traditional Muslim' values, which are shaping cultural trends. Observing the adjustment of *women's status and the major sociological shifts in family life* helps to understand the dynamics of changing paradigms in the region. According to Joseph & Slyomovics (2001:14), gender differences are historically and culturally constructed and reproduced through complex moralities, idioms and power structures.

---

[4] According to Taylor (2000:9), "The majority of Christians – whether in the West or the non-West- do not have an adequate theology of suffering, much less of persecution and martyrdom. But we must develop one soon!"

Women's Status

Women's status was a central topic in the political hurricane that endured in *Tunisia* three years after the revolution. The Personal Code Status in Tunisia is, along with the one in Turkey, the vanguard for the region.[5] After three years of hard political battles against more conservative Islamic forces, the rights of women were confirmed by the new Constitution in January 2014.[6] In spite of this, there are some steps backwards, like the revival of the illegal "*orfi*"[7] marriage, which started among radical young Muslims. "New-old" models come-up!

In Morocco, the major changes to woman's status stipulated by the Reformed Family Code of 2004 point towards the restriction of polygamy, place the minimal age of marriage at 18 years for both women and men, abolish the need for a tutor (father, uncle, brother...) for women, and give adult women the freedom to marry without parental permission. Furthermore, the new *Moudawana* gives both husband and wife the "shared responsibility" for their family.[8]

Family Changes

The 'Arab' family is undergoing multidimensional transformations because of economic, political and social issues. Some factors are: the nuclearization of the family as a consequence of rural exodus and urbanization, the rise of women's education, and their entry to labour markets, the influence of communications media, migration, contraception...

Rampant male unemployment has restructured power relationships in families. Women have become bread-winners and economic heads of households, but these achievements are not reflected statistically,[9] because of 'informal' work. Morocco has the highest rate of vulnerable informal employment in the region for both women (65 percent) and men (47 percent).[10]

---

[5] In Tunisia, immediately after independence (1958), polygamy and repudiation were abolished, and the age at marriage limited to women and men at 18. Abortion and adoption are legal. Habib Bourguiba and Ben Ali governments have enacted woman's rights quite similarly to Western countries (except women' heritage).

[6] The Constitution of 26 January 2014 assures in Article 46, "The State is committed to protect the acquired rights of women and ensures consolidate and promote them [...]".

[7] *Orfi* is a customary marriage without legal contract. It is starting to be practised on campus and in shanty towns. The woman and child born out of wedlock are not protected.

[8] Art 51-3 speak of the wife, with the husband, as responsible for the management of household affairs and the protection of the children.

[9] According to World Bank, Women's 'formal' labour force remains at about 20 percent – by far the lowest among all regions.

[10] Source: World Bank. Regional Highlights World Development Indicators 2012 – World Bank data.worldbank.org/data-catalog/world-development-indicators

In spite of this, violence against women remains high: 64% of women between 18 and 64 years old have experienced some form of violence in 2011.[11]

How does the local Church support women, and fight discrimination and violence again women? Considering the evolution of women's status, how has Church included new ministries to women?

Versatile Models

These political and sociological shifts create versatile models. When people overthrow governments, they are contesting the established models and institutions. The revival of political Islam is a manifestation of non-conformity to the *status-quo*, a way to fight inequality and injustice, a quest for identity and meaning, mixed with powerful economical claims. Otherwise, the social questions that existed before the 'Arab Spring' were taboo, like sexual issues. Now they are part of public debates and discussed in social networks, showing that new moralities make visible the gap between norms and practices. So, the modern "Muslim" woman no longer fits old stereotypes of the quiet, uneducated submissive, silent women, reflecting Youssef Courbage's statement that there is no "*Homo Arabicus* or *Islamicus*".[12]

How does the Church in the region confront these peoples' claims' and respond to social shifts? What kind of culture is transmitted in the Gospel that western missionaries bring? Which models are we passing on?

Modeling through Kingdom Values

Kingdom values can help to reflect on models:

> Elise worked among prostitutes in the south of Tunisia. She met Butheina, a single mother with four children, who came to the association to ask for help.[13] Elise encouraged her to do something on her own. The association helped Butheina with a microcredit and she made beautiful carpets for sale. Butheina's life was transformed. She became a Christian, and a new sense of dignity and worth empowered her to stop her old style of life and favored her economic autonomy.

Work experience among marginalized women and children shows that values like *amal* (hope) and *karama* (dignity), shared in the practice of

[11] Statistics: With a prevalence of 35.3% of women, 3.4 million, have suffered an act of physical violence since the age of 18. HCP "Principales résultats de la prévalence de la violence à l'égard des femmes » http://www.hcp.ma/downloads/Violence-a-l-egard-des-femmes_t13077.html, Retrieved on 05/08/2015.

[12] According to Youssef Courbage, demographer , Institut National d'Etudes Démographiques (France), in the seminary "Familles et politiques publiques dans le Monde Arabe" , in Institut d'études de l'Islam et des sociétés du monde musulman (IISMM), in Paris, Avril 5 2013.

[13] Single mothers in Muslim societies are social marginalised.

Christian witness, have a tremendous impact on people's lives. According to Chris Sugden, in a Christian view, dignity assumes identity. "God's grace is the source of identity and humanity in relationships is the context for affirming dignity. The new identity in Christ empowers people to believe that God's purpose for them is that they be stewards and that all the power of God is available to them to overcome the forces of evil that prevent them from exercising and fulfilling stewardship" (1999:238, 258)

Sharing Christian faith, in contextual ways through word and acts has a humanizing influence, as they collaborate to transform communities. Araujo argues that missions today can still perform a significant service to the nations by giving them a new set of values (Araujo:68). It is not about Western values, but to promote the values of the Kingdom, founded on the Scriptures. This includes equipping believers to judge the patterns of their community according to the patterns of the Kingdom.

Modeling Kingdom values, means walking alongside people, sharing life, and "sacrificial love" as observed by Moyra, in a way that people may see God's grace through our loving service, done in humility. I remember two experiences that transformed my life as I saw God is at work beyond my expectations. Lilia is a psychologist who used to work amongst cancer patients in a regional hospital in Tunisia. She invited me to work with her to develop a project to improve the condition of those patients, children and adults. We spent two years working together at the hospital. One day she said to me "I had a dream. I dreamed that we were praying together in your house, so can we pray this afternoon?" She became a follower of the Messiah. Meanwhile my close friend Emna found Jesus through a vision. She 'gave her life to Him' while praying below a flourishing almond tree in her garden. We used to meet to pray and to read the Gospel together, after reading the Scriptures we knelt down to pray. What wonderful moments for both of us! She became a professional storyteller and now she is visiting Arab countries to tell stories and passing on the values of the Kingdom.

Our model is Jesus Christ; we are being shaped by Him. I appreciated the notion of "Mimesis" in Moyra's paper because to be a disciple requires modeling His image. Let us be constantly transformed by Him.

(Re)interpreting Liturgies, Texts and Music

Moyra's paper explains that the Qur'an and Hadiths, in scriptural and oral forms, have a sacred role to shape the practice of Muslim faith, formatting peoples' worldview, liturgies, and daily life. I got a glimpse of this during my first years in Morocco, when a new Christian believer who never met another Christian explained how he imagined a "Christian" church: "*If we are going to make church here, we should first take all the furniture out of the room, put down a big carpet, and people will come in white 'shylabas'; they will take off their shoes, and wash themselves before entering to hear God's Word. We'll burn perfume (incense). The person who will read the Bible will sit on a floor but higher than others [...].*" He had described a mosque! Once the foreign friend invited Mohamed to go to the Anglican Church in Casablanca, he adapted immediately to the western worship style. Later he understood that if he continued to go to a public church, he would be at risk.

When churches are planted by non-locals, they borrow foreign models during the first period and may continue to carry them on. It takes time until the *Church "wears local dress*" and develops worship and liturgies that correspond to cultural patterns and are more adapted to meet peoples' desires and loves. The Early Church gives a good example of cultural adaptation adapting the worship and teaching styles of the synagogue: reading the Sacred Text, preaching, singing psalms and hymns and breaking bread.

How to be church in a context of persecution, where it is forbidden for Christians of Muslim background to join 'public cults'? Which style of liturgy should be reproduced in the context of limited liberties?

Texts and Globalization

The power of digital forms of interconnections have been evident during the regional upheaval, especially in Tunisia, where women and men organized forms of resistance. Similarly, through social networks and Christian programs many people in North Africa are getting in contact with Christian faith. The Word of God can be shaped differently, to new audiences without frontiers. This is seen in the cases of Lilia, and Gael, two students who heard about Jesus through TV Christian programs and online forums. Both decided to go to a public church meeting in the capital city of Tunis. Lilia said, "I *was impressed with the level of spirituality and modesty of the preacher, who discussed the difference between Islamic and Christian teachings. After a year reading the Bible and attending the Church service, I decided to follow Al-Messiah [...]*

The use of storytelling and Gospel audio-cassettes has a double justification: first, people like tales and proverbs, because they talk in a practical way and facilitate application to daily life; and second, illiteracy among women is still high, especially in rural areas. Furthermore, memorizing Scriptures should be emphasized as a culturally adapted form of learning.

> Mahdia lives with her family in the mountains of Sidi Bouzid. She has three children; two of them are physically disabled. She has never been to school, but she needed to do something to change her family's situation, so she started a micro-project financed by a Christian organization. One day, Ilse visited her to see how the project was going. The conversation turned to spiritual issues. Ilse told her a story about Sidna Aïssa Al Messiah. Mahdia wanted to know more, then she received an audio cassette of the Gospel in derija and a small cassette recorder to hear it. She loved to listen to Gospel stories while watching over her sheep. One day she was in the mountains with one of her disabled children, and a big storm arrived. She prayed to Sidna Aïssa to stop the storm until she arrived home… and the Lord did it! She was excited when she said to Ilse "I believe in Al Messiah, he hears me and helps me!" God's Word came to Mahdia in the middle of the desert hills!

The Bible, as a book, should not only have symbolic relevance in lives of believers but also be given an honorable physical place and treatment, including the way that it is handled because the Word links with the Author, who is the Awesome, the Holy One and the Greatest.

Music and Belonging

Music is, in some Christian communities, a sign of contextualization of the Gospel. The style of music should be 'part of the heart' of the people, and lyrics should convey appropriate values and doctrine. Worship Music helps to implant the Gospel in our bones,[14] and because Music is formative, it should transmit an appropriate theology based in God's Word.

Today, globalization and the crossroad of people produce hybridization of styles of worship. Some identify Christian worship with Western culture and completely reject the Gospel because of that. Others are attracted by a Western style of music and enjoy Christian multicultural fellowship. Nevertheless, as Moyra notes, the development of local worship is one important factor of church growth. The Tunisian Church has appreciated the development of a local style of worship in "Voices of Carthage" with a local sound.[15] Furthermore, 'doing' church should be adapted to respond to a sensible and changing context and to hardship, seeking alternative forms of worship, having flexibility in forms and spaces for fellowship. The centrality of God's Word alongside indigenous worship create significances and shape the lives of those who are discovering God's way.

Indeed, many questions emerge when considering this important subject like: What kind of worship should be adopted in house-churches? How many people can meet in a house without attracting attention? Should songs be translated or created in their own national language and dialects? ... These are questions that should be responded to locally.

Conclusion

Moyra explored the complex process of the formation of identities among women in Islam and raised how communal allegiance constrains personal choices and practices, as well as the importance of right and adapted (contextual) models and liturgies in order to form a *telos*.

In this paper, we have seen that God's grace and love confers an identity that is not based on classifications of gender status, class or merit, but which conveys to new Christians a sense of dignity and self-worth. People are enriched by this new identity as child of God belonging to God's family, it doesn't mean to break family allegiances or personal identity, but to prioritize

---

[14] James K. A. Smith How Worship Works: Implications for Practice – - "Imagining the Kingdom" https://www.youtube.com/watch?v=69ybkrbExb4, consulted 29/07/2015.
[15] http://lavoixdecarthage.com/en/songs/voiceofcarthage#p

telos in God. Thus, Church Community is relevant, as an extended loving family, caring for people through welcoming fellowship and supportive service, and in this way to avoid isolation, so people can feel as part of the imagined Christian Ummah, belonging to a Community that exceeds the temporal situation, with an eternal perspective. This is more relevant where people are confronted by social and political instability, pauperization and displacement. Church has the challenge to respond in practical and holistic ways, with a contextual theology of suffering to help people to face persecutions and hardships.

In my response, I underline sociological shifts in North Africa and in 'Arab' families in MENA region that modified women' status and gender issues, which are changing cultural trends. Even if the family is the primary model for women, as Moyra argues, other factors also influence the construction of identities, like social networks, digital media, and globalized values and ways of being. Thus, the models are not unique, but versatile and fluctuating. 'When narratives or liturgies collide, when identities and allegiances clash' , the grace and love of Christ restores and motivates to (re)think our own identity and inspires us to tell another story. This internal transformation can be experimented in discipleship through genuine relationships of sacrificial love. The community Church should accompany new Christians building-up their new identity in intimate relationship with Christ through teaching (kerygma), fellowship (koinonia), and service (diakonia), with liturgies of bipolar, *inward* and *outward,* orientations (Bosch, 1991:119).

The 'Word became flesh' in a context; our challenge is 'fleshing out' the Gospel in our own societies.

References

Araujo, Alex. 'Globalization and World Evangelism', pp. 57 - 70 in *Global Missiology for the 21st Century: The Iguazzu Dialogue*. Edited by W. Taylor. Grand Rapids: Baker Academic, 2000.

Auge, Marc. *Le sens des autres: Actualité de l'anthropologie*. Paris: Fayard, 1994.

BECKER, Howard S. *Outsiders: Studies in the Sociology of Deviance*. New York: Free Press, 1966.

Bosch, David. *Transforming Mission: Paradigm Shifts in Theology of Mission.* American Society of Missiology Series, N°16. New York: Orbis, 2004.

Boissevain, Katia. « Le baptême adulte de chrétiens tunisiens: rituel public d'un engagement privé », *Cahiers d'études du religieux. Recherches interdisciplinaires* [Online], Numéro spécial | 2014, mis en ligne le 22 septembre 2014, consulté le 01 juillet 2015. URL: http://cerri.revues.org/1408.

Castel, Robert. *Les métamorphoses de la question sociale. Une chronique du salariat.* Paris: Fayard, 1995.

Courbage, Youssef. "Familles et politiques publiques dans le Monde Arabe", in *Institut d'études de l'Islam et des sociétés du monde musulman* (IISMM), Avril 5, 2013.

Charrad, Munira. 'State and Gender in the Maghrib'. pp. 62 - 71 in *Women and Power in the Middle East.* Edited by Suad Joseph and Susan Slymovics. Philadelphia: University of Pennsylvania Press, 2001.

Chekir, Hafidha. Conférence *Les droits des femmes et les spécificités culturelles: l'attitude des Etats arabes* in the seminary Genre, politiques et sexualités. Orient/Occident, 31/03/2011, Paris: Fondation Maison des Sciences de l'Homme (FMSH).

Haut-Commissariat au Plan, Royaume du Maroc, "Principales résultats de la prévalence de la violence à l'égard des femmes [Online: http://www.hcp.ma/downloads/Violence-a-l-egard-des-femmes_t13077.html, Retrieved on 05/08/2015.

Joseph, Suad and Slyomovics, Susan (eds.) *Women and Power in the Middle East.* Philadelphia: University of Pennsylvania Press, 2001.

Mernissi, Fatema, *Islam et démocratie*. Paris: Albin Michel, 2010.

Samuel, Vinay and Sugden, Chris (eds.). *Mission as Transformation: A Theology of the Whole Gospel*. Oxford: Regnum Books International, 1999.

Smith, James K. A., *How Worship Works: Implications for Practice*, "Imagining the Kingdom" https://www.youtube.com/watch?v=69ybkrbExb4, consulted 29/07/2015.

Stahl, Paul Henri. Soi-même et les autres: quelques exemples balkaniques, in Lévi-Strauss, C. *L'identité*, pp. 287 – 303. Paris: PUF, 1977.

Sugden, Chris. 'What is Good about Good News to the Poor?' Pages 236 – 260 in Samuel, Vinay and Sugden, Chris (eds) *Mission as Transformation: A Theology of the Whole Gospel*. Oxford: Regnum Books International, 1999.

World Bank. Regional Highlights World Development Indicators 2012 – World Bank data.worldbank.org/data-catalog/world-development-indicator

4

Do Muslim Women Need Saving? Cultural, Theological, and Missiological Perspectives

Do Muslim Women Need Saving?
Cultural, Theological, and Missiological Perspectives

Miriam Adeney

How do we speak God's Word with our Muslim sisters? With great respect, and with great confidence.

Too often, Christian witnesses have not respected Muslim cultures. We have suffered from an inadequate theology of culture. Furthermore, spurred by our Western modern value of pragmatic efficiency, we have defined Muslim women as victims needing help. Then, for solutions, we have promoted salvation from sin along with expanded human rights and education, health care, and microenterprise programs.

In anthropologist Laila Abu-Lughod's book *Do Muslim Women Need Saving,* she warns against emphasizing Muslim women's problems more than their strengths. She laments "pulp non-fiction" books, like *Infidel* by Ayaan Hirsi Ali, which select negative data to cultivate "sexual titillation and moral horror…a gendered Orientalism…subjects known only by deficits…with the remedies known in advance by others" (2013,:88, 223). Do not be quick to interfere, she advises. "Rather than clicking on a website to donate $10, or flying to distant lands to bring school supplies to girls, and certainly before calling in military troops, we should take time to listen" (2013:202).

If we do, we will see that Muslim women are not primarily victims. In many spheres, they are active decision-makers who demonstrate competency and creativity. Their cultures are normal systems that provide functioning patterns for family life, finance, governance, art, etc. Most women in Bible times lived in cultures with similar laws and customs regarding women.

Yes, Muslim cultures are marred by patterns of exploitation and idolatry. So are our own cultures. Therefore, we are in no position to bring "civilization" to Muslim women. We just bring Christ. He is as much a shock to us as to them. Yet Christ did not come to annihilate their cultures. He came to fulfill their communities' highest aspirations.

We begin with sincere respect for their heritage, their families, their communities, their markets, their celebrations. We speak humbly. At the same time, we speak with confidence in the power of God. "Aggressoletics" – speaking with conviction – may be more attractive than apologetics among Muslims.[1] We therefore communicate with vigour, with joy in the power of God, and with deep respect.

---

[1] Personal communication from an Egyptian.

Social-Relational Patterns in Culture

We show respect by paying attention to our friends' cultures. Every culture is composed of patterns of meanings, organized into social- relational patterns, material-economic patterns, and worldview patterns. Yet these cultural patterns are not all-powerful. Within each culture there is movement, variety and even contradiction. Human beings make choices, sometimes unexpected ones. As Kierkegaard observed, every person is an exception. Still, although cultural patterns are not absolute, they do provide order and meaning – cognitive frameworks, associational ties, familiar action patterns, and memorable celebrations with tastes and aromas and music and performances and joyful crowds. Cultures provide individuals with a personal place in the long human story.

Some cultural patterns empower women more than others do. In the social-relational sphere, for example, the bilateral kindred of Southeast Asia empower women more than the patrilineages of East Asia, South Asia, and the Arab world. Such patrilineages work well for creating corporations. They do not work so well to strengthen the position of women. But where bilateral kindred are strong, as in the Philippines and Indonesia, daughters and sons matter equally. They inherit equally. Women can speak up in councils, and do. When they are educated, women are active in all the professions – even women with ten children. Admittedly, Spanish Christian and Asian Muslim powers brought codes and customs that limited women. Still, a great many Southeast Asian women are managers, doctors, bankers, professors, pharmacists and leaders in their families and communities, empowered from childhood because of their bilateral kindred family systems.

Aisha and Faridah are middle-aged sisters in Southeast Asia who live in the Muslim communities where they were born. Both follow Jesus. Aisha has brought about twenty people to Jesus, and Faridah has started a chain that includes about fifty disciples. These sisters demonstrate how the Spirit gives wisdom to believers with very little training.

Aisha is the cook and Faridah irons clothes for a foreign family. The household studies the Bible together once a week. Afterwards, one of the women will take the Scripture pages that they have studied and make copies at a local copy shop. That weekend when they go home to their villages they will use those pages as they lead Bible studies and prayer and praise meetings.

When Faridah is in the village, the men who drive motorcycles with sidecars come to her door every morning. They ask for prayer, because their jobs carry risk and they sense that God is with her.

Faridah has developed prayers that teach theology. First, she prays the Lord's Prayer over the drivers. Then she prays a Trinitarian prayer that she has devised:

> In the name of God, the Creator, the Sustainer, the Judge, the Holy, the Loving, the One True God who comes close to us in the person of Jesus…I ask blessing on these drivers this day.

> In the name of Jesus the Messiah, the Word of God, who had a virgin birth, who died for our sins, who rose in power, who will come back to judge, who can protect us from the powers of darkness, who calls us to be his disciples...I ask blessing on these drivers this day.
>
> In the name of the Holy Spirit...

Every morning Faridah teaches through her prayers.

After villagers believe and evidence sustained commitment, the women baptize them, pouring water on them three times, once to mark forgiveness of sins, once to mark the righteousness Jesus gives and once to announce that sin no longer has dominion over them.

Ten men from this chain of disciples have moved across the country to work in a big construction project for a year. They take turns returning home to visit their families and bring the month's salaries to all the wives. In exchange, the wives send back ten copies of the Bible texts they have been studying. As a result, the church is growing on the opposite side of the country. Aisha and Faridah have been empowered by their bilateral kindred structure to be channels of God's grace to their people.

Social-relational patterns – family and community arrangements – are profoundly important for Muslims, however these are structured. Women do not make decisions in isolation, Abu-Lughod notes. Individual rights are balanced by the wellbeing of the group. Healthy living means consultancy and concessions, expressed in culturally specific ways. "Choice" and "consent" will be affected by context. Autonomy is a fantasy. If individualistic Western NGOs suggest otherwise, "we ought to have as little dogmatic faith in secular humanism as in Islam" Abu-Lughod comments (2013: 46).

Yet sometimes, individual Muslims come to Jesus by themselves, apart from their group. Then their choices should be honoured and their lives and faith nurtured. At the same time, though the group may disapprove, some kin may continue to provide community for these Jesus-followers, even in patrilineal societies. Vahida, for example, trusted Jesus while she was a university student in India. After her graduation, her father began to arrange a marriage for her, as was his responsibility. Vahida requested Viju for her husband. This made her father furious because, while their families were business acquaintances, Viju's family was Christian. Vahida's father confiscated her Bible and sent her off to live with her aunt. However, her brother stood by her. In time, he was able to persuade their father, and Vahida and Viju did marry.

Group relationship and identity are important. Whenever possible, these connections should be respected. However, they do not determine destiny. A culture is a complex continuum, continually changing. There may be space for negotiation.

Consider this case. In North Africa, several professional single women became followers of Jesus. The Arab fellowship group met on Fridays, the normal day for worship. Yet on Fridays, these young women felt that they should be at home to help their mothers prepare food and serve guests. They requested that the worship meeting time be changed. The fellowship's male leaders disagreed. "This is part of the cost of following Christ," the elders decided. So the young women left the Arab church and moved down the street to the French-language international church. Although they valued the Arab group, they had other options. Culture is not a straitjacket.

Worldview Patterns in Culture

Social-relational patterns matter. So do economic-material patterns, although we will not discuss them in this paper.[2] Worldview patterns – values, beliefs, ideas – are equally crucial.

There is variation in Muslim women's worldviews. Some are strict fundamentalist Wahabis. Others are syncretistic folk believers or Sufis who visit shrines and revere Muhammad as an eternal cosmic power. Others are professionals who identify most with modern scientific understandings. Others are victims of war, and their thinking is dominated by suffering. Others are pleasure-seekers who delight in transgressing discretely against Muslim standards. Each of these groups of women prioritize values differently.

In spite of these differences, we will suggest three broad themes in Muslim women's worldviews that may provide bridges for communicating the gospel across these categories.

What women can do for their communities.

A few years ago, I was asked to speak at an all-day evangelistic picnic for Muslim women in Indonesia.[3] Sixty women arrived. I began:

> *Assalamu Alaikum.*
>
> It is an honor to talk with you about women.
>
> Why do we exist? Let us begin with Eve (Siti Hauwa).
>
> Nabi Adam and Siti Hauwa were created by God to be his *khalifa* – to take care of his earth.
>
> That is why we too were created. We do not exist for our own pleasure.
>
> We are created to worship God,
>
> To take care of our community,
>
> To be God's *khalifa* in our neighborhoods.

---

[2] The material-economic dimension of culture affects women significantly, and must be studied thoroughly. Missiologist Karen Scott has demonstrated the relationship between empowering women through microloans and their growth as Christian disciples in her dissertation, *The Influence of Community Development and Micro-Credit Programs on the Status and Role of Rural Bangladeshi Muslim Women: A Paradigm for Discipleship*, Fuller Theological Seminary, 2007.

[3] This evangelistic women's picnic event was organized by a network of Indonesian and foreign Christians who had sustained relationships with Muslim women.

> Now, we cannot do this alone. We need each other's help. That is how women usually have contributed to their communities. Working together.
>
> In the world of Islam, there are many kinds of women – rich and poor, fundamentalist and folksy, noisy and quiet, calm and fussy.
>
> Consider rich women, for example. Of course there are many lazy rich women, selfish, rich women.
>
> But there are others who realize they have been blessed in order to be a blessing. They serve their communities.
>
> In the nation of Tunisia, 25% of the judges are women…

I went on to talk about Bedouin women, and poor urban women who were recipients of microloans and used them well, African market women's cooperatives, segregated Saudi women serving women clients, even courageous Afghan women educators. I concluded:

> So here we have seen rich women, poor women, nomad women, and segregated women all learning to take care of their communities.
>
> This is our calling as well.
>
> Why do we exist?
>
> To worship God, to care for his earth, and to bless our neighborhoods.
>
> *Assalamu Alaikum.*

The women divided into groups and excitedly talked about how they could improve their own immediate environments. Eventually we spread banana leaves on the floor, set out our potluck lunch offerings, and feasted. Songs and games followed. Then once more I began:

> *Assalamu Alaikum.*
>
> This afternoon I would like to tell you the story of Habiba, a woman from Egypt.
>
> This morning we talked about how we women can bless our communities.
>
> Why women are important to one another.
>
> There is power in women working together. Power for good.
>
> Our neighborhoods have so many needs. Jobs. Housing. Water. Education for the children. Health for our bodies. Peace in our families. Tranquil hearts.
>
> Now we women, as we work together, may be able to overcome some of these needs. Together we have strength.
>
> At the same time, we ourselves also struggle. We sin. We become discouraged. We cry.
>
> It is true that we can help our communities. At the same time, we ourselves need help. We need encouragement. Forgiveness. Empowering.
>
> We need to know God truly as merciful and compassionate.
>
> Habiba is an Egyptian woman who wanted to help her community. She came from a very religious family. At the age of seven she was veiled…

Then I told the story of a socially active Egyptian woman who found God's justice and righteousness, mercy and compassion in Jesus. She experienced new birth, and was empowered to serve her society even more. I concluded:

We are created to be God's *khalifa.*

Yet, we must admit, in ourselves we are very inadequate.

How can we bless our communities

Unless first of all we fall on our knees and cry out to God

until he pours his blessing on us?

After that picnic, several women joined Bible studies. Some have come to faith in Jesus as Lord. The concept of bridging as something they can do for their communities caught the women's attention.

The Mercy of God

Smart women realize that we need all the help we can get. We are not victims, but troubles sometimes pile up until we are almost crushed. Then we find ourselves crying out, "Have mercy!" This is the second theme in Muslim women's worldviews that can be a bridge for the gospel. For Muslims, the mercy of God is a key concept. They speak of it every day – *al Rahman, al Rahim,* the mercy and compassion of God. We experience God's mercy as He blesses us with family and friends, with the beauties and produce of nature, and with his Word transmitted through his holy prophets. Muslims consider Jesus to be one of those prophets, an expression of the mercy of God.

But,I say to Muslim friends, the mercy of God extends further and is more radical than we imagined. I recite John 1:1-14 about how the eternal Word of God took on human form and lived among us. This is the great mercy of God – not only to create the universe and hold it all together, not only to maintain human history to its final conclusion, not only to communicate with us through prophets and scriptures and the designs of nature, but most of all the mercy of God is expressed when God comes close to us in the person of Jesus, enters into our human vulnerability and pain, and then explodes out the other side of death. This is amazing mercy, and it is the kind of mercy we need.

The Substitutionary Lamb

Two years ago, I was invited to speak to a women's conference in a mosque in the U.S. During my talk, I told a story that is both in the Bible and the Quran:

Ibrahim (Abraham) had a son who was his joy.

But one day God said to Ibrahim, I want you to show your loyalty to me, I want you to sacrifice your son.

In the religions at that time, people did offer their children as sacrifices to their gods.

So Ibrahim obeyed. He prepared to kill his son.

> Then God said, "Stop! I see your heart. I see your obedience. I myself will provide an animal for the sacrifice. God did provide an animal, and Ibrahim offered that.
>
> Every year the *Id al Adha* feast celebrates this. Abraham's son did not have to die because God provided a sacrifice.

The women all smiled, because they had just cooked for this feast. I continued:

> Now what happened to Ibrahim's son points to Jesus.
>
> In the gospel, Jesus is called the lamb of God.
>
> The gospel says he died so that we human beings do not have to pay for our own evil.
>
> He died in our place.
>
> God *provided* a sacrifice by becoming the sacrifice.
>
> But death could not hold him. God absorbed death into himself and burst right out of it. God made death insignificant. Because – of course – God is great. *Allahu akbar!*
>
> God is so great that he can afford to be tender. Vulnerable. Loving.
>
> This is the true greatness of God.
>
> This is why women can cry out "Have mercy!" and find grace to help in time of need.

One woman came up to me after that talk and asked, "Did I hear you right? Did you really say that Jesus died for *us?"* This was amazing good news to her.

Here we have seen three themes that tie into Muslim women's worldviews: (1) helping our communities (2) experiencing God's mercy, and (3) connecting with the sacrificial lamb. Other themes include healing (physical and emotional), visions and dreams, and – for some – liberation from poverty and injustice. Face-to-face prayer and sharing the Bible remain extremely powerful bridges, particularly Bible stories of women and even more the stories of Jesus. In other words, if we want to be effective witnesses, our first call is to be women of God, his Spirit, and his Word.

Teaching and Learning Patterns in Culture

How should the Word be shared for greatest effectiveness? What teaching methods or media should be used with Muslim women? There is a South Asian community where two foreign women ministered for thirty years. Over that time, 640 Muslims came to faith in Christ. Most of these Jesus-followers have stayed true, and a number of the youth have grown up to become pastors. Memorization of the Bible has been key. New believers were required to learn 34 specific verses from the gospel of John. Oral learners picked these up from other believers. As a result, they felt that they owned the message. It was inside them. Some have become excellent evangelists, even though they are illiterate.

(Through contests with prizes, literate teenagers in this community have been inspired to memorize whole epistles!)

Amid a variety of media, curricula, and discipleship programs, simple memory of Scripture should not be marginalized. Eunice, who lives in a very dangerous city, has a reputation for reciting Scripture beautifully in the local language. At gatherings of her Muslim friends, she will be called to stand and recite, which she does with aplomb. By contrast, Myrna saw several young women friends jailed for their faith, and mourned that she had taught them through inductive Bible studies rather than Scripture memory. "Their Bibles were taken away! But if they had memorized the Scirpture, they would still have God's Word with them in their cells!"

Local oral art styles and performance etiquette should be noted when we prepare to teach. Who tells stories in this society? Where and when? Do people of different ages or social classes or genders discuss matters together, or do they need separate groups? And what about art style? Many cultures have sophisticated multidimensional criteria for oral genres. Consider Bedouins. Whether they are male or female,

> Bedouins are sensitive to the graces and evocative power of oral textual elements such as sound, alliteration, intonation, and rhythm...metaphors and new images...even familiar and ordinary images...derive great connotative richness from subliminal intertextual comparisons. Individuals know so many poems that each new one undoubtedly evokes image-traces and feeling-traces from others with shared words, phrases, or themes.. (Abu-Lughod, 1988:173)

Stories, poems, and songs are arenas where a multiplicity of meanings collide. We may never master these arts, but we can acknowledge their richness and keep learning, keep alert to the connotations. This will enhance the quality of our teaching.

Contextualized *methods* are not enough, however. Comprehensive, balanced biblical *content* must be planned. There is so much biblical ignorance, so much superficial and skewed understanding among Jesus' people around the world. John Stott once said, "All our preaching, week in and week out, should gradually unfold the 'whole counsel of God' and so contribute to the development of Christian minds in the congregation." If we are teaching Muslim-background women, we have a similar call. From Genesis to Revelation, from God to Jesus to the Holy Spirit to human nature to the church to last things, what do they know? Balanced teaching of the whole counsel of God must be our goal, not just snippets of stories, as we speak the Word respectfully and confidently with our sisters.

Maximizing Missional Impact

Finally, if these ideas matter, how do we increase the impact of women's voices in missiological circles? Consider the experiences of David, Kathy, and Janice.

"Is it right for single women missionaries to serve in Muslim countries?" David asked me. A Central American mission leader, he had just returned from visiting 70 Latin American missionaries scattered across India. He found that some Latin sending churches were withdrawing their single women and replacing them with married couples. In one case, two women had served for thirteen years. They spoke the language and their ministry appeared to be effective. But they were being called home and in their place an inexperienced husband and wife were being sent out.

My student Kathy hoped to be a missionary among Muslims. One summer she was part of a short-term team to a country where a well-known missiologist served. Having read his books on Muslim ministry, she hoped to meet him. But when her team advisor tried to arrange the meeting, the missiologist asked, "Tell me something. Is she engaged? Or does she have a boyfriend?"

"No," the advisor said.

"Well, let her bring her fiancé, and then I'll meet her," the missiologist said. He had no time for a single woman candidate.

Kathy is not in Muslim ministry today. Nor is Janice. When Janice was serving on a short-term team in a Muslim country, the leader told her, "Janice, your main ministry will be in the homes and neighborhoods, because that's where the women are." Yet Janice knew the head of the department of engineering at the national university was a woman. Who would reach such women?

Today Janice and Kathy both have Ph.D.s and are making a contribution in the world, but not in the field of Muslim missions, partly because missiologists blocked them.

To their credit, these male missiologists aimed for contextualization. Since it looked like men were the leaders in Muslim communities, the missiologists focused here. In so doing, however, they missed (1) the dynamic worlds of Muslim women and (2) the realities of change, negotiation, and confrontation in the Muslim world. Incidentally, we women sometimes overlook this dynamic, reality, too. For example, in some countries we may be distressed about female genital mutilation. Rather than setting up our own protest project, we should investigate whether there is a national women's group that is confronting this. We ought to join them, even if they are Muslims. This will honor the culture, as well as providing us with new friendships.

How, then, can women's voices in missiological circles be encouraged? There are several practical steps. We must participate in general missiology conferences. We must speak up graciously and articulately on topics on which we are informed. We must volunteer for projects, especially writing projects. In churches, in parachurch events, and in civic events, we must volunteer to talk on appropriate topics (like immigration) and must write and publish in diverse venues. We must study how to do these things with excellence, and must do them habitually. Learning marketing techniques may help.

We must take initiative to converse informally with male missiologists, and must present a serious and positive mien so that we are perceived as valuable and competent conversation partners. Toward that end, we must keep abreast of missiological and general journals in order to understand current theory. We would do well to cultivate good relationships with senior missiologists (male or female) so that we can ask them to make introductions or open doors for us on occasion. We must learn how to procure grants from donors. (Getting a grant greatly impresses male colleagues). We must choose our battles, and not worry about small slights.[4]

For mutual encouragement, wisdom, and contacts, a network of women can pursue these goals together. An example is the North American Institute of Indigenous Theological Studies, which is a program of evangelical American/Canadian Indians. Ten years ago a handful of Indians from different tribes across the continent decided that if they were going to lead their peoples into a cutting-edge, contextualized Christian future, several would need to get Ph.D.s. At least six began Ph.D. programs, both men and women. At least two have finished so far. Meanwhile they started an annual conference, resulting in periodic publications of serious papers, and procured grants to support this. After almost ten years, NAITTS found a physical home when George Fox University welcomed it as an independent part of their M.A. program in 2013.

Another example of the power of a likeminded network is Mary Webb's humble Cent Society in Boston in 1800. This eventually gave birth to a movement of 40 missions founded by women, governed by women, financed by women, supporting 2,500 women missionaries, 6,000 indigenous Bible women, and hundreds of schools and hospitals and Bible teaching programs throughout Asia and Africa. Still other examples are the communities of women who were drawn together by Mariam Bawardy and Marie Alphonsine Bhattas to serve the needy in God's name. In May 2015, these two Palestinian nuns were canonized by Pope Francis. They are the Catholic Church's first Arabic-speaking saints. The centers they founded stretch from Egypt to Syria to Bethlehem and emphasize prayer, literacy, children, the elderly, and health. As we encourage female voices in missiological circles, we too may find it useful to cultivate a network of likeminded women.[5]

Do Muslim Women Need Saving?

What is a woman? Property? A sex object? Cheap labor? A cook and housekeeper? A mother for some man's children? A community connector and stabilizer? Or, more negatively, a costly bit of baggage? Or a dangerous spiritual pollutant?

None of these definitions is adequate. Rather, we must view a women as a person made in the image of God, potentially liberated by Jesus' death and

---

[4] However, we should not assume that education will lead men to be more open-minded about women in leadership. On the contrary, when churches move from pioneering to consolidating phases, women tend to be marginalized. That sociological dynamic simply makes our task more challenging.

[5] Christians for Biblical Equality is a Jesus-centered, biblically-based, international network with many curricular and human resources.

resurrection, potentially empowered by the Holy Spirit, and commissioned for active service in God's world.

Although historic theologians have marginalized women, Jesus affirmed women. His story opens with the faith of a woman, Mary. Soon after his birth, the prophetess Anna witnessed about him. As an adult, Jesus commended a woman named Mary for focusing on spiritual things, and her sister Martha for giving words to one of the very first christological confessions. He commended another Mary for her courage in anointing his feet. He served Peter's mother-in-law, a woman taken in adultery, Jairus' daughter, a woman with a flow of blood, the Samaritan woman at the well, the widow of Nain, and a woman crippled by a spirit for 18 years.

Through it all, he never demeaned women. He never put them down. Instead, his stories show women making choices, such as the woman who lost a coin, the widow who donated two cents, the persistent widow, the wise and foolish bridesmaids, the woman using yeast, the queen of the South who will rise in judgement on this generation, and two women who are grinding grain together when the Messiah returns.

Women were important figures at the cross, and women were the first to receive the news of the resurrection. Women are woven throughout the story of Jesus.

Do women need saving? Yes, if the Savior is someone like Jesus. As we seek to understand our Muslim sisters' social-relational patterns, material-economic patterns, and worldview patterns, as we speak God's Word respectfully and confidently in their contexts, and as we nurture skills to increase women's voices in missiological circles, we will do well to keep our eyes on Jesus.

References

Abu-Lughod, Laila. *Do Muslim Women Need Saving?* Boston: Harvard University Press, 2013.

Abu-Lughod, Laila. *Veiled Sentiments: Honor and Poetry in a Bedouin Society.* Berkeley: University of California Press, 1988.

Scott, Karen. The Influence of Community Development and Micro-Credit Programs on the Status and Role of Rural Bangladeshi Muslim Women: A Paradigm for Discipleship, Pasadena: Fuller Theological Seminary, 2007.

Do Muslim Women Need Saving? Cultural, Theological, and Missiological Perspectives Response 1

Farhana Nazir with Margaret Powell

Do Muslim women need saving? Miriam Adeney affirms the need for all women to be saved through the Saviour, Jesus Christ. God has created all women (and men) in his image; he has given his daughters gifts for use in his mission. Therefore, their value to God and standing before God transcends their culture and religion.

The theological perspectives outlined in Miriam's paper (namely the faith Muslim women have in God's mercy; the substitutionary sacrifice of Jesus Christ; God's grace) are powerful insights. However, I would like to examine the cultural and missiological perspectives more closely and broadly.

Miriam reflects on the book by anthropologist Laila Abu-Lughod (*Do Muslim Women Need Saving?),* who argues against the need to help Muslim women because of the sexual culture, morality and gendered Orientalism that characterises descriptions of Muslim culture. Miriam claims that Muslim women should not be regarded primarily as victims who only need to be given civilization and dignity. According to her, Muslim culture deserves our consideration despite the cultural pattern not being absolute in terms of 'providing individuals with a personal place in the long human story.' Miriam notes that within Muslim culture there are cultural patterns that do empower women, e.g., some Southeast Asian cultural patterns empower woman more than East Asia, South Asia, and Arab culture. I wish to examine this supposition more closely.

In many countries, cultural values are shared between Muslim and Christian female groups and communities of South Asia (India, Pakistan, and Bangladesh). Among such communities, there are various cultural values that are still practiced despite the separation of these countries. For example, some cultural shared practices have been seen in marriage ceremonies and seasonal festivals like Besakhi and Basant, and the *zanana* pattern of providing space to woman. Though some of them have modulated and modernized with the passage of time and migration to western countries, it can be said that the communal acceptance and practice is deeply rooted South Asian history and culture.

In the past, such practices opened the missiological door to the Muslim neighbourhood. *Zanana'* women's place, from the Persian word '*zan*,' a woman, and '*ana*,' place is the part of the house of native women, entirely separated from that occupied by men (Weitbrecht, 1875). It can be said that this cultural practice has been used to bring Christ to the Muslim women. *Zanana* Mission is the best example in the history of South Asia where an opportunity was provided to Christian women (both local and women missionaries) to share the Gospel with Muslim women neighbours.

Today, such practices unite Christian-Muslim communities.

Miriam draws our attention to the political and professional achievements of women in South Asia. For example, Benazir Bhutto, the first woman Prime Minister of Pakistan was popular among Muslim and Christian communities alike. Such examples reveal the empowerment of women through 'bilateral kindred family systems'. The Arab culture could provide further examples.

It is encouraging to see that women who are new believers in Christ in SE Asia not only escape persecution, but are able to use their culture to share with others the good news of Jesus Christ. However, in many parts of the Islamic world, the culture is not so conciliatory and Muslim women who begin to follow Jesus are not so easily accepted or listened to.

Difficulties of interfaith marriages are not easily overcome. The children of a marriage between a Christian man and Muslim woman will be officially seen as Muslim. They commonly suffer a confusion of identity and lack of acceptance in either culture.

Since the 1980s, Pakistani Muslims (male and female) have been legally allowed to convert to any religion, even for marriage. However, in practice, a disgruntled Muslim can easily accuse a Christian of blasphemy with detrimental results for the individuals concerned as well as the Christian-Muslim communities. For example, Robert Fanish (19), a Christian from Jatheki, Sialkot Punjab, known to be having an affair with a Muslim woman, was accused of committing blasphemy in September 2009 (Zafar, 2009:19). Before his arrest, the local church, its religious books and Bibles was set on fire. Fanish was later arrested and, before any trial and inquiry, he was found dead inside his jail cell. The offence of blasphemy and its application to all religious communities such as Ahmadis, Christians, Hindus and some Muslims is one of the most critical issues in Pakistan today.

Disagreements of any kind may be labelled blasphemy in South Asia because mutual cultural respect between Christians and Muslims has been fractured. Accusations of blasphemy may be prompted by insult or personal advantage or animosity. Such friction has become a matter of life and death in Pakistan. This results in the Christian women of South Asia having little confidence to speak with their Muslim neighbours.

I experienced this when I found myself unable to answer questions about Christianity in some religious discussions with fellow students who were Muslim and Ahmadi. We were a happy group of young women enjoying and celebrating Christmas and the Muslim Eid. Of course, I was regarded as the one lacking true religion. They raised various apologetic questions: the Bible is not pure but is an altered and corrupted book; Jesus did not die on the Cross and did not rise from the dead; British and American Christians (with whom I usually associated) do not keep themselves in *parda* veil, and similar issues. I was unable to answer freely and if I attempted to respond, I deliberately kept my voice flat, especially when comparing Christianity to other religions.

I was shocked one day when one of my friends brought me an Urdu book comparing Christianity with Islam. I read the book and saw that many references were misquoted. I took that book back and asked whether misquoting the Bible was a religious offence or not? They were somewhat embarrassed, but no one answered. I was aware that if any Christian had commented in such way with respect to Islam without taking care and respect, the situation would have been different. Misquoting or changing the context of some biblical references was not important to my friends, but it hurt me and changed my life. I began to learn more about Christianity and the social issues Christians face in Pakistan. I started to research the historical causes of religious conflicts among religious communities. I concentrated on how to connect with Muslims and what missiological tools were available in this context.

Further analysis needs to be done when considering mission in a hostile context. The use of culture missiologically may not be as simple or as positive in all Muslim contexts. Where possible there is a need to respect Muslim culture and to use it missiologically as Miriam commends. However where there is no mutual respect using culture missiologically is not possible. In fact, South Asian culture makes gospel proclamation, freedom of belief and the independence and dignity of women more problematic. The society, law, rules and regulations have segregated Christian women from Muslim women and prevent Christian women bringing the Gospel to Muslim women.

As well, church leaders have difficulty in accepting women wholeheartedly in the church. To many leaders it is inappropriate for women to use their gifts in the mission of the church. In addition, Miriam notes that a woman's single status can be an obstacle for mission in an Islamic society. To Miriam, various women in East Asian and South Asian communities have been neglected by the church leaders and have chosen a different vocation (like Janice and Kathy who chose higher educational field rather than mission). However, many highly educated Christian and Muslim women in South Asia are trying to bridge the gap.

What is needed is 'mutual encouragement, wisdom and contacts [with] a network of women [who] can pursue a mission goal together' as Miriam suggests. Here women can realize what they can do for the community. The neighbourhood still needs their help. There may be some parts of Islamic regions where women cannot speak directly about the gospel such as Pakistan but loving their neighbour will be the best missiological approach to show the love of God and Christ.

References

Weitbrecht, Mary, *The Women of India,* (1875) BiblioBazaar, 2009

Zafar, Emmanuel (ed.) *The Minorities' View.* September 2009.

Do Muslim Women Need Saving?
Cultural, Theological, and Missiological Perspectives
Response 2

Ruth Nicholls

Taking her title from Laila Abu-Lughod's book, Miriam Adeney's paper *Do Muslim Women Need Saving?* asks the same question but specifically from *Cultural, Theological and Missiological Perspectives.* However, even with the subtitle the core question needs a context: the word 'saving' conjures up many alternative connotations, so there are plenty of Muslims who, hearing the question from their perspective, would question a woman's need of 'saving'. For Adeney, though, 'saving' finds its meaning and context in the Christian gospel.

Adeney's treatment of the topic is primarily practical, informed by her training, study and experiences as an anthropologist and as a Christian. Whilst from the title one might have anticipated section headings such as culture, theology and mission, the subject is approached in terms of *socio-relational patterns in culture*, *worldview patterns in culture, teaching and learning patterns in culture,* and *maximizing missional impact.* Reflecting the title, her categories are rather more nuanced and focused on specific examples. This is helpful but can limit practical application.

Both Abu-Lughod and Adeney warn of the dangers of stereotyping because it fails to recognise the uniqueness, individuality and distinctiveness of each specific person and situation. Stereotyping can lead to oversimplification of challenges and result in trite solutions to problems. Even so, both Adeney's paper and this response inevitably take something of a generalising approach, whilst drawing on specific examples, to illustrate the application of ideas in specific cultural situations.

Adeney's well-chosen introductory sentence, "Paying attention to our friends' cultures", sets the theme for the section "Social-Relational Patterns in Culture". Within the context of a Southeast Asian Muslim culture, Adeney provides the example of two Christian women who are ministering in effective ways within the limitations of their cultural setting. She shows that respect for a culture requires recognising the decision-making process within that culture. For Muslims decision-making is usually done corporately rather than by an individual alone. The role of the individual and of the group can vary immensely. In some instances an individual decision is affirmed by the group adding its approval. In other situations, the group is the sole decision maker and may not even consult the individual. Consequently, the way a decision is made in any situation may lie anywhere along that continuum. The degree to which the individual accepts the decision of the group also lies somewhere along a continuum, this time ranging between unquestioning submission to active rebellion and disregard. People within a culture play the system: some conform while others push at the boundaries.

Having promoted respect of 'other's cultures' in her first section, in her second section, *Worldview Patterns in Culture,* Adeney narrows her focus. She recognises the great diversity of worldviews, which she identifies as being found in 'values, beliefs, ideas', but in relation to this she chooses 'three broad themes': what women can do for their communities; the mercy of God, and the substitutionary lamb – each of which are applied within a specific Muslim context; Indonesia, an undisclosed country, and North America. Why these three categories were chosen, or the justification for their choice, is not indicated. However, once again Adeney provides practical illustrations of how she uses these themes.

Her third section, *Teaching and Learning Patterns in Culture*, emphasises the 'culture of others' by recognising the distinctive patterns of learning that are associated with oral cultures, with their emphasis on stories, poems and songs, all of which are committed to memory. Again, Adeney is practical. She also indicates that content, that is biblical content, is paramount.

At the beginning of her presentation, Adeney shared Abu-Lughod's wariness of stereotyping in relation to women, especially Muslim women. In the penultimate section, *Maximizing Missional Impact,* she comes back to the topic by considering the difficulty for Christian ministry to Muslim women which arises from of a 'stereotypical' understanding of ministry in Muslim contexts. Such an understanding effectively denies Muslim women the opportunity to be 'brought Christ'. Adeney briefly suggests some ways in which this can be countered.

Finally, Adeney returns to the question *Do Muslim Women Need Saving?* Like Abu-Lughod, Adeney rejects defining their need to be rescued in terms of a reductionist socio-economic characterisation. However, as she indicated from the beginning and has practically suggested throughout her presentation, Adeney insists they must be 'brought to Christ' 'if the Saviour is someone like Jesus'.

So, by reusing the provocative title, *Do Muslim Women Need Saving?* Adeney clearly wants to suggest that there may be another angle to the question that needs consideration. In responding to Adeney's paper, I reflect on her question in terms of cultural context, theological perspectives, and missional response, from that same angle. I then extend the application by placing emphasis on their significance for the primary task of Christian discipleship.

Cultural Context

Adeney's presentation very importantly places each Muslim woman within the dynamic, living context of her specific culture and society, recognising individual uniqueness within that context. As she indicates, from a Christian perspective it is a context, like all contexts, that is marred (by sin) and flawed. However, the degree to which there is 'self-awareness' of how much women and girls are honoured and valued, or not, within the wide diversity of Islamic cultures varies immensely. Some claim that there is 'nothing wrong' on the basis that, through its holy Qur'an and Hadith, Islam has assigned the highest value to women and girls.[1] Indeed, as a Western foreigner who lived in an Islamic country for many years, I was confronted and told on several occasions that it was I who needed saving. I was the one who was to be pitied; who needed to be brought into true freedom and experience the value of being a woman!

On the other hand, the report on *Britain's Forgotten Women* paints a very different picture: one of abuse, forced marriages and isolation. And from another context, Ibu Aisjah Dachlan of Indonesia tells of their hopelessness, lack of education, their lack of rights and voice and at times abuse (van Doorn-Harder, 2006:208; cf., Armstrong 2002:182). The stories of honour killings,[2] female genital mutilation,[3] and child brides[4] are considered by many as devaluing women. Having to live with the sense of shame that you were born a female and not a male, that your freedom is determined by the males in your family, that in some cases of law your voice has only half the value of that of a male, strongly suggests that many women in the Islamic world are offered and experience very limited 'value' and 'worth'.

---

[1] See for example Badawi, Jamal, *The Status of Women in Islam*, https://islamswomen.com/articles/status_of_women_in_islam.php. Cited 3 July, 2016

[2] For example: "Honour killings in Pakistan are more common than one might assume. The Pakistan Human Rights Commission 2014 annual report states that more than 3,000 women (PDF) have died in so-called honour killings in Pakistan since 2008. The Aurat Foundation, a rights group in the country puts estimates even higher and maintains that these incidents claim the lives of 1,000 women every year." *Defending Pakistani Women against Honour Killings* http://www.aljazeera.com/indepth/opinion/2016/03/defending-pakistani-women-honour-killings-160307075135769.html cited 9 May, 2017.

[3] More than 200 million girls and women alive today have experienced FMG in 30 countries in Africa, the Middle East and Asia where FGM is concentrated World Health Organisation Fact Sheet, http://www.who.int/mediacentre/factsheets/fs241/en/ cited 9 May, 2017. However, it must noted, that FGM is not restricted to Islamic societies. Nevertheless, while the Qur'an is silent on the topic, there appear to be Hadith which suggest the practice. On the other hand, there are those that question that interpretation (cf. Haifaa A. Jawad, *The Rights of Women in Islam, An Authentic Approach,* p58).

[4] While countries with the highest prevalence of child marriage are concentrated in Western and Sub-Saharan Africa, due to population size, the largest number of child brides reside in South Asia. https://www.icrw.org/child-marriage-facts-and-figures/ cited 9 May, 2017. While child marriage is not limited to some Islamic societies it is a common practice in others.

So, the Islamic socio-cultural context of which Adeney speaks is complex and multifaceted, impacting the lives of individual Muslim women to varying extents. Among those women, some genuinely seek to understand the Qur'an and its injunctions, desiring to live a life that reflects that of the prophet, and\or his wives, which for them is the essence of being a Muslim (Dale, 2016:83-110). Some, within the confines of their cultural milieu rise to levels of significance and find their voice within that context: Asma Jahangir, a respected lawyer in Pakistan, was one such example. On the other hand, there are those, some of whom have been influenced by Western feminism, who are challenging traditional interpretations of the Qur'an and Hadith and are exploring the roles of women within the traditional boundaries of Islam (see van Doorn-Harder, 2006; Dale. 2016) as well as creating opportunities to have their own voice.[5] Currently, many are being disturbed and shaken by the rise of ISIS and its brutality toward those who claim to be Muslims.[6]

As Adeney noted, the socio-relational dimension is an important facet of culture for many women in a Muslim context. However, it isn't the only significant dimension. Increasingly, the education-economics dimension is equally, or even more, important, for it can result in women negotiating, exploring and in some cases pushing the boundaries that lie along the community/communal- individual/independent continuum.[7]

Somewhat related to this, is the degree to which Muslim women understandingly participate in their religious heritage. Some give blind adherence to religious traditions and the explanations they are given, while at the other end of the spectrum there are women who are diligently studying the Qur'an and Hadith, including those who are questioning traditional explanations and adopting roles that push the current boundaries. Amongst the most influential are Asma Barlas, Amina Wahud and Fatima Mernissi (van Doorn-Harder, 2006: 207ff; Dale, 2016: 138).

Christian Theological Perspective

Within her explanation of the significance of the cultural context, the most important feature was Adeney's emphasis on the women themselves. These women, as all women, need respect: they need to know that they have value and honour, especially where they are subjected to shame even for being born a woman. From a Christian perspective, every woman needs to know and experience what it is to have been created in the image and likeness of God.

---

[5] *In the Shadow of Islam, The Women's Movement in Iran* lists some thirteen major women's organisations as well as mentioning ten smaller ones.

[6] Dave Cashin, *How ISIS is spreading the Gospel,* Zwemer Centre for Muslim Studies, http://www.zwemercenter.com/articles/page/3/cited 1/12/2016

[7] The micro-financing of women's projects is having a similar impact to that of the formal education of women and the opportunities of taking up various roles within the economic sector.

That is, women are uniquely created: they are precious in God's sight. More than just knowing this, they need also to experience that they are loved by God and that it was for them Jesus died and rose again. Every woman needs to be able to look in the mirror and say "God loves me" (John 3:16; 1 John 4:9-10). Even more importantly, every woman needs to know that, in Jesus Christ, her shame has been taken away and that she is blessed with all the honour associated with His Name. For women who have fears,[8] they need to hear the message "Do not fear". They also need to experience the sure and lasting refuge that a loving Father God can truly offer.

Any Christian who sees their goal as the proclamation of the message to the exclusion of considering those with whom the message is being shared needs to learn again from Jesus. Jesus, who is both the message and the model, had the ability to balance both perspectives. Certainly, in the context of the Christian Gospel, the answer to the question "Do Muslim women need saving?" is 'yes'. However, the Christian theological foundations of that question lie not only in the Christian doctrines of sin and salvation but they also include the reality of Jesus' death on the cross and his resurrection. The Gospel message is not merely that everyone, man and woman, needs to accept what is proclaimed but that they are to participate in the gift of salvation that Jesus Christ offers. It is of primary importance to note that salvation is a gift from God, and is only available through the activity of the Holy Spirit. Human beings cannot save a person from sin. Though God has entrusted to us the message of salvation, ultimately the work of salvation is God's work. We need to also remember that acceptance of the message of salvation is not the endpoint. Sadly, there are those who seem to have made it the goal. Questions like, "How many people have you saved?" or the similar "How many people have you brought to Christ?" perpetuate that focus. Rather, biblically, a person is saved so that they can go on to spiritual maturity or more specifically grow in their relationship with Jesus Christ (Eph 4:11-13; Phil 3:12-16). Using the terms of Eastern Orthodox theology,[9] it is participating in the divine nature (2 Pet 1:4). Arguably, not least because of their proximity to Islam from earliest times, the Eastern Orthodox emphasis on salvation as relationship and experience is a more important emphasis for women from a Muslim background than the western focus of salvation in terms of guilt and righteousness. For Muslim women whose experience means they know what it is to be 'property', who experience shame at many levels, who have many fears, who feel trapped and

---

[8] Some of Muslim women with whom I have interacted have voiced the following fears: their husband taking another wife because they haven't given birth to a son; lack of harmony in the home; sons failing to take advantage of educational possibilities; the effect of the 'evil eye' and/or evil spirits on their home and children; finding good marriage partners for their children; the fear of failing to live 'righteously' and its consequences; the fear of not reaching her potential.

[9] Since much of that Christianity has been lived within a Muslim context that aspect of salvation takes on a greater significance.

bound, the Christian gospel has a powerful message – a message that can speak deep into their hearts. It is a message that brings salvation to the whole of her person.

So, the question "Do Muslim women need saving?" of itself, cannot only come across as reductive in its attitude to an individual woman's culture: it can also fail to recognise the uniqueness of that specific individual woman to whom the gospel is presented.[10] Significantly, Jesus' command to his disciples was not 'go and save'.[11] He commanded his disciples to 'be witnesses' (Matthew 28:18-20; Acts 1:8) and 'to make disciples' (Matthew 28:18-20). Now whilst the testimony of the witness might lead to salvation (but often 'a witness' dies), and is primarily through words, the term is actually a call for the whole of life to reflect that of Jesus Christ. The early Christians were distinguished by their love for one another. That is, their witness was love in action. Alongside this, they were to 'make disciples' (Matthew 28:18-20).

One might ask, 'when were the disciples of the Lord Jesus saved?' It's a question that raises a lot of debate. Similarly, at what point do our Muslim brothers and sisters experience salvation? Is a Muslim saved when he/she begins the journey of discovering what Christianity is about? Is it that moment when they realise that the Bible is the Word of God? Is it when they admit that Jesus is more than a prophet? Is it when they see a vision of a 'man in white'? Surely, a Muslim's journey, be they male or female, is one of a thousand steps. What did Jesus do? He selected a group of people, both men and women, and chose to disciple them. Jesus' method of operation was to faithfully lead his disciples along a road to spiritual maturity.

Missional Response

Do Muslim women need saving? Yes, from a Christian theological perspective they do, but that is not the endpoint. They need discipling, which is to be taught to obey all the Christ has commanded (Matthew 28: 18-20).[12] So how then does one disciple them? In light of our previous discussion the answer must be, as individuals who have been uniquely created in the image, in the likeness of God, living within a dynamic culture with its unique societal shape, who need mentoring on their own journey towards maturity in Christ. Be assured, the Holy Spirit will bring them to a point of salvation when it is the right time for

---

[10] Even a superficial glance of the Gospels shows Jesus ministering to each of the women mentioned in a way that was specific to that woman's need (cf. Matthew 8: 14, 15:21-28; Mark 5:21-43; Luke 7:11-17; John 4).

[11] Jesus did call his disciples to 'fish for people' (cf. Mark 1:17) – fishing of itself does not involve saving; it focuses on gathering in.

[12] It is interesting to note that Islamic teaching also focuses on 'obedience'. Obedience in that context is virtually synonymous with 'imitate' which has the sense of 'mimic' (cf. Dale 2016:84-85). However, the type of 'obedience' that Jesus Christ desires is a 'willing attitude of heart which expresses itself in action'.

that person. Ministry to people begins where they are and encourages them on towards Jesus Christ in a living growing relationship.[13]

This, then, raises the question 'How does one disciple?' In the days of its infancy, the Church itself was learning how to disciple. The only model it had was that of Jesus Christ. Little is written of the processes that He used. Here I sense a touch of God's wisdom. In discipling a person, one needs to respect the spiritual journey which that individual is encountering. That journey is distinct to that uniquely created individual. It is also a journey taking place within a dynamic cultural context. That person needs to grow spiritually and develop Christ-likeness within their own personal, social and cultural context. Because of this, I believe we have not been given a one prescriptive model that fits all. Indeed, I suggest that Paul's letters reflect the ways in which he disciple: if nothing else, those letters reflect the individual-ness of the discipling process. No two letters are alike. Several are similar but each one is different. Still we have been entrusted with the task of discipling, with the Holy Spirit as our instructor and guide. That, of course, calls for the discipler to be walking closely with the Lord, seeking His guidance while responding to the Holy Spirit's promptings in the life of the one they are discipling.

In this respect, Adeney's paper draws attention to one of the most important factors that impacts ministry to individuals within their personal, social and cultural context. It is that of worldview. Worldview is one of the most complex and possibly one of the most difficult aspects of a person's life to fully grasp. The term describes an emotionally grounded, culturally shaped, personally experienced understanding of the world and of life that has been moulded in a particular social milieu, and which is evidenced in the beliefs, attitudes and behaviours that emanate from the very core of a person's being (Kraft, 1996:55-58).[14] It is like the gossamer of a spider's web. At times, it can appear irrational and illogical.

Adeney picked out three aspects of worldview, which she has been able to engage effectively in ministry. Of these, the Christian understanding of *being loved by God* is most notably counter-cultural, giving a woman value and respect in a context where she's often merely the slave, treated as being nine parts sexual desire, with a devalued life story. What does the Word of God say to a woman whose fears and insecurity are growing as she faces an uncertain future as death looms large? What would bring comfort to the woman who has been shamed into feeling that her religious failures have resulted in the ongoing evil eye curses which are plaguing her son's life? It is as we work with women on that one-to-one level, within their cultural context, discipling them on the road of a spiritual journey to Christ that we discover more of their own

[13] *Patterns of Discipleship in the New Testament*, ed. Richard N. Longenecker 1996 identifies the various patterns of discipleship that are found in the New Testament providing in addition an excellent resource for various forms of discipleship.
[14] Charles H Kraft deals more fully with the subject in his book *Worldview for Christian Witness*, 2008.

worldview and in turn can respond scripturally to the needs of their hearts; scratching them, as the saying goes, where they itch. Do Muslim women need saving? Let us rest assured that the Saviour will meet Muslim women at the point in their lives where they seek Him in their need. Without a doubt, the Holy Spirit will engineer the circumstances since the Lord Jesus has left us with the responsibility of witnessing to them. Our responsibility is to encourage them to continue to walk with Him on their personal spiritual journey.

Fostering the Spiritual Journey: Some Specific Proposals

Adeney provides some helpful practical suggestions for fostering a person's spiritual journey toward the Lord Jesus Christ. She is discerning in picking out the significance of orality.

Most Muslim societies are still significantly oral. That orality must be honoured and used to the glory of God and for the spreading of His kingdom. Of course, there are a significant number of women within Muslim communities who have been educated and hold positions of varying importance and significance within universities, business and government: as already acknowledged, whether in relation to variations in religious practices or the recognition of differing education, gifts and abilities, there is no 'catch all' single method of approach to ministering amongst Muslim women. However, there are common practices which can be mirrored. From a religious perspective these include:

- memorizing the Qur'an;
- reciting the creed;
- knowing the prayer liturgies;
- reciting the chants (*dhikr*);
- saying prayers (*du'a*);
- telling stories at group meetings for teaching and discussion.

Adeney emphasised the importance of memorizing Scripture – 'the hiding of God's word in one's heart so one doesn't sin against the Lord' (Psalm 119:11). This Scriptural injunction seems to have largely been lost in Western cultures. However, the memorising of Scripture gives individuals opportunities to meditate and contemplate (Joshua 1:8; Psalm 1:2) on the words they are reciting. As the discipler walks alongside an individual this meditation and contemplation can lead to developing affirmations of faith. These are statements which summarise truths (see attached example based on selected verses from the Psalms) that have been learnt, take the role of credal type statements. Taking the example provided, it is possible to explore with the individual what she understands by 'refuge'; what a 'fortress' means for her and what 'trust' involves. Many verses of the Scriptures read like creedal statements. Such verses can be easily turned into prayers (*du'a*) and, in being recalled over and over, become a '*dhikr*'. '*Dhikr*', which has an important role in Islamic religious life, has as its base meaning, 'remember': essentially it is remembering over, and over again, and for one walking on the Christward journey it can be verses or phrases from the Bible that sheds light on their life path.

Within Islam, the '*salat*' or formal prayer liturgies, create the regular rhythm to their day. Within Christianity, the daily office has for many, and over many years, established the regular rhythm of people's day. For someone who is walking the Christian journey what better way could there be than encouraging the disciple to develop their own daily liturgical practices based on Scripture? If at least some of this can be done in a group format, as happens at some mosques (Dale, 2016), it assists in forming the bond of Christian community, which provides the relationship dimension, expressing the church on earth, that is so important for Christian growth and the development of spiritual gifts. Some might benefit from using the set liturgies that are already part of Christian worship practices, but always with the caveat that, while these provide models, they may not be relevant for the spiritual journey of a specific individual. It ever remains important to respond to where people are. Adeney provides an excellent example of this in the case of the woman who teaches liturgical prayer forms to the 'taxi drivers'. So too let us allow the Holy Spirit to be creative within us, and assist women to create prayers for themselves based on Scripture for the situations in which they find themselves. The Scriptures are full of prayers – some of them prayers of women (e.g., Hagar, Miriam, Hannah, Esther) – which can be used as they are or as models for other prayers. Likewise, the Psalms too are human prayers that have been recorded for our benefit and use.

Alongside this, many of the Islamic cultures are replete with stories – many of them rooted in the Qur'an. Story telling as a means of sharing the Gospel is becoming increasing recognised (Wong, 2015), as Adeney also indicates. Indeed, in contrast to the Qur'an, the Bible, and in particular the Gospels, contain many stories featuring women which reflect their importance and their place within God's scheme of history and salvation. Holy songs also have a significant role in some Islamic contexts – why not encourage the women to create their own where this is appropriate.

Where to From Here?

Adeney raised the question 'Do Muslim women need saving?' Her answer within the context of the Christian message was 'to bring Christ'. Her paper outlines ways that this might be achieved: recognising the unique patterns of their culture; taking advantage of their worldview patterns, and by utilizing their own teaching and learning models. She also explores how effective sharing of the message has been undermined by Christian stereotyping and through particular Christian theological interpretations.

The travesty of this is that in the beginning God created men and women in His image, in His likeness, and loved them both so much that He was prepared to send Jesus to die for them, so that ultimately both men and women would experience His love, His life and His likeness. Such is the heart of the Christian message. Do Muslim women need saving? Yes, they do, as do all women everywhere, and they need to know that they are loved by God and that He desires to have a relationship with them. But the question 'Do Muslim women need saving?' can reflect an understanding of salvation that limits it to a narrow goal of ministry. In sharing the message of salvation with Muslim women, the uniqueness of their createdness and the socio-cultural-religious environment in which God has allowed them to live, grow and develop must be recognised. Consequently, the message of God's love needs to be presented to them in ways that enable them to grow to maturity through spirituality flourishing in their personal relationship with Christ. How can that be done? It can be done by recognising their uniqueness and their identity, and by leading them onwards using Scripture through the forms of memorization, remembering (a form of chanting), creed-like statements and liturgical forms that will enable them to develop spiritual disciplines and gifts that make up the road to spiritual maturity – a journey of a thousand steps fostered in a culturally appropriate way through a discipler\mentor\sister in Christ.

GOD IS OUR REFUGE

God is our refuge.
He is a strong tower.
He is a rock and a shield.
The eternal God is our refuge.
He is ready to help us in our troubles.
He will guard my life and He will rescue me.
And underneath me are His everlasting arms
And I can take refuge in the shadow of His wings.
His way is perfect and His Word is flawless
No one who takes refuge in Him will be condemned.
Have mercy on me, O my God, have mercy on me
For in you I take refuge.
I will take refuge in you till the danger has passed.
Blessed are all those who take refuge in you.

References

"Child Marriage around the World," International Center for Research on Women, https://www.icrw.org/child-marriage-facts-and-figures/. Cited 9 May 2017.

UNICEF'S DATA WORK ON FGM/C https://www.unicef.org/media/files/FGMC_2016_brochure_final_UNICEF_SPREAD.pdf. Cited 9 May 2017.

Adeney, Miriam. *Daughters of Islam: Building Bridges with Muslim Women.* Downers Grove: InterVasity Press, 2002.

Armstrong, Sally. *Veiled Threat, the Hidden Power of the Women of Afghanistan.* Toronto: Penguin-Viking, 2002.

Badawi, Jamal, *The Status of Women in Islam.* https://islamswomen.com/articles/status_of_women_in_islam.php. Cited 3 July 2016.

Bodman, Herbert L & Nayereh Tohidi. *Women in Muslim Societies, Diversity within Unity.* Boulder: Lynne Rienner Publishers, 1998.

Cashin, Dave, *How ISIS spreading the Gospel,* Zwemer Centre for Muslim Studies, http://www.zwemercenter.com/articles/page/3. Cited 1 December 2016.

Dale, Moyra. *Shifting Allegiances: Networks of Kinship and Faith: The Women's Program in a Syrian Mosque.* Eugene: Wipf & Stock, 2016.

Dyer, Emily. *Britain's Forgotten Women, Speaking to Survivors of 'Honour'-based Abuse, Case Studies and Policy Recommendations.* London: The Henry Jackson Society, 2015.

Heyzer, Noeleen. "Promoting Gender Equality in Muslim Contexts – Women's voices must on be Silenced," *UN Chronicle: the Magazine of the United Nations*, XLIV: 4 (2007). http://unchronicle.un.org. Cited 29 June 2016.

Kraft, Charles H. *Anthropology for Christian Witness.* New York: Orbis Books, 1996.

___________. *Worldview for Christian Witness.* Pasadena: William Carey Library, 2008.

Jawad, Haifaa A. *The Rights of Women in Islam: An Authentic Approach.* London: MacMillan Press, 1998.

Longenecker, Richard N., ed. *Patterns of Discipleship in the New Testament,* Grand Rapids: Eerdmans, 1996.

Nicholls, Ruth. 'Liturgy to Focus Mind and Heart: Fostering Spiritual Growth among Muslim Seekers'.pp. 205 – 216 in *Longing for Community, Church, 'Ummah', or Somewhere in Between.* Edited by David Greenlee. Pasadena: William Carey Library, 2013.

Tabari, Azar & Nahid Yeganeh, (compilers).*In the Shadow of Islam: The Women's Movement in Iran.* London: Zed Press, 1982.

Van Doorn-Harder, Pieternella. *Women Shaping Islam: Reading the Qur'an in Indonesia.* Urbana: University of Chicago Press, 2006.

Wong, Mary. "Building Bridges through Stories", *Centre for the Study of Islam & Other Faiths Bulletin 2013/14*, Issue no. 6/7, May 2015; 46-57.

5

Fire-words: Voicing the Pain

Fire-words: Voicing the Pain

Ida Glaser

> 'Pain shakes the very foundation of our existence, yet God sustains those of us whose foundation is shaking, when we participate in his pain' (Kitamori, 1966:149)
>
> 'I assess the power of a will by how much resistance, pain and torture it endures and knows how to turn to its advantage' (Nietzsche, 1901)

I invited one of my Muslim colleagues to speak to a group of Anglican ordinands about 'Questions that Muslims want to ask Christians'. His most challenging question was, 'Why do Christians not care about Muslim suffering?' If he had heard more women's voices, and if he had seen the many Christian women who are pouring out their lives for suffering Muslim people, would he have asked that question?

There are many Christian voices on Islam in today's world, and a large proportion express fear and anger about perceived threats. Yet, I think that most Christian women who really try to get to know Muslims and to think about Islam are more aware of the pain that they see than they are of political threats. Perhaps one of the things that women can contribute is a concern for the pain of Muslims as well as for the pain of Christians – and of many others – caught up in the tensions of today's world.

In 2003, I was involved in organising a conference that was full of bishops and other leaders from around the Anglican Communion.[1] We worked in groups, and I wanted to be in 'Mission, plurality and pluralism', which would have fitted with my work on the theology of religions. My fellow organisers (all male) insisted that I should, instead, join the 'Conflict, suffering and mission' group. I found myself as the one white Westerner, and one of only two women, in a group of church leaders from such war zones as Congo, Northern Nigeria, Northern Uganda and South Sudan. We shared our stories, and I was able to contribute some theological reflection – on my use of Psalm 137 to voice the grief, fear and anger of a people torn from their land.[2]

The group was expected to make a report to the conference; but to what conclusion can you come when you are all looking at situations of long-term instability and agony? We decided to take our clue from the psalmist – we would not try to 'report', but we would lament, and we did, in front of all those

---

[1] The Evangelical Fellowship in the Anglican Communion conference, *Anglican Life in Mission*, held at Limuru, Kenya, 12-18th July 2003.

[2] See 'We sat down and wept: Biblical resources for conflict situations', in *The Round Table: The commonwealth journal of international affairs*, Issue 382 (2005) 641-52.

bishops and leaders, we one by one stood and poured out our grief and fear and anger aloud before our Lord. The most memorable to me were the Ugandan woman ululating her grief over the slaughter of villages and the kidnapping of children to be made soldiers; and the Muslim background Kenyan bishop (now dead) bewailing the church's lack of love for his Muslim people.

My contribution was the last. I talked over with God the suicide of my aunt, who had not been able to cope with life as dreams of Holocaust times erupted into her old age. I moved on to my questions about that Gentile (Christian?) destruction of my Jewish people, and my anguish over people who imply that I am not a proper evangelical if I do not think that God was shovelling my family into hell as the Nazis were shovelling them into the gas chambers. From there, I moved to the tensions of being a Jewish Christian working in a department of Islamic and Middle Eastern Studies and hearing the grief and fear and anger of Palestinian Muslims, as well as the concerns of my Israeli sister-in-law for her family. We ended with my arms outstretched – torn between the Jews and the Muslims – and with someone reading Colossians 1:19-23 and my responding with verses 24-25. Unplanned, the Ugandan woman and the Kenyan bishop had come to stand on either side of me during the reading, and they held me and helped me back to my seat. I needed the help!

I remember it vividly, and I guess that everyone else who was there remembers some aspect of that presentation – I have certainly never seen so many bishops in tears! The published conference report says:

> Conference members wept as they shared the confusion and anger of those who feel that God had abandoned them in the face of conflicts and persecution. ... The participants of the track on suffering overwhelmed the rest when they spoke to the rest through a series of prayers, complaints and petitions to God.[3]

I also remember what it taught me: the power of voicing our pain before God and before one another. It should not have been a surprise: the Psalms give us a model. So often, the Psalms speak to us through the voicing of pain. They set us free to voice our pain to God and to ourselves, and so to discern when and how to voice that pain to others. Without the psalms of agony, we might be afraid to own our pain and unable to bring it to the only one who can carry it, and our unowned pain could be projected onto others in unacknowledged and destructive ways.

I also learnt that I, as a woman with a particular history of pain, am not helpless in the face of the agonies of the world. God can use us, provided that we offer Him our pain. The key is, I think, to somehow align my pain with His. This is more than a hermeneutical circle between Bible, theology and lived pain: it is, as Kitamori suggests, using our pain as a deliberate participation in God's pain. Paul describes it in the verse I used at that conference in Kenya: 'In my flesh I complete what is lacking in Christ's afflictions' or, as Tom Wright

---

[3] 'Anglican life in mission: Evangelical fellowship in the Anglican Communion International Consultation July 12-18 2003, Limuru, Kenya', *Transformation*, 20: 4 (October 2003), 254.

translates it, 'I'm steadily completing, in my own flesh, what is presently lacking in the king's afflictions on behalf of his body, which is the church. I became the church's servant, according to the terms laid down by God...' (Colossians 1:24-25).

An alternative is that of Nietzsche: to acknowledge and embrace our pain, but to focus on how we can use it to strengthen our own selves. Nietzsche's views of pain are notoriously complex,[4] but he saw the deliberate bearing of one's own pain as a way of empowering the self, and inflicting pain on others as an effective way of controlling them. Such views, albeit out of their original context, are notorious for having fed the thinking of Hitler and led to some of the agony which I was expressing in my lament. On a very different basis, we might see them echoed in the mentality that seeks martyrdom as it inflicts as much damage as possible on the enemy in the advancement of a movement that sees itself as an 'Islamic State'. Are these but logical uses of pain in world-views that have no cross, no place where pain is carried and transformed in love?

Pain is powerful. It has consequences, and it has huge potential either for salvation or for destruction. One of the most urgent needs in our world is for right understandings of pain and right direction of pain – into prayer and the service of the triune God and His world. Do we, as women, want to serve the church and its king? One starting point is to look hard at God's pain and our own, so that we can take our place in completing His afflictions. We cannot voice pain without looking at it. This paper looks at God's pain and our own pain before going on to seek a theology of human trauma that finds its place in the *missio dei*.

Looking at God's Pain

Since I first started to explore my own pain, I have had in mind the phrase, 'the theology of the pain of God'. I found it in the title of a book by the Japanese theologian Kazoh Kitamori, written in 1945 in the aftermath of Hiroshima. He writes, 'The heart of the gospel was revealed to me as "the pain of God"' (1945:19); and he found that heart in Jeremiah 31:20:[5]

> Is Ephraim my dear son?
> Is he my darling child?
> For as often as I speak against him,
> I do remember him still.
> Therefore my heart yearns for him;
> I will surely have mercy on him,
> declares the Lord.

---

[4] See L. O'Sullivan, 'Nietzsche and pain', in *Journal of Nietzsche Studies* (Spring 1996): 13-22.

[5] Another key verse for Kitamori is Isaiah 63v15.

Kitamori sees God's pain as the sum of His holy response to sin and His love for human beings, which results in the cross on which His heart of pain is revealed and on which His 'love rooted in pain' saves the objects of His love and leads to resurrection. The 'grace of God's pain' can then give value to human pain – more than that, pain can be the most precious of all our experiences, since it is necessary to enable us to witness to God's pain. 'The theology of the pain of God can be pursued only when we participate in it through our own suffering' (1945:149).

Re-reading Kitamori in writing this paper, I realise how deeply some of his ideas resonated with my own experience and have stood as a foundation for my thinking. In recent years, I have explored what I call 'the pain in the heart of God', and have come to summarise my Christology as 'Jesus is the pain in the heart of God'.[6] Kitamori does not quite say that, but he sees God's 'will for salvation... manifested in the person of Jesus as his pain', and concludes, 'Our task... is to comprehend the depths of Christ's love as God's pain' (1945:146).

What do I mean by saying that 'Jesus is the pain in the heart of God'? I mean that Jesus is that of God which responds to the pain caused by human sin with unconditional commitment, and eventually deals with it by coming to us and by bearing the pain of judgement by being, Himself, the sacrifice that is the alternative to the flood (see below). Jesus did not become that when He was conceived in Mary: He has always been that, because God has always had 'a heart'.

The eternity of Jesus as the pain in the heart of God has been well expressed by two friends of mine:

- A Muslim teenager with whom I was discussing the forgiveness and love of God. I explained that I believed that such forgiveness and love were intrinsically linked with what Jesus had done on the cross, and she responded, 'You mean, if it weren't for Jesus, God wouldn't be like that?'[7]
- A Christian poet, in a poem that ventures to express God's thoughts on the beginning of Jesus:

> My own necessary death determined my design for sunlight. (Peace, 2008:11)

Kitamori reached his conclusions in the context of Japanese tragedy: I have done my thinking in the context not only of my own journey through Jewish tragedy and personal trauma but also in the context of Islam. All my theology is in cross-reference to Islamic thinking. In that context, the pain of God is often a scandal or a conundrum, but it can also be the heart of the good news.

---

[6] See my *Thinking Biblically about Islam: Genesis, transfiguration, transformation*, Langham, 2016:42.

[7] Shabana Choudhry Marshall, who now works for the Holocaust Educational Trust – a Muslim woman helping British school children to understand what happened to the Jews.

My own theology of the pain of God begins in Genesis 6:6. I read the flood story as God's own response to the problem of evil. He sees His good world being wrecked, as the powerful 'sons of the elohim' exploit the good daughters of Adam[8] and produce monstrous children. He sees the wickedness of humankind: 'how every plan devised by his mind was nothing but evil all the time' (Genesis 6:5, JPS). We then get the first glimpse into the heart of God – the heart which is not, for the Genesis writer, the seat of the emotions, but the seat of the will. It is the place where God speaks with Himself.

> 'The Lord regretted that He had made man on earth, and His heart was saddened' (JPS)

We notice that, unusually, the Genesis writer uses 'Lord' (Yahweh) in chapter 6:1-8, emphasising that this the loving and steadfast god of the covenant. We overhear His discussion with Himself, as His regret leads Him to the judgement of the flood. We will again glimpse His heart in chapter 8:21-22, when He sees that the human heart is as evil as ever it was, but says to Himself, 'Never again….'

These two responses to the evil in the human heart lead us to a deeper reflection on the heart of God – the tension that we see in the second half of Genesis 6:6, 'His heart was saddened', which is also translated, 'His heart was deeply troubled' (NIV) or 'it grieved Him to His heart' (ESV) or even, 'It broke His heart' (New Living Translation).

What is this sadness or grief in the heart of God? The Hebrew has, *yit'atsev el-livo*. The root *'tsv* can also be found in Genesis 3:16, where it twice describes the pain in which the woman will bear children, and in 3:17 where is describes the painful toil with which the man will work for food. It occurs again in 5:29, describing the painful toil from which Noah's father hope to be released. I do not think that we would push the text too far if we concluded that God's heart in 6:6.

Genesis 6 was reflecting the human pain that resulted from the 'fall'. Genesis 6:6 is a glimpse of pain in the very heart of God: it is pain that somehow participates in human pain, and it is this pain that is His response to the problem of evil in His world.

We can go further, and infer that the pain that we glimpse in God's heart in Genesis 6:6 can be associated with the 'never again' in God's heart in Genesis 8:21-22. Both are His responses to the evil that He sees in human hearts. The regret that leads to judgement, the pain, the commitment to all of creation despite the wickedness of the human race… these are the three divine responses that Genesis shows us. The pain is at the centre, and I would agree with

[8] This is my own interpretation of Genesis 6:2-4. There is some discussion as to whether *elohim* here refers to gods or to human leaders – I prefer the latter. The Hebrew word translated 'beautiful' in Gen 6:2 is *tov* – the word translated repeatedly as 'good' in Genesis 1. The word for 'men' in verse 2 is the plural of *adam* – the name of Adam is the word for a human being.

Kitamori here that the pain is in the tension between the holy decision for judgement and the passionate commitment to steadfast love.

The resolution of this tension is to come, as Kitamori insists, on the cross. However, here in Genesis we have a picture of what is to come. It is as God 'smells the aroma' of Noah's sacrifice that He makes the covenantal commitment to His creation. It is the 'one full, perfect and sufficient sacrifice, oblation and satisfaction for the sins of the whole world'[9] that enables God to be committed to a sinful world, because that sacrifice will deal with the sin that would otherwise need a flood to cleanse it.

The Noah story, then, offers us two ways in which the pain in the heart of God deals with the wickedness of humanity: flood or sacrifice. And it tells us that God's priority and commitment is to the way of sacrifice rather than to the way of the judgement of the flood, because God's pain is a consequence of His love for His creation. This is a lens for the reading of all the follows in the Bible.

I have developed this theological basis 'in conversation with' Islam. The qur'anic Noah story has much in common with the biblical Noah story, in that it presents a wicked community that is judged by God. However, it has more in common with the way that Noah is taught in Sunday School than with the actual Genesis account. Children are often told stories of how Noah warned people of the coming judgement and called them to repentance. There is not a hint of that in Genesis, but there is much more than a hint of it in the Qur'an. Indeed, the qur'anic Noah is primarily a prophet who argues and pleads with his people, just as Muhammad argued and pled with the people of Mecca (See Sura 72 and Sura 11:25-49). He is a paradigm for a series of other prophets – Hud, Salih, Lot and Shu'aib (Sura 7:59-93; 11:50-95). In each case, the prophet preaches to the people; some believe but most reject him; and there is a cataclysmic judgement in which the unbelievers are destroyed and the believers are saved.

The qur'anic Noah, then, gives us the pattern for the qur'anic picture of God's response to evil. As in the biblical story, we see both judgement and mercy. The judgement is, as in Genesis, a flood that destroys the wicked along with their wickedness. The mercy is, in contrast to Genesis, sending a prophet to warn people, and preserving those who accept the message. The preaching of the prophet divides people into those who will be destroyed and those who will be preserved.

In Genesis, the people who are preserved are not necessarily good or even believers: they are simply the family of Noah, and, by the end of the story, we know that at least one of them was bad and was cursed. In the Qur'an, too, Noah has an unbelieving son, but he is drowned: Noah pleads for him, but God rebukes him, and tells him that unbelief has removed the son from his family (Sura 11:42-47). In Genesis, God looks at the people who have survived the flood and sees that their hearts are no better than the hearts of those who were

[9] *Book of Common Prayer*: 601.

destroyed (Genesis 8:21). It is very clear that the world is not divided into 'good' and 'bad' people, so that evil cannot be dealt with by destroying the bad and keeping the good.

In Genesis, God's mercy is in His covenant commitment to all of His creation – bad and good, believing and unbelieving. And what makes that commitment possible seems to be the sacrifice. The Qur'an has no sacrifice. It tells us of Noah's distress at the judgement of his son, but has no suggestion that God is grieved. The Qur'an has no glimpse of pain in the heart of God.

We can trace these differences through the Qur'an's treatment of themes and characters that are also treated in the Bible:

- **Most of the sacrifices are missing from the Qur'an**. The exceptions are Abraham's near-sacrifice of his son (Sura 37: 101-106) and the sacrifices of Cain and Abel (Sura 5: 27-32). Perhaps most striking is the omission of all the details surrounding the sacrifices given in the Mosaic covenant. The Qur'an gives a great deal of space to Moses, and the qur'anic Moses is remarkably like the biblical Moses. The Qur'an reflects many aspects of the Mosaic personal, family, civil and criminal law; but it has only hints of the tabernacle, the priesthood and the sacrifices that take up so much of the Pentateuch. This leads to the observation that the Qur'an removes the *shekinah*, because it removes the place of the *shekinah* and the sacrifices that make possible the presence of the Holy God amongst His people.
- **The qur'anic world-view produces Islamic thinking that has no room for 'pain in the heart of God'.** First, the Qur'an gives little idea of the motivation behind God's words and actions. Indeed, traditional Islamic thinking insists that God's motivation is inaccessible to human knowledge, as is His essence. For example, if we say that God is merciful, 'merciful' cannot be understood as meaning the same as it would mean if we said that a human being was merciful, because God is unimaginably other than humanity. It might mean that His actions are those that could be seen as a result of mercy were they to be done by a human being, but we cannot go further than that. Second, we cannot say that God suffers, since suffering would imply weakness or imperfection, and God is perfect and all-powerful. Third, we cannot say that God suffers as a result of human sin, since He is far above being affected by anything in His creation. In short, we need Him but He does not need us; and pain in response to anything in His creation would imply that He depended on us in some way.

It comes, then, as no surprise that Islam removes the Cross. (It is, of course, a matter of contention as to whether the Qur'an itself does this.) The Cross brings together the *shekinah* in Jesus the Messiah and the sacrifice that opens the way for *shekinah,* and the pain caused by the sin that separated God from His creatures.

Of course, Islam does not remove pain from its understanding of the world. Pain is a common human experience, and all religions need a way of dealing with suffering. In much Islamic thinking, the focus is on avoiding pain in the next world, and that may involve accepting and even embracing pain in this world – for example, by accepting pain as the will of God, and embracing the pain of martyrdom. Shi'ite Islam adds a focus on pain in this world, as people look back on the pain of Hussain, of the holy family, and of the Shi'ite community through history. There are some aspects of this pain that are seen as redemptive.[10] However, this is not the pain of God, and it has no resurrection. Shi'ites look forward to the coming of the hidden Imam for release from injustice and pain and look back in grief and, often, in anger, at the injustices of the past. We hear the cry of, 'Death to Yazid!' – death to the enemy who killed Hussain, and to the enemy who is the current threat to our community. The Gospel calls us to look back to the coming of Christ who has already dealt with injustice and pain even as we look forward in hope. The resurrection calls us to a cry of 'Life!' – Jesus' death brought life to His enemies, including us, and He wants it to bring life to all.

The Cross makes a difference to how we voice our pain – do we align it with the loving pain of Jesus, or with anger at ongoing injustice?

Looking at Our Own Pain: The Bible as a Mirror

Aligning our pain with the cross and voicing it implies a journey: it is a journey into understanding both our pain and that of God in Jesus, and into finding words and other ways of voicing the two together. In my experience, a key to this journey is exploring our own pain by looking into the mirror of the Bible. This can help us to see that our pain is neither a strange thing nor peculiarly 'ours': it is something that is part of the world that we see in the Bible, and we share in the pain of fallen humanity. Seeing our pain in this way can then help us to relate our pain to God's pain, because pain seen in the Bible must be pain that God cares about, and it is just this pain His pain in Christ redeems and transforms. It can, therefore, transform our crippling voicing of personal pain into a shared song which offers hope to others. I offer here some 'tasters' from my own journey.

Women's Voices

Of the many women's voices in the Bible, not a few are voices of pain, whether put into words or acted out in life. We hear of the pains of competition and childlessness through Rachel and Leah (Genesis 29-30), of patriarchal injustice through Tamar (Genesis 38), of parental power and foolishness through

[10] See Mahmoud Ayoub's *Redemptive Suffering in Islam, A Study of the Devotional Aspects of Ashura in Twelver Shi'ism*, De Gruyter, 1978.

Jephthah's daughter (Judges 11:29-40), of savage exploitation through the silent body of the Levite's concubine (Judges 19) and of widowhood and destitution through Naomi (Ruth 1). We see Hannah voicing her pain before God (1 Samuel 1:12-13), and then erupting into praise as she witnesses to His answers (1 Samuel 2:1-10). We could continue, but we pause here to recognise how many women down the centuries have also rejoiced with Hannah, not least Mary, and the generations of Christian women who have repeated her song of praise (Luke 1:46-55) in the midst of their own pains. The biblical portraits of all these women give us fellowship in our particular pains, and encourage us to place them within the providence of God and to look onwards towards worship.

All the pains mentioned in the above paragraph are women's pains, and can be seen in different ways in different contexts throughout the ages – we might say that, in this fallen world, they are normal, and that they echo the pre-flood exploitation of the daughters of Adam by the mysterious powerful male figures. Over the past decade, I have been trying to voice a different category of pain, which in English is called 'trauma'. I have been reflecting on my own experience of 'Post Traumatic Stress Disorder' (PTSD), and, as I have voiced it, I have realised its relevance to today's fraught world of Christian relationships with Muslims.[11]

Trauma

Trauma is a Greek word, meaning 'wound'. In English, 'trauma' can refer to traumatic events – that is, events which combine the experiences of great danger and complete helplessness – or to the sort of wounding which those events produce. There is a range of normal responses as people process what has happened to them: for some, the processing gets 'stuck', and long-term PTSD results. Instead of the memories being processed and receding into the past, they remain in the present and are anticipated in the future, and the body as well as the mind keeps on reacting to them, often through the adrenalin-driven responses of freezing, fleeing or fighting. In more serious cases, people can suffer states of 'dissociation', that is, they are switched out of their present situation into the past experience or some other place of escape.

The word *trauma* also appears in the New Testament, in the context of Jesus' explanation of 'love your neighbour': it was into the *trauma* of the beaten Jew that the Good Samaritan poured his oil and wine (Luke 10:34). As a verb, *traumatizo*, it appears twice: first, in the parable of the wicked tenants who *traumatize* their master's final messenger (Luke 20:12), and second in Acts 19:16, when the sons of Sceva are *traumatized* by the man with the evil spirit. If, as many of us have argued, the relationship between Jews and

[11] Some of the material below originates in my *Trauma, migration and mission: biblical reflections from a traumatised Hebrew*, Crowther Centre Monograph No. 2, Oxford: Church Mission Society, 2008. Later reflections can be found in my blog, https://atraumaobserved.wordpress.com/

Samaritans in New Testament times is parallel to the relationship between Christians and Muslims in some of our contexts, the parable of the Good Samaritan encourages us to minister to wounded Muslims and to be ministered to in our own wounding. The other two passages affirm that the world is a dangerous place, where human beings can wound us if we do our mission in God's way, and evil powers can wound us if we do it in our own way. The 'mirror' of the Bible is, I think, showing us not only that we are called to minister to the traumatized, but also that our shared humanity means that we, too, are in danger of trauma, and that the missionary calling increases the danger.

Axes for Analysis

In trying to develop a biblical understanding of PTSD, I have found it helpful to keep two axes in mind:

Axis 1: Between trauma caused by events originating in human sin, and trauma caused by events originating in the natural order.

'Natural' disasters and human atrocities raise different theological issues, largely related to the question of who or what might be blamed; and the Bible has much material related to both. For example, Matthew 24 speaks of persecutions and wars which originate in human sin and of earthquakes and famines in the natural order.

Actual situations are more complex, and may lie between the two extremes of the axis. Many apparently natural disasters are aggravated or even caused by human agency – for example, by environmental damage, by economic factors leading to vulnerability, or by mishandling of the aftermath of the events. What about a car crash, such as that which features in my own PTSD? On the one hand, we call it an 'accident', implying an uncontrollable chance, and therefore, perhaps, a 'natural' event. On the other hand, there were particular human errors which caused the crash. It seems to me that such an event is therefore situated right at the centre of the axis, along with events caused by other man-made devices that unwittingly let loose the destructive powers of nature. The greatest potential for trauma is when human attempts to control the natural order are directed towards evil ends; but there can also be enormous damage when human beings find their attempts loosing powers beyond their control.

Axis 2: Between individual and ethnic trauma.

There is *individual trauma*: each person's experience is different, and trauma symptoms depend on the particular experiences that triggered them. There is *trauma that affects families* – nuclear and extended. Even a trauma that apparently affects only one person affects family and friends because it affects the person's relationships with them. Many psalms voice individual and family pain, but perhaps the greatest biblical resource here is the book of Job. Job's agonies are the result of both human wickedness (the attacks of the Sabeans and the Chaldeans) and natural disaster (the fire from heaven and the destructive wind).

Perhaps less understood but more pervasive in our world is *trauma that affects whole communities and ethnic groups.* My own experience as the daughter of a Czech Jew, named after his mother who died in Auschwitz, makes the 'holocaust' and the long Jewish experience of exile and persecution part of my make-up, despite the fact that it all happened before my birth. I personally inherit the sort of terror and rage expressed in Psalm 137, and I can see its aftermath affecting Jewish people world-wide. Some such *trauma has world-wide effects.* Today, this is often due to media coverage and to migration, but there have been many past events which have affected many countries and peoples and have changed the course of world history. I would include the Holocaust here, with its lasting heritage of publicity and guilt, and its ongoing effects on literature, theology and psychology as well as on nationhood and politics.

With the notable exception of Job, all the Bible's accounts of trauma are embedded in the history of Israel or of the early Christian community. I see the experience of the Jewish people recorded in the Bible as a key mirror for understanding communal trauma, and as offering key resources for dealing with it.[12] Psalm 137 is where I often begin. As it invites readers into the experience of Israel, it enables sufferers to understand that their experience is not so unusual, and that their terrified and terrifying responses are normal. And it does this in the context of the psalms of covenantal worship which surround it.

That points us in two directions: recognising the commonality of traumatic experience, and moving towards recognising the greatness and goodness of the God who is in control of His world and who is the place of ultimate safety.

Two Key Concepts

> 'The core experiences of psychological trauma are disempowerment and disconnection from others. Recovery, therefore, is based upon the empowerment of the survivor and the creation of new connections.'[13]

This professional approach to the treatment of PTSD relates to two underlying problems. First, there is the dissociation which makes the sufferer feel that she is not quite part of the world around her – that the traumatic experience has somehow cut her off from present reality, from her fellow human beings, and even from God Himself. Second, there is the feeling of helplessness which is the result of having actually been helpless in a situation of terrifying danger. Our biblical resources speak into these problems.

---

[12] See my paper, 'We sat down and wept: Biblical resources for conflict situations', in The Round Table: The Commonwealth Journal of International Affairs, Issue 382 (2005), 641-52.

[13] J. Herman, *Trauma and Recovery: The aftermath of violence – from domestic abuse to political terror* (New York: Basic Books, 1992), 133. This section owes much of its understanding of the dynamics of trauma to Herman.

The Normality of Trauma

The 21st century Western world breeds the myth that safety is the normal human condition, which occasionally gets violated by dangers that someone ought to avert. Biblically, we recognise that God created a good and safe world, so this is what we long for. However, safety disappeared very rapidly as sin appeared, and the hard facts are that danger is now normal, and that we are often powerless to counter it. On the one hand, such a passage as Psalm 137 expresses normal outrage at violence and exile. On the other hand, it reminds us that traumatic events are part of the regular human experience in a fallen world.

So, in Matthew 24 (and Mark 13 and Luke 21), Jesus He prepares his disciples to face traumatic events. Traumatic events are, we learn, to be expected. Traumatic experience can often lead to feelings of disconnection, isolation and the 'why should this happen to me/us?' anger: this passage assures us that we are not alone, and that our experience is not so very unusual, and so can help people to deal with those feelings.

More than that, Jesus tells His disciples that their experience are meaningful: they have their places in mission, in God's judgements, and as part of the last days and therefore of the ultimate aim of creation. Traumatic experience can call all our foundations into question and result in a sense of meaningless: this passage gives hope and tells us that, in the midst of it all, there is something good that will never crumble (Matthew 24:35). And the hope is not only for ourselves: for disciples who are properly prepared, these events become meaningful as the place of witness, particularly when they are caused by human sin (Matthew 24:14; see also Luke 21:13). As explained in Mark's account, it is in places of helplessness that the Helper, the Holy Spirit, speaks through us (Mark 13:11). The place of trauma becomes the place of mission.

Part of the hope is the knowledge that these events are limited. The terror will not last forever, and the eventual result will in the coming of the Son of Man to put everything right (Matthew 24:29-31). Despite all appearances, God (and only God) is in CONTROL (Matthew 24:36); and Jesus assures us that those who 'endure to the end' will be SAFE (Matthew 24:13).

Safety and Control

Since PTSD is a response to situations which combine danger and helplessness, it is not surprising that, as memories are being processed, therapists see the need to

- Help the client to find a place of safety to counter the pervasive feeling of danger
- Help the client to gain a measure of control of their situation to counter the feeling of helplessness.

From a biblical perspective, these are forlorn efforts: the world is fallen and therefore not a safe place; and trying to be in control is the original sin. I agree that safety and control are of key importance in dealing with a condition rooted in danger and helplessness, but God is the only one who can safely be in control, and the only ultimate safety is in God Himself. It is salutary to remember that 'salvation' is about being safe; and that opens vast biblical resources for finding a safety which endures beyond the inevitable dangers of this life. Of course, finding as much physical safety as possible, and the realization that one is responsible for one's own recovery and not a helpless victim, are still important. However, the recognition of God as the place of safety and control not only offers ultimate security but also puts self-control into perspective.

One of the therapeutic techniques used in coping with traumatic memories is for the client to imagine a 'safe place;' to which she can return at will. I have found it impossible to find such an imagined safety since I neither rationally nor emotionally believe that this world is a safe place. But I do believe that there is a safe place in God. Indeed, one of the rabbinic names for God is 'Ha Maqqom' – 'The Place'[14] This is associated with the 'place near God' in the cleft of the rock, where Moses could safely stand as the glory passed (Exodus 33:21-2), and of the picture of God as dwelling-place (*ma'on*) in Deuteronomy 33:27 and Psalm 90:1; and Psalm 121 is put into Jacob's into mouth as he lies down in The Place:[15] 'You will go your way safely and not injure your feet. When you lie down you will be unafraid; you will lie down and your sleep will be sweet. You will not fear the sudden terror or the disaster that comes upon the wicked, for the Lord will be your trust; He will keep your feet from being caught.' (JPS translation). His feeling of helplessness is not countered by taking control of his life: on the contrary, he learns that it is the Lord who is in control.

More than that, God's control is, ultimately, safe[16]. In fact, He is the only one who can safely take control, because He is the only one who has both complete goodness and complete wisdom. His control deals with both ends of our first trauma spectrum: He made the natural order, and His management of potentially destructive forces is without the weakness of human limitation or the taint of human sin. It is this God who is the safe Place, the Helper of the helpless.

Worship

Books on PTSD speak of the need to empower the trauma victim; that is, to replace the sense of helplessness with a sense of control. I would argue instead that we need to realise that we are small, but that God is in control. It is only as I have struggled through my own trauma that I have seen the significance of

---

[14] The idea is explored in the Midrash on Genesis 28:10, where Jacob, setting out for Haran, 'came to a certain place' (*Genesis Rabbah* 48:9).

[15] Genesis Rabbab 48:1-2.

[16] The rabbis recognise that this is not always apparent, and that it often appears that the righteous suffer more than the wicked. Genesis Rabbab 48:5 notes that apparent ease of Esau and suffering of Jacob at this time, and observes: 'Thus we learn that the Holy One, blessed be He, hastens the happiness of the wicked and delays that of the righteous.'

Job 40:43, 'Behold, I am of small account.' (ESV[17]). Trauma can produce a survivor guilt which makes us feel that we ought to be able to do better, to change things, to make the world safer. It can produce anger which drives us to do something – whether constructive or destructive. It can produce a general feeling that, if only we could get things 'right', disaster would be averted. It is not accidental that God's response to Job was to overwhelm him with a vision of His total control over all the natural forces which had so destroyed Job's family. Job's realisation of his smallness does not, I think, squash him. If my experience is anything to go by, it does quite the opposite: it releases him from the need to do anything to put matters right, and even to get the answers to all his questions. It is enough to get himself into perspective – as a very small person, part of a very big world, and with an infinitely powerful God. And that God is good, and cares enough about little Job to come and talk to him. The unbearable burden of control, which we know that we cannot carry, shifts, at last, onto the shoulders on the One who made us.

That brings us to the theme of worship. We can but guess what Job understood through the voice from the whirlwind; but we do know that He was satisfied and worshipped. The book of Revelation, opening up future traumatic events for churches under huge pressure, makes things much more clear: from the first vision of Jesus, through the worship around the throne, and to the final vision of heaven, we see the wounded and risen Messiah at the heart of God. It is He who is the first revelation to the exiled John, and who says, 'Do not fear!' and 'I know, I know, I know, I know, I know, I know, I know.' (1ohn:17; 2:2, 9, 13, 19; 3:1, 8, 15). It is He, who is the missionary and the survivor, who is in control (Revelation 1:5).

The traumatized are invited, then, to worship. As I concluded in an early reflection on my own trauma, 'It is not enough to know that God is in control: we are invited to be glad that He is in control, to address Him, to enter into relationship with Him. Like Job, we can acknowledge His greatness and our smallness as we respond to His coming to us. Like John, we can fall down before the crucified. As we worship, we will find that worship is actually something needed for recovery, because we need to reconnect to God in order to reconnect to ourselves and to the world. Worship puts life into perspective: it enables us to take the focus off the traumatized self, and focus on the traumatized Messiah. As we face our ongoing vulnerability and the fact that we will never be the same again, we recognize the scars that remained after the resurrection and into heaven. Those scars tell us that Jesus' trauma accomplished something – that He is now our Safe Place.

'Jesus, who has power over winds and waves, systematically refused the obvious power of material goods, political status and wrong use of the miraculous throughout His ministry. The way to resurrection power was, for

---

[17] The Hebrew root, qll, means 'to make light (not heavy)', so related words have to do with diminishing or despising. Hence the range of translations of this verse such as 'I am vile' (KJV) to 'I am unworthy' (NIV).

Him, a very literal stripping and wounding. As the LXX helpfully uses the Greek translates Isaiah 53:5, 'He was *traumatized* for our transgressions.'' (Glaser, 2008: 23, 22)

That brings us back to mission. Why was the Messiah wounded? To ransom not only us, but also people from every tribe and language and people and nation (Revelation 5:9). It is this that provokes the worship of heaven. Maybe wounding is necessary to mission, because there is pain in the heart of God.

Trauma and the *Missio Dei*

What are my qualifications for teaching about Christian-Muslim relations? In a western college, I will probably include my experiences of teaching in Muslim countries and of living and ministering amongst Muslims in inner city UK, and then add my teaching experience, academic qualifications and publications. In The Theological College of Northern Nigeria, where students are regularly getting news of family and friends suffering from 'Boko Haram' attacks, I present myself quite differently. I start with my Jewish Holocaust heritage (I am called after a grandmother who died in Auschwitz); go on to my sudden loss of both parents in a car accident at the age of 15, my inner city experience of living with crime, deprivation and racist violence, my personal journey through head injury and post-traumatic stress disorder; and then add my experience of life and ministry amongst Muslims and my academic qualifications.

The Nigerians may learn my lectures verbatim in order to pass exams, but they will not learn anything for their lives if I have not entered their world, ready to share my own journey and to align myself with theirs. My pain is my major qualification for ministry.

The writer to the Hebrews said something similar about Jesus: 'He himself has suffered, you see, through being put to the test, and that's why he is able to help those who are being tested right now.' (Hebrews 2:18, NT Wright). If we want to 'complete what is presently lacking in the king's afflications', an obvious way of doing it is to enter the world of the Muslims for whom Christ died and share their pain; but we can also voice our own pain in a way that serves people by entering their world.

I use the phrase 'enters their world' very deliberately. It is popular in missiological circles to speak of sharing the *missio dei* – of being aligned with God as a sender. God sends prophets, God sends His Son, God sends His Spirit, God sends His Church… and I am sent as part of that pattern of sending. In the Islamic context, I want to turn this around and say that the heart of God's mission is not His sending nature but His coming nature.

Muslims can agree that God sends – indeed, in the qur'anic economy, sending is His primary activity in revelation and in dealing with the human condition. Even as He sends Adam and Eve out of paradise onto earth, He tells them, 'when guidance comes from Me, as it certainly will, there will be no fear for those who follow My guidance nor will they grieve (Sura 2: 38; 20:123). Elsewhere, the Adam story is followed by this exhortation:

> Children of Adam, when messengers come to you from among yourselves, reciting My revelations to you, for those who are conscious of God and live righteously, there will be no fear, nor will they grieve. But those who reject Our revelations and arrogantly scorn them are the people of the Fire and there they will remain. (Sura 7: 35-36)

In the Qur'an, God's mission to His world can be summarised as sending – sending a long series of prophets and messengers with guidance for humankind. The Arabic word usually translated 'messenger' is *rasūl*, and it literally means 'apostle', 'one who is sent'.

In the Bible, God does indeed send individuals, but most of the 'prophets' of the Qur'an are not (or are only marginally) prophets in the Bible. Adam, Enoch, Noah, Abraham, Isaac, Jacob and Joseph all find their places in Genesis not as prophets but as patriarchs. They and their wives (few of the latter get more than a mere mention in the Qur'an) are important not for the bearing of messages but for the bearing of children, and hence for the establishment of one special people amongst all the peoples of the world. That is, it is not a series of individuals that is 'sent', but a whole people – the people of Israel – that is 'sent'. Israel is God's *rasūl.*[18]

We might ask what is the *risalah*, the message, that Israel is to carry. The answer is that it is nothing less than *the presence of God*. From the Garden of Eden to its achievement as the new earth comes down from heaven (Revelation 21:3), it is God's desire to live amongst human beings. That is why God's revelation is seen in His coming rather than in His sending. The problem with the human condition is not that it can prevent people from getting back to paradise, but that it can prevent a holy God from living amongst them. We sometimes think of the pain of human beings in being separated from God: maybe we can tiptoe into the awesome idea that God might be pained in being separated from us. He wants to come, so He finds ways of coming.

He comes to Adam and Eve hiding in the garden; He comes to Noah's sacrifice; He comes to see and to judge Babel; He comes to Abram and to Hagar and to Sarah and Abraham; and He comes to wrestle with Jacob and to name him 'Israel' (Genesis 32:25-29). Exodus sets up Israel as the locus for the presence of God in the tabernacle, with the sacrifices and the priesthood to make a pure place for the Holy One, and God comes to dwell there. The theme continues throughout the Old Testament, notably through God's presence in the temple and then with the exiles to its fulfilment in the coming of God in the Lord Jesus Christ – surely the *risalah*, the Word, that Israel carries.

We see, then, that God does not just send His Son – He comes in His Son. He does not just send His Spirit: He comes in His Spirit. It is therefore logical to say that He does not just send His Church: He comes in His Church.

[18] There will be a chapter on this idea in the book I am currently writing for Routledge.

Christian mission is not so much about God sending people as about God coming to people. Wherever two or three live in the Name of Jesus, God's has come; and the job of that two or three is to prepare others for His coming into their lives, their families and their communities.

This is, I suggest, where we can understand our pain as our opportunity for 'completing what is presently lacking in the king's afflictions'. As we take our pain into the world of Muslim people, or into the world of non-Muslim fears of Muslims, we can align it with the pain of God. We can, very deliberately, offer it up in worship, and embrace it – not as a way of empowering ourselves, but as a way of participating in the Lord Jesus and His cross. As we pray in our twos and threes, we can begin to see our pain as a pale reflection of the pain of God, and the pain of God will be present amongst the people whose world we have entered.

Perhaps, as we do this, we can help other people to see their pain as a step towards the coming of God in their own lives. I have recently been re-reading Job with the questions of this paper in mind,[19] remembering that Job was a non-Israelite, separated from the people who carried God's presence. The first scene of Job is reminiscent of a caricature of an Islamic world-view – with God as transcendently above His world, sending angels and the 'satan' down to earth to do His will and to report back. Job is, then, an excellent Muslim, carrying out all his religious and familial duties.

Why, we wonder, does God provoke the 'satan' into making Job suffer? The key question of Job from the human point of view might be, 'Is a God who lets people suffer worthy of worship?' But what might be the key question from God's point of view? My analysis suggests that the key question from God's point of view might be, 'How can I come and dwell amongst these sinful human beings?' In other words, as far as God is concerned, the scenario of Himself up in heaven and Job as a perfect servant down on earth is just not good enough. The whole point of the book is that, at the end, God bridges that gap, and COMES!

This is the most important re-connection. This is the only empowerment that we need.

Pain is powerful. It can shake the very foundations of our existence. Trauma changes our world so that our signposts tremble and all meaning is put into question. Pain shook Job's world. His neat religious life and the neat religious world of his friends no longer fitted reality, and, bit by bit, he was pushed to the edge where all he wanted was to meet God.

True, he had no idea what that might mean, and perhaps he still wanted to meet God on his own terms, but he was getting to the stage where he didn't even care about that. Read in this way, Job shows us that, for people outside the covenant community who do not have the temple and the priesthood and the

---

[19] This reflection was also stimulated through reading Tim Davy's thesis, 'The Book of Job and the Mission of God: An Application of a Missional Hermeneutic to the Book of Job', University of Gloucester, 2014.

sacrifice, the way of pain can open the way for God to come to them. This makes sense if the pain in the heart of God is, from eternity, dealing with the sinfulness that prevents His dwelling amongst human beings.

Could we conclude that God not only permitted the 'satan' to test Job, but even provoked the 'satan' to push Job to the place where God could come to him? How many testimonies have you heard from Muslims who have got to that stage, and cried out to God, and the pain in the heart of God has responded to their pain? May we discern how God is using the power of pain, and may we offer Him our own pain to be caught up into His purposes!

How better to finish this reflection than with the voice of that great missionary woman, Amy Carmichael?

I cried and said, "O God, my words are cold!
The frosted frond of fern or feathery palm
On whitened window wrought
As near to burning are, as these my words;
Oh that they were as flames!"

God answered me: "Thou shalt have words
But at this price, that thou must first be burnt,
Burnt by red embers from a secret fire,
Scorched by fierce heats and withering winds that sweep
Through all thy being, carrying thee afar from old delights.
Doth not the ardent fire
Consume the mountain's heart before the flow
Of fervent lava? Wouldst thou easefully,
As from cool pleasant fountains flow in fire?

Say, can thy heart endure
Or can thy hands be strong
In the day that I shall deal with thee?

For first the iron must enter thine own soul,
And wound and brand it, scarring awful lines
Indelibly upon it, and a hand
Resistless in a tender terribleness
Must thoroughly purge it, fashioning its pain
To power that leaps in fire.

Not otherwise, and by no lighter touch,
Are fire-words wrought."[20]

References

'Anglican life in mission: Evangelical fellowship in the Anglican Communion International Consultation July 12-18 2003, Limuru, Kenya', *Transformation*, 20: 4,

[20] Originally published in *Made in the Pans*, Edinburgh: Oliphants, 1917.

October 2003.

Ayoub, Mahmoud. *Redemptive Suffering in Islam: a Study of the Devotional Aspects of Ashura in Twelver Shi'ism*. Berlin: De Gruyter, 1978.

Carmichael, Amy. *Mountain Breezes: the Collected Poems of Amy Carmichael.* Fort Washington, PA: CLC Publications, 1999.

Glaser, Ida. 'We sat down and wept: Biblical resources for conflict situations', in *The Round Table: The commonwealth journal of international affairs,* Issue 382, 2005.

Glaser, Ida. *Trauma, Migration and Mission: Biblical Reflections from a traumatised Hebrew*. Church Missionary Society, 2008.

Herman, J. *Trauma and Recovery: The aftermath of violence – from domestic abuse to political terror*, NY: Basic Books, 1992.

Kitamori, Kazoh. *The Theology of the Pain of God*. Richmond: John Knox Press, 1945.

O'Sullivan, L. 'Nietzsche and pain', in *Journal of Nietzsche Studies*, Spring 1996.

Peace, Barbara Colebrook. *Duet for Wings and Earth*. Winlaw, British Columbia: Sono Nis Press, 2008.

Fire-words: Voicing the Pain
Response 1

Guli Francis-Dehqani

I want to begin by expressing my gratitude to Ida Glaser for her paper and by thanking her and the organisers of this conference for inviting a response from me. When I was approached, I hesitated and expressed some doubt. Having been involved in academic research a number of years ago and having been born into a Muslim context and lived amongst Muslims in my formative years, neither of these things is (at the time of writing) part of my present life. I'm an Anglican priest in the Church of England, currently neither involved in research nor participating in active dialogue or living in relationship with people of other faiths. I say this not by way of apology (as women we do have a tendency to begin with apologies) but by way of explanation. The experiences of my early life in the tiny and much persecuted church in Iran and later living as an exile, together with my research on the role of missionary women in Iran, have shaped me – they inform the person I am and the way I practice my ministry. My faith, the things I hold dear and the issues I'm passionate about arise very much out of my experiences as a woman who is the product of two cultures, languages and religions – this is often uncomfortable and has led to suffering through painful experiences but it has also been and continues to be a source of richness and blessing. So I can echo Ida's words when she writes about her credentials for having worked in Nigeria, that academic qualifications and practical experience counted for little but rather it was pain that was her major qualification, enabling her to make connections, understand people and be understood in return. Similarly, I guess my response to Ida's paper is less scholarly, growing rather out of my own pain and the suffering of the church in Iran.

In reading Ida's paper, I was interested by her use of the word trauma compared with the more familiar Christian terms: woundedness, pain, suffering. Of course it makes perfect sense in relation to Ida's own situation and, moreover, I found it helpful because a change of language can often allow us to think afresh about a subject that may have become overfamiliar. At the same time, I wonder if there are distinctions which remain unexamined in the paper. Trauma implies emotional, psychological or in response to a *specific* experience, which may or may not be repeated, and which causes abnormal stress and perhaps involuntary physiological symptoms such as PTSD. Whereas what I understand by words such as woundedness and suffering imply something broader that relates more to living with pain at a deep level – more like an ache which doesn't necessarily have traumatic or post traumatic implications in quite such an acute way. This is the way I would express my own experience of suffering.

Now of course there is crossover between how I've described trauma and suffering, but they do seem to express somewhat different facets of pain with different implications for what survivors might need in order to deal with their particular situation. Ida's paper is a highly personal and moving testament of how she has dealt with trauma and post-traumatic stress. Though there is of course a broader backdrop which is her family's experiences during the holocaust and indeed the suffering of Jewish people more generally. From these personal experiences she has drawn conclusions (aided by biblical illustrations) which she suggests may be applicable more widely, for survivors of trauma generally.

Ida speaks of analysing trauma along two axes. Firstly, she differentiates between trauma caused by events originating in human sin (war and persecution), and that caused by natural events (earthquakes and famine). Ida of course recognises there is a spectrum here and uses the incident of her parents' car accident to make the point that sometimes events don't sit easily in one or other category. Secondly, she distinguishes between what she calls individual and ethnic trauma. This is particularly interesting to me, as I think *context* – and especially the social and political context of a traumatic experience – might have an impact on how people respond. If a particular experience is part of a wider social or political backdrop, it might be easier for survivors to find meaning in what has happened and to strive for a response that speaks into the situation.

Stephen Cherry in his book, *Healing Agony* touches on this, using the example of Gordon Wilson, whose daughter Marie was killed in Northern Ireland by the IRA in 1987. Wilson's comments in the aftermath of the murder were in contrast to much of the rhetoric of hate associated with Northern Ireland at the time. He said, "I have lost my daughter, but I bear no ill will, I bear no grudge. ... Dirty sort of talk is not going to bring her back to life." (Cherry, 2012:95-6). Cherry argues that it isn't just character or strength of faith which enables such generosity of spirit but that Wilson's words were contextual and political, giving a clear message into an environment where all the pressure was to stoke up hatred and incite yet more violence. (2012:96-103). With his comments, Wilson was saying, "not in my name will vengeance be sought. Let my daughter's death provide no excuse for further violence. Instead, let this tragedy contain the beginnings of hope and something positive."

My family's situation in Iran was similar. During the Islamic Revolution in 1980, my brother's car was ambushed and he was shot dead. He was 24 and his crime was association with the church and being his father's son. My father (who was at the time Bishop in Iran) responded by writing a prayer in which he spoke of forgiveness.[1] Like Wilson, he was speaking into a volatile and violent context, pleading for an end to hatred and looking for something positive to come out of an almost unbearable tragedy. All this is to say that context can be highly significant for those dealing with trauma. The situations I've described seem to me to be very different from one in which an apparently random accident leaves a family devastated and where it might be far more difficult to find a positive message to speak into a wider context. I'm not saying that some tragedies are easier to cope with but that it's difficult to generalise about trauma and people's response to it. Each person and situation is highly individual and the response depends on a whole range of things, but wider family, social and political context may have some relevance.

In addition to these two axes which Ida outlines, I'd like to propose a third and crucial one and that is the distinction between a traumatic event that has passed and one which is ongoing for example living in a war zone, being in an abusive relationship or living with a chronic, painful illness. This axis offers an even more nuanced analysis of the subject under discussion and may also have

---

[1] "O God, we remember not only Bahram but his murderers,
Not because they killed him in the prime of his youth
and made our hearts bleed and our tears flow;
Not because with this savage act they have brought further disgrace on
the name of our country among the civilized nations of the world:
But because through their crime we now follow more
closely thy footsteps in the way of sacrifice.
The terrible fire of this calamity burns up all selfishness
and possessiveness in us.
Its flame reveals the depth of depravity, meanness and suspicion,
the dimension of hatred and the measure of sinfulness in human nature;
It makes plain to us as never before our need to trust in thy love
as shown in the cross of Jesus and his Resurrection.
Love that makes us free from all hatred towards our persecutors:
Love which brings patience, forbearance, courage, loyalty, humility,
generosity and greatness of heart;
Love which more than ever deepens our trust in God's final victory
and thy eternal designs for the Church and for the world:
Love which teaches us how to prepare ourselves to face our own day of death.

O God,
Bahram's blood multiplies the fruit of the Spirit in the soil of our
souls: so when his murderers stand before thee on the Day of
Judgement remember the fruit of the Spirit by which they have
enriched our lives, and forgive."

This prayer has been published in several different places. See, for example, George Appleton (ed.), *The Oxford Book of Prayer* (Oxford: Oxford University Press, 1985), 458. and H.B. Dehqani-Tafti, *The Hard Awakening* (New York: Seabury Press, 1981), 113-14.

some relevance for mission alongside those who suffer. The distinction between a past traumatic event and one which continues touches in particular on the part of Ida's paper entitled "safety and control". Ida recognises the accepted wisdom that the process of recovery requires the establishment of a place of safety for the survivor, and also that feelings of helplessless must be countered by an element of being in control. At the same time, she posits that from a biblical perspective these are forlorn efforts. She talks of the normality of pain in a post fall world and of our attempts to be in control as sinful, arriving at the conclusion that only God is in control and only God provides the place of ultimate safety. If I've understood correctly, for Ida it seems to have been embracing this that aided recovery. She does stress that this has been her own personal experience and I have no wish to invalidate that. Nonetheless, I remain wary of over emphasising divine control and safety *particularly where the trauma may be ongoing* – hence the importance of my 3rd axis. Crudely, what good is it to a woman regularly beaten and sexually abused by her husband that God is in control and offers her a place of safety? Is it right for those of us living in relative comfort and safety to speak of God's safety to someone experiencing daily violence and hostility in a war zone or constant physical pain because of illness?

Of course, I do understand what Ida is expressing and yet in missional terms as we seek to share the pain of others and express our concern and care, I think we have to be careful about our language. I'm a great fan of paradox as essential to faith. A paradox is the holding together of apparent opposites in a kind of creative tension; and I think I recognise a paradox here. For us as women of faith, God is indeed ultimately in control and the greatest place of safety. Both the psalmist and later St Peter in his second epistle express something of our lack of understanding and the narrowness of our perspective compared to God's all-encompassing vision when they speak of a thousand years in God's sight being like a day in ours.[2] And we need to hang on to that. With Paul we might say, "Now we see in a mirror dimly, but then face to face. Now I know in part; then I shall know fully".[3] And yet, it seems to me, that some people have had enough suffering and trauma, and where it continues, the message about not fully understanding the ways of God who is in fact in control, offering safety, may be offensive or harmful at worst and meaningless at best. I reiterate, it's impossible to generalise or have rules about the correct response to trauma or suffering. But for me the idea of God being in control is less significant than perhaps it is for Ida. In the longer version of her paper, which was the one I first read, she writes, "The pain in the heart of the God who is in control and who accepts the sacrifice is what, for me, makes the existence of trauma bearable".[4] By contrast I think what I want to say is, "The

---

[2] See Psalm 90:4 and 2 Peter 3: 8.

[3] 1 Corinthians 13:12.

[4] See longer version of conference paper by Ida Glaser, *Fire-words: Voicing the pain*: 12-13.

pain in the heart of God who is steadfast and comes alongside us in our pain, is what makes the existence of trauma bearable." There is a difference of emphasis here. The one stressing God's control and the other God's presence" and for me, that difference is crucial. Like Ida, I don't have the answers and I seek to live with the questions but for me part of the mystery is that in his very helplessness on the cross – the point at which he has relinquished all control and is in the place of greatest danger – it is there that Christ's suffering touches our pain and connects us to the heart of God.

There was much that I appreciated in Ida's paper. I value, for example, her emphasis on the importance of voicing pain and of lament as part of this process. Without this, we might fail to move on from the trauma or transform the suffering. Many writers speak in some form or other of having to face the pain, expose its rawness and perhaps even rage angrily against it before it is possible to move forward. Marion Partington in her extraordinary book, *If You Sit Very Still,* which recounts the dreadful events surrounding the torture and brutal killing of her sister Lucy, says that the point of recovery began with her expressing feelings of "murderous rage". (Parrington, 2012:106) Stephen Cherry, to whom I have already referred, writes of entering the "wilderness of hurt" which is a place of utter desolation but also the place where "struggle can be rewarded with wisdom and hope". (2012:13-4)

This reminds us of the importance not only of exposing the pain, but of giving it due attention. In her book, *Resilient Pastors,* Justine Allain Chapman explores the role of suffering and woundedness in developing both empathy and resilience for pastoral ministry. She draws on Henri Nouwen's famous image of Christ as the wounded healer but warns against the dangers of overemphasising the woundedness rather than the healing and the damage that can be caused by those she refers to as unhealed wounders. (2012: 107, 116) She talks of resilient pastors (we may insert missionaries) needing to be self-aware enough to recognise their own woundedness (ie voice the pain) and to attend to those wounds. For wounds of themselves do not heal. They lead to healing only when they've been uncovered and dealt with; otherwise they are festering sores, destroying our health and the health of those with whom we deal. (Chapman, 2012:107)

I enjoyed Ida's scriptural analysis with the parallel accounts of the Noah stories as related in the Bible and the Quran and what each of these tells us about the nature of God and God's pain. I loved her emphasis on the incarnation, reminding us that God is one who comes to us rather than one who in a more dispassionate way sends us and that this has implications for how we might understand mission.

There was, however, one topic I felt was notable by its absence in a paper dealing with pain, suffering and trauma and that is the theme of forgiveness. (It is mentioned once in a quote on p. 3 but not explored further) Forgiveness is of course a huge and complex subject not to be approached lightly. Nonetheless, it is a central Christian theme and one which deserves attention in relation to coping with hurt and pain. Furthermore, it seems to me to be intrinsic to the pain in the heart of God and the way in which Christ exemplified and bore his suffering. The way in which God's pain was transformed into love (a theme picked up by Ida in her paper) is surely through his will to forgive the creation that causes his pain. There has been much that is crass and insensitive written and said about forgiveness in Christian tradition. Indeed, we are often accused by secular society of not taking justice seriously and talking instead of a glib kind of forgiveness. In reality, forgiveness is far from the easy option and can involve a lifetime of searching and heart ache.

Recently there has been growing recognition that the subject is immensely complicated and cannot be defined or summarised easily. Endeavours such as the international Forgiveness Project and books such as Partington's and Cherry's to which I've already referred, indicate a developing interest in the topic and an increased awareness that it's not a subject to be approached lightly. Certainly, there is no prescriptive route towards forgiveness nor a clear path with a beginning, middle and end. Each person's experience and circumstances make their response unique and it is unhelpful and harmful for Christians to impose forgiveness on the traumatised and suffering as a prerequisite for the life of faith.

The corollary to forgiveness is perhaps justice. Two sides of the one scale – both of which must be held together in some kind of balance. Again, there is a paradox – we see many times in the Bible and especially the New Testament, God's endless capacity to forgive without counting the cost nor demanding anything in return. That is, I believe, the scandal of Christianity – forgiveness for all. And yet, we also see a God who loves justice and demands righteousness and calls us to speak up wherever there is injustice and suffering. In my own story, my brother's murderers were never brought to justice and what followed his death was for me and the remainder of my family exile and separation. I have had a lifetime of grappling with the theme of forgiveness and what it looks like for me without the comfort or resolution that I imagine may come from some kind of justice. Perhaps it is that which has made me passionate about justice in all areas of life. At any rate, it seems to me that forgiveness and justice have the potential to open up the study of trauma and suffering further. They are central to Christianity and ones we cannot avoid. I would have been interested to hear Ida's thoughts on these in relation to her experience of trauma.

I'd like to end by picking up on Ida's ideas about pain as intrinsic or somehow necessary to mission. This is a rich and interesting theme, resonating with the writings of Richard Rohr who in his book *Falling Upward* uses the term "necessary suffering" as an essential ingredient for maturing in Christian life. (2012:74) Rohr writes about spirituality in the first and second half of a Christian life, relating these not to age but to levels of maturity. He suggests that a degree of suffering is necessary to take us from one stage into the other. That suffering, which may come from tragedy or failure or a falling of some kind, opens the eyes of faith and understanding, giving us tools to mine the richest depths of our spirituality. There is not time here to unpack Richard Rohr further, but I commend his writings to you.

Whilst I warm to the theme of necessary suffering or necessary trauma as Ida has it, I remain cautious about her suggestion that these are things willed on us by God. With Ida, I agree that since we live in a fallen world suffering is the norm and that we should not be surprised by it. And yet some people seem to have so much more of it to bear than others and I resist the notion that that is because God has singled them out for the purpose of testing and purifying. What I do believe instead is that somehow, mysteriously God can use our pain and transform it into something beautiful and wonderful and that when we allow it, suffering can enhance our lives, help us connect with others and in the process take us right to the heart of God.

References

Allain Chapman, Justine. *Resilient Pastors: The Role of Adversity in Healing and Growth.* London: SPCK, 2012.

Appleton, George [ed.]. *The Oxford Book of Prayer.* Oxford: Oxford University Press, 1985.

Cherry, Stephen. *Healing Agony: Re-Imagining Forgiveness.* London: Continuum, 2012.

Dehqani-Tafti, Hassan. *The Hard Awakening.* New York: Seabury Press, 1981.

Partington, Marion. *If You Sit Very Still.* Bristol: Vala, 2012.

Rohr, Richard. *Falling Upward: A spirituality for the two halves of life.* London: SPCK, 2012.

Fire-words: Voicing the Pain
Response 2:
The Pain of God as the Beginning of Good News

Eva M. Bergmann[1]

Um Muhammad, a Syrian refugee in Jordan, told me in tears how her nephew was slaughtered by ISIS. He was stopped at a roadblock and asked to recite the confession. In his panic, the teenager could not remember the words correctly. Um Muhammad ended her account with *shukr 'ala kill shi* – Thank God for everything.[2]

What does the experience of pain mean for our ministry as women who are sharing the gospel with Muslims? This question has been one of the underlying themes of my work since I left Syria in 2011, just as the country that I loved fell apart. For me, each of the different fighting sides bore the faces of beloved friends. Last year, I returned to the region to work with Syrian refugees. As I sit with grieving family after grieving family, this question is becoming even more urgent. Accordingly, I have read Ida's paper with immense interest and benefit, and have not stopped thinking through some of the issues that she raises. In this paper, I will reflect on the correlation of lamenting or praising God in suffering and how I apply this to evangelism. However, before I do that, I have a theological question concerning the Christology that Ida Glasser touches on in her paper.

Is the Pain of God Eternal or Transitory?

I appreciate that the theology of the pain of God Ida presents is an important correction to some of the evangelical theology that has a one-sided focus on God's sovereignty and tends to empty the revelations of God's pain of their meaning, interpreting them as mere anthropomorphisms, sometimes missing the continuity between who God is in the Old and the New Testament.

However, I am struggling with an understanding that identifies Jesus as God's eternal pain, which would be similar to saying that pain is part of God's being. Ida also writes that the pain of God is the response to our sin, the tension between his holy wrath that leads to judgment and love that leads to his commitment to sinful people. Is this not a contradiction? It also seems to

[1] This is a pseudonym.

[2] Visit in Amman, Jordan, March 2015.

contradict Scripture, which begins with the account of God's delight at everything that He has made.

Stating that God's love is "rooted in pain" seems to give prevalence to God's pain over God's love. However, does not 1 John 4 suggest that His pain is rooted in His love in the first place even if this love is only able to persevere in pain as long as sin exists? The way I understand it, His pain is an essential response of His love to sin, that makes us unlovable. It is not alien to God's being, but it is not God's being. It is transitory because, as Martin Luther put it in the 28th thesis of the Heidelberg disputation: "The love of God does not find, but create, that which is lovable to it."[3]

Consequently, scripture is looking forward in even stronger terms than Gen 1, to the day, when God will purely delight again in his holy people, with whom he will dwell:

> On that day it shall be said to Jerusalem:
> "Fear not, O Zion;
> let not your hands grow weak.
> The LORD your God is in your midst,
> a mighty one who will save;
> he will rejoice over you with gladness;
> he will quiet you by his love;
> he will exult over you with loud singing. (Zephaniah 3:16, 17)

This seems to me to say that not only our tears will be wiped away, but also God's pain will be no more when our sin will be no more.[4]

Is Lamenting Necessary to Thanking God in Suffering?

I am aware that since starting my work with Syrian refugees I have more unanswered questions. The thoughts I am presenting in this paper still need to be examined and tried, and I am looking forward to hear your responses. However, the subject of pain confronts us not only in horrendous situations such as the Syrian civil war, but in more ordinary experiences as well. Especially in coming to terms with how Muslim women relate their pain to their personal faith, I also return to my observations previous to the current crisis.

According to my observations, there has been a recent change in the way this topic is perceived among evangelical Christians in Europe. A couple of years ago, I taught a workshop on evangelism among Muslims in Germany. The participants were initially a bit irritated when I chose to discuss suffering rather than an apologetic topic. More recently, I have come across high expectations that God would use the state of suffering in the Middle East to stimulate Muslims to ask questions about God's presence in their pain, thus leading them to Christ.

---

[3] Amor dei non invenit sed creat suum diligibile. WA 1.365.2.
[4] Comp. Jeremiah 31:32; Isaiah 62:4&4; Hosea 14:4 et al.

But are they asking these questions?

Ida briefly touched on the subject of pain in Islam and the way that Muslims may embrace pain now in order to avoid it in the hereafter. I would like to further develop this idea. I believe a better understanding of how lamenting and praising God are interrelated both for Muslim women and for us as Christians could deepen our ministry of Christ to them.

Last December, I started visiting with Nadia and her two relatives. The three families had fled from Syria a few weeks earlier, after their homes were destroyed by barrel bombs. We were still doing the introductory small talk when one of the women started sobbing: her little daughter had died ten days ago. "Don't cry, don't cry" the others tried to calm her down. "Say *al hamdu lillah,* praise God", "It is what God has willed", "Thank God for everything!"[5]

Shukr 'ala kill shi – Thank God for everything: Even though pious blessings and invocations were very much part of daily discourse in pre-war Syria, in my observation the use of this short prayer seems to have increased under suffering. It is particularly noticeable whenever the conversation takes a religious turn. Expressions of thankfulness combined with invocations of God's sovereignty seem the main reaction. Of course, strong emotions like sorrow, anger, or fear are expressed, tears are wept, and sometimes the enemy is cursed – but more often than not faith related sentiments like the call to praise and thanks are used to stop the voice of pain.

In traditional practice, a death in the family used to be lamented loudly, but with the Islamic revival, these practices have become less prevalent and the ideal of a measured response to suffering more dominant.[6] The understanding that dramatic displays of grief oppose and displease God, are based on traditions like the often quoted "The eyes are shedding tears and the heart is grieved, and we will not say [anything] except what pleases our Lord."[7] Thankfulness in suffering, on the other hand, makes sense if suffering merits forgiveness of sins, as the following *hadith* promises: "No fatigue, nor disease, nor sorrow, nor sadness, nor hurt, nor distress befalls a Muslim, even if it were the prick he receives from a thorn, but that Allah expiates some of his sins for that."[8]

If suffering is explained as a way to gain forgiveness or a test of faith which is successfully "passed" when the believer patiently praises and thanks God, lamenting has no rightful place. At first sight, this rationalization of suffering apparently can help Muslims to cope in admirable ways. One of my Syrian

---

[5] Visit in Ta'labaya, Lebanon, 09.12.2014.

[6] Comp. Katharina Lange: "There Used To Be Terrible Disbelief": Mourning and Social Change in Northern Syria, in *Ethnographies of Islam: ritual performances and everyday practices*, ed. B Dupret, et al (Edinburgh: Edinburgh University Press, 2012). 31-39.

[7] Sahih al-Bukhari, Vol. 2, Book 23, Hadith 390, as quoted in: http://sunnah.com/bukhari/23/62 [accessed 07.09.2015].

[8] Sahih al-Bukhari, Vol. 7, Book 70, Hadith 545, as quotes in: http://www.sunnah.com/urn/52930 [accessed 07.09.2015].

friends, for example, explained to me, how the patience of the prophets and the hope of reward helped her in the middle of her pain and anger when she felt pressured to get married to an abusive man. God's testing of her faith through her difficult life circumstances made sense to her. Learning to thank God became a way to deal with her situation. Understanding personal suffering as punishment for sin has helped another friend to cope with the pain of infertility after an earlier abortion. Feeling that she knew the reason why God did not give her a child helped her to come to an acceptance of her circumstances, and to focus on gaining forgiveness through supererogatory prayers rather than on her pain.

If our culture tells us that safety is normal, and suffering is not normal I have observed that there is at least a strong counter tendency in Muslim culture to accept trials as God's method to divide good people from bad. This idealizes the measured response in which thanksgiving quickly follows the tears, as an expression of true faith.

At the same time, these typical reactions of Syrian Muslim women remind me of Job's "The LORD gave, and the LORD has taken away; blessed be the name of the LORD." (Job 1:21), words that have echoed through the centuries as the good Christian response to suffering. Shying away from lamenting is not only a Muslim reaction, but a natural religious response that sees lamenting as dangerously close to doubting God. However, in my observations, there is a deeply rooted fear among the Muslim women that I work with, based on the teaching of Islamic sources, that protesting against suffering that is God's will would place them in opposition to God himself. In a similar vein, Muslims may voice consternation at the lack of patience and thankfulness of biblical prophets.[9]

There are, of course, alternative ways in which Muslim women try to cope with suffering. Various practices, both orthodox and heterodox, promise protection and provision of needs by means of visits to shrines, use of amulets and the Qur'an to gain blessings. Though I am not focusing on these practices here they do reveal that merely thanking God in suffering often does not bring real peace of heart to the believer.

In the Bible, the sovereignty of God and lamenting cannot be seen as a contradiction because God himself laments the evil of human kind in the prophetic literature. I wonder if we could even go so far as to understand some of the texts about human cruelty, that seem to lack theological meaning or even the mentioning of God, in the sense that they are texts in which God remembers the pain. – Taking scripture as the word of God seriously, maybe we can even say that God voices his pain at the senseless evil that is committed in making these texts part of his word. One example is the texts that record the violation of women, such as the rape of Dina, or Tamar. In the latter case, distressingly,

[9] As for example Muhammad Abdel Haleem in: The Story of Joseph in the Qur'an and the Bible, in *Understanding the Qur'an* (New York: I.B. Tauris and Co Ltd, 2001), 138-157.

David refused to acknowledge and act on what had happened, leaving Tamar desolate - but God remembers her and her suffering to this day.

The Muslim women with whom I work seem to see lamenting as contradictory to praising, whereas the psalmist often laments and praises in the same breath. This is only possible because biblical lamenting does have the opposite function from the praising that I have observed among Muslims. Rather than showing strength of faith and earning forgiveness through perseverance, coming before God with lamenting is an expression of our weakness. Rather than passing the test of faith, in our lamenting we express that we are riddled with doubts about God's presence, about whether He is still for us or against us. We pour out our lack of understanding asking why, voicing the apparent senselessness of the suffering of the innocent while the godless prosper. Yet lamenting leads to praise because of who God is – a God, who obviously wants us to pour out our hearts before him in unrestricted, totally honest ways; who can be asked because we expect him to answer. That God should be there with us in the pit of despair, when we fail the tests of faith – this realization brings us to wonder and praise.

In this sense, lamenting that leads to praise is only possible because of God's pain. It says in Hebrews, that we should come to God without holding back, because Jesus' compassion with us is based on his own experience. Lamenting has a different quality, as we believe that we are addressing the One who understands all pain in total depth. Lamenting becomes praise with the amazement at God's closeness and being with us, based on His pain, he *knows*.

Ida has written about the pain of God because of His desire to be with us, loving what cannot be loved, that is expressed throughout scripture in God's laments for his people and found its ultimate expression in the cross. I wonder whether God's lamenting isn't actually the necessary condition of our lamenting. God, by revealing his heart to us, enables us to pour out our hearts to him. Thus, the laments of God in scripture draw us closer to God in our pain.

I have started with the question whether the experience of pain is a bridge for us as we share the gospel with hurting Muslim women. I wonder whether one way of doing so could be to invite Muslim women on a journey to learn to lament before God. This process would teach them about God's heart.

How Does Lamenting Prepare the Way for the Gospel?

Syrian refugees have so many needs. I am often overwhelmed, and sometimes I wonder – and sometimes I'm challenged by others – whether studying scripture is really something that they need now. Will it do any good? Are we just adding some biblical material to the religious knowledge of these broken people? Or even worse, do we portrait Christianity as a quick solution to their pain? I think that reflecting on the pain of God and our pain is important because it points to one of the huge challenges in evangelism: how to get to deeper levels of what Muslims hold true concerning God and humankind, by starting a process that changes the ways they think and practice faith. The main method that I use is chronological inductive Bible studies and storying with families or small groups of women. In my experience, these are great tools to make the salvation story known, but obviously our own understanding shapes the way we teach how to read the texts we choose. For example, one of the recurring discussions among my co-workers is, whether the story of Noah should be part of our chronological study set because of the Qur'anic version. The argument is, that the Genesis account teaches nothing new to Muslims. Others suggest that we start the study in verse 9 to avoid offending Muslims with the description of God's regret. A third group likes to include the Qur'anic account of Noah's unbelieving son to emphasize the message of salvation through obedience. Ida's reading of the Genesis account helps to focus our understanding of this text as a text about who God is, first of all.

Another text that comes to my mind is the account of Abraham's sacrifice. For many Muslims Abraham is one of the main examples of God inflicting pain on believers to test them. While the Qur'anic account is relatively short with a focus on the son's complicity, Islamic traditions have recounted heartrending dialogues between Abraham and his son. They reflect on how the sacrifice could be done in a way that Abraham would not be overcome by his pain and thus fail to obey.[10] Pain is undoubtedly a theme in the Genesis account, too, as Isaac is described more than once as "the son, whom you love". Here, as father and son walk up the mountain, and Isaac asks about the sacrifice, Abraham cannot bear to tell his son what he is planning to do. Where is God in this story of painful willingness to obey? The Sufi Farid al-Din Attar (d. 1221) writes, that God inflicts pain because he does not love. He tells the story of a Christian merchant whose beloved son dies. In his pain, the father converts to Islam, arguing that God cannot have a son or he would never have afflicted him so terribly. (Kermani, 2008:191) The theology of the pain of God, on the other hand, suggests to read the story of Abraham's sacrifice as a story of God's love, helping us to catch a glimpse of what it means that the Son sacrificed himself for us, the pain of Abraham becoming a type for God's pain that we can only – partly – understand because human parents also love their children. If we are studying scripture chronologically, the way we understand who God is from Gen 6:5-8 and 8:21 helps us to understand who He is in Gen 22.

We discover God as the One who loves us with real love, who responds to our sin with pain, so that He does not destroy us. This vital message shows the cross of Christ as essential to who God is. By applying this to reading Old Testament texts with Muslim women, my question is, whether those, who are learning to lament before God, may be more ready to embrace Him who suffers in response to our sin?

---

[10] Al-Tabari, e.g., recounts the tradition that Isaac said to Abraham: "Do not lay me down on my side for I fear that if you gaze into my face, weakness will overtake you and that will come between you and the command of God concerning me." Quoted in: Andrew Rippin and Jan Knappert, eds. & trans, *Textual sources for the study of Islam.* (Manchester: Manchester University Press,1986), 65.

Since beginning my work with Syrian refugees, I have often considered how to study the Bible as a book that talks about being a refugee. Consequently, before I start to read the Bible with them as a story of redemption I have started to read it as a book about God's care for and presence with displaced and grieving sinners.

The Biblical accounts of Hagar's flight from Sarah and later expulsion, for example, do not give us any hints that Hagar called to God in her distress, nor that she had great faith in Him. Even though she experienced God being with her during her earlier flight, apparently she had not learned to cling to God's promise to prosper Ishmael when they were facing death again after their expulsion. Yet God heard the weeping and saved her.

The story of the exodus is another text that speaks especially to refugees in the Middle East who share the experiences of oppression in foreign countries and the fear of violent death. However, scripture is very clear that neither their suffering nor their faith redeemed them but God's compassion and faithful love of the covenant with their forefathers. Maybe this is common place theology, but in practice, compassion and feelings of inadequacy in the face of suffering so easily leads us down the road of reading these passages as texts about good suffering people and bad oppressors.

These stories prepare for Bible studies of texts of lamenting. My goal is that women, encouraged by God's merciful response to weeping, will move from the religious pressure to praise, to embracing a text like Lamentation 5. I think that this prayer can only be prayed to the God of the Bible, even if the women with whom I study have only just started a journey to know Him. Learning how to lament and to pour out their hearts to God with all their terrible experiences means learning to express that their pain has no redeeming qualities because lamenting is a confession of our absolute weakness. That is why I hope that overcoming the opposition to express questions, doubts and feelings of abandonment before God will prepare their hearts for the gospel.

Conclusion

Sharing our experiences of pain and lamenting with Muslim women can make us feel very vulnerable, because it looks – and sometimes is judged – as "less spiritual" than the ubiquitous thanksgiving and reminders of God's will. However, studying Biblical texts of lamenting is hugely liberating indeed. My hope is that suffering Muslims will recognize their true hearts in the biblical texts about pain and lamenting, and that the courage to be real before God, because he cares and knows, could give them a great desire to know Him, who saves people who constantly fail the test of suffering.

References

Abdel Haleem, Muhammad. *Understanding the Qur'an*. New York: I.B. Tauris and Co Ltd, 2001.

Kermani, Navid. "Das Buch der Leiden", *Der Schrecken Gottes. Attar, Hiob und die metaphysische Revolte*. Munchen: C.H. Beck Verlag, 2008.

Lange, Katharina "There Used To Be Terrible Disbelief": Mourning and Social Change in Northern Syria. In Dupret, B., et.al.: *Ethnographies of Islam: ritual performances and everyday practices,* Edinburugh: University of Edinburugh Press, 2012.

Rippin, Andrew and Jan Knappert (eds. & trans.) *Textual sources for the study of Islam*, Chicago: Univeristy of Chicago Press,1986.

6

When Women Speak: A Missiology of Resistance

When Women Speak: A Missiology of Resistance[1]

Cathy Ross

Introduction: Silencing Women

This chapter will explore in some detail the impact of violence enacted against women globally simply because of their gender. It will then offer an analysis of this violence through the lens of Iris Marion Young's five faces of oppression. It will consider the place of patriarchy and sin in colluding with this oppression. Finally, it will consider a range of missiological responses concluding with a call to resistance and renewal.

Women have been silenced and rendered invisible throughout the ages. Sexism, silencing of and violence against women are longstanding problems and are universal. They happen everywhere in our world. Let me give you a high profile example from the UK to introduce this phenomenon.

In 2013, the Bank of England announced that Winston Churchill would replace social reformer Elizabeth Fry on the £5 note. This meant that every bank note issued would have a man on the reverse side – all male luminaries. Christine Criado-Perez decided to challenge this and naively assumed that the Bank would cave in immediately as it was so clearly an unnecessary and unhelpful decision.

This campaign ran for three months with petitions, legal challenges, meetings until finally the Bank gave in and announced that they were issuing a new £10 note with Jane Austen on it. The campaigners had won. However, the day after the Bank's announcement, Caroline received her first rape threat by Twitter. Then another. And another. By the end of the first weekend, the police had 300 A4 pages of vitriolic and vicious threats against her. Her (incorrect) address and phone number were posted on the internet. She had a panic button installed in her flat. After two months of constant abuse, she closed down her twitter account.

In her book, she quotes a study from the University of Maryland where fake accounts were set up and sent into chatrooms. "Those with female names received an average of 100 messages every day that included "sexually explicit or threatening language."" (Criado-Perez, 2015:124) Criado-Perez concludes

---

[1] Parts of this paper were first published in my article "Marvellous Makanaka: Contextual Mission, Women and the Holy Spirit in the Church" in Thomas Hughson (ed) *The Holy Spirit and the church: Ecumenical Reflections with a Pastoral Perspective. (*Abingdon: Routledge, 2016), 73-98. It is reproduced here with the permission of the publisher.

that women are being told to shut up and be silent. She theorises that many of the threats that she received and much of the violence perpetrated against women focuses around the speech area. Research conducted by Professor Lorna Martin of the University of Cape Town into the injuries suffered by femicide victims found that a large proportion of the injuries were in the face and neck area. Criado-Perez sees this as a clear message – that women are to be shut up by any means necessary. She claims that this silencing starts early – boys interrupt at almost three times the rate of girls according to some research.

Gendercide

Issues of gender affect all of us, are systemic and deeply embedded within our societal structures, so that often we are not even aware of how this injustice plays out. Let me offer an example from the UK. The annual UK *Sex and Power Report* shows a distressing absence of women from senior positions in public life. The 2011 edition claimed that 'it will take another 70 years to achieve an equal number of women directors in the FTSE 100 and another 45 years to achieve an equal number of women in the senior judiciary. It will take another 14 general elections – that is up to 70 years – to achieve an equal number of women MPs.'[2] That is a shocking and revealing indictment regarding representation of women at senior levels.

This points to issues of lack of representation and invisibility but it is even more depressing and distressing when we consider global violence against women and girls:

> The global statistics on the abuse of girls are numbing. It appears more girls have been killed in the last fifty years, precisely because they were girls, than men were killed in all the battles of the twentieth century. More girls are killed in this routine 'gendercide' in any one decade than people were slaughtered in all the genocides of the twentieth century. In the nineteenth century, the central moral challenge was slavery. In the twentieth century, it was the battle against totalitarianism. We believe that in this century the paramount moral challenge will be the struggle for gender equality around the world. (Kristof and WuDunn, 2009:xvii)

The term 'gendercide' was first used by feminist writer Mary Anne Warren in her 1985 book, *Gendercide: The Implications of Sex Selection.* The term gendercide is helpful in raising consciousness because it names and defines the problem for what it is – violence, prejudice and bias against women and girls based on their gender.

In 2013, the WHO called violence against women a 'global health problem of epidemic proportions.' (Criado-Perez, 2015:202-3)

The statistics about violence against women are difficult to absorb so this is well labelled as gendercide to give us an awareness of the massive nature of the

---

[2] http://www.equalityhumanrights.com/sites/default/files/documents/sex+power/sex_and_power_2011_gb__2_.pdf, p3.

problem. 'Misogny rooted in historical, cultural and religious belief systems continues to fuel crimes and practices that target women and girls.' (Criado-Perez, 2015:52) This is expressed in many forms throughout the world. In China, for example, through the one-child policy which has resulted in the forced sterilization of women, prenatal sex identification resulting in the abortion of female foetuses and tens of thousands of baby girls being abandoned. In 1990, Indian economist, Amartya Sen estimated the number of Asian females missing aborted, killed, neglected or put to death at one hundred million.[3]

Human trafficking is another form of violence against women and girls. Although trafficking of persons affects all people, the US Department of State reports that approximately 80% of those trafficked are women and girls of whom 50% are minors. (Gerhardt, 2014:47) Traffickers take advantage of natural disasters and target the most vulnerable – women and girls because of their gender and marketability. Sex tourism and child pornography are global industries made more accessible by the internet.

FGM is one of the most disturbing gender-related atrocities against women. It comprises all procedures that involve partial or total removal of the external female genitalia, or other injury to the female genital organs for non-medical reasons. It has no health benefits and can harm women and girls in many ways. It is normally performed as a rite of passage ceremony and is an attempt to control a young girl's sexuality and to ensure her virginity for marriage. In December 2012, the UN General Assembly adopted a resolution on the elimination of female genital mutilation. More than 125 million women and girls are living with the consequence of FGM.[4]

Early or child marriage is another violation against women. Child marriage threatens girls' lives and health, and it limits their future prospects. Girls pressed into child marriage often become pregnant while still adolescents, increasing the risk of complications in pregnancy or childbirth. These complications are a leading cause of death among older adolescents in developing countries.[5] Moreover, young girls who marry before the age of 18 have a greater risk of becoming victims of intimate partner violence than those who marry at an older age. This is especially true when the age gap between the child bride and spouse is large. Like FGM, this is a complex cultural issue but ultimately one that is harmful to women.[6]

Rape of women and girls in war-torn areas has now been defined as a war crime. However, 'an estimated 20,000 rapes were committed in the war in Bosnia, yet they resulted in only 27 convictions; 64,000 rapes in Sierra Leone

---

[3] http://www.nybooks.com/articles/archives/1990/dec/20/more-than-100-million-women-are-missing/

[4] http://www.who.int/mediacentre/factsheets/fs241/en/

[5] http://www.unfpa.org/child-marriage

[6] http://www.who.int/mediacentre/news/releases/2013/child_marriage_20130307/en/

yielded six convictions; and 500,000 rapes in Rwanda, eight convictions.'[7] An Oxfam report in 2010 conducted in the Democratic Republic of Congo revealed that 60% of rape victims were gang raped by armed men and that there was a seventeen-fold increase in rapes against civilians between 2004 and 2008. The report also describes the stigma of rape for the women. Only 1% of women went to the hospital with their husbands and wives are often abandoned because of the associated stigma.[8] Rape, 'honour killings', sexual assault – these forms of oppression as violence are endemic and the numbers are simply overwhelming.

In their now familiar scenario of reducing the global population to a village of 1,000 people, Amnesty International has depicted the plight of gender-based violence against women to help us grasp the enormity and scandal of this issue.

> In this village, 500 are women. It would be 510, but 10 were never born due to gender-selective abortion or died in infancy due to neglect. 300 are Asian women. 167 of the women will be beaten or in some other way exposed to violence during their lifetime. 100 of the women will be victims of rape or attempted rape in their lifetime.[9]

This is a brief analysis of gender injustice with particular reference to violence against women. Feminist theologians analyse this epidemic of systemic and structural violence against women in different ways. Some analyse pornography, for example, as an expression of a power relation in which women are depicted as submissive objects that men desire to dominate. This then helps to embed distorted power relations in society at large. Julia Kristeva analyses violence through the lens of psychoanalysis and 'claims that the social desire to brutalize and efface women's bodies is tied to a social unconscious that secures its masculine identity by wounding or destroying the metaphoric "body of the mother/feminine."' Others use Rene Girard's scapegoat theory which says that groups achieve coherence and meaning through ritually enacted sacrifices of victims. They argue 'that communities create a feminine victim whose body becomes an acceptable and accessible site for this definitive act of sacrifice.' (Jones, 2000:90)

Five Faces of Oppression

Clearly, the issue of violence against women and the fact that women are over represented in statistics and issues of poverty, war, illness, unemployment, homelessness, migration, morbidity, invisibility all point to a common theme of women's oppression. Broadly defined, this refers to dynamic forces —personal, social and systemic – which diminish or deny the personhood and flourishing of women. In fact, we need many theories of oppression. We need to

---

[7] http://articles.latimes.com/2009/aug/13/opinion/ed-rape13

[8] https://www.oxfam.org/en/pressroom/pressreleases/2010-04-15/new-report-shows-shocking-pattern-rape-eastern-congo

[9] http://www.amnesty.org.au/svaw/comments/2370/

understand economic exploitation where women may be underpaid, and theories about sexual violence; we will need to understand cultural oppression such as Female Genital Mutilation (FGM). We need to acknowledge the dynamics of power and domination in which women may occupy the subordinate place and therefore exercise diminished control over their lives. And, of course, the personal plays a role in the dynamics of domination.

'When feminists say that 'the personal is political' they are saying that what happens in the bedrooms, kitchens, workstations and interior dialogues of women must be included in the theories of oppression.' (Jones, 2000:74) If we depersonalise oppression too much, then we fail to see the ordinary places where women can try to challenge their oppression and encourage resistance to enact social change.

Iris Marion Young, who was Professor of Political Science at the University of Chicago, offers the following analysis of oppression. She describes five faces of oppression: exploitation, marginalisation, powerlessness, cultural imperialism and violence.

Oppression as Exploitation

In the West, this is most clearly seen in the split between the public sphere and the private sphere. Historically, this idea emerged after the Industrial Revolution with the rise of a capitalist economy and the creation of the nuclear family. 'Public and private', 'the angel in the house', and the cult of true womanhood are also part of the language and concepts which attempt to describe and analyse the state and role of women in 19th century Britain and America. The ideal Anglo-American woman of the 19th century was to be pious, pure and domesticated – able to present her home as a model of pious domesticity and a spiritual haven from a materialist world. The 'proper' sphere of women was to be in the home while men were to be in the world. We see the legacy of this still in the West today. We find this public/private split elsewhere leading to exploitation in the labour of slaves, children, indentured labourers, servants, migrant workers – even the sex industry, polygamous families, and child brides.

Oppression as Marginalisation

According to Young, '*Marginalisation* is perhaps the most dangerous form of oppression. A whole category of people is expelled from useful participation in social life and thus potentially subjected to severe material deprivation and extermination.' (Young, 1990:53) Young Lee Hertig from Korea gives a good example of marginalisation in her article on 19th century Bible women and 20th century evangelists in Korea, "Without a Face" because they remained "invisible and faceless." (Hertig, 2002) Yet despite this, they "carried the gospel from house to house and were sacrificially devoted to their labour of love." She claims that once the church began to become institutionalised, "masculinization of the Korean church took place, and the hard labour of the Bible women remained invisible and faceless. Patriarchal leadership took over and continued to harvest the Bible women's work with women's labour credited to male leadership." (2002:186) Chung also confirms this claiming that the new Christian movement became "a new version of confinement and bondage" as women were once again marginalised and so the "Korean church became, and remains, male dominated." (Chung, 2012:227)

Oppression as Powerlessness

'*Powerlessness* is the inhibition in the development of one's capacities, lack of decision-making power in one's working life, and exposure to disrespectful treatment because of the status one occupies.' (Young, 1990:58) This particular face of oppression is linked to not having a voice. A sense of powerlessness can make us feel trivialised and silenced. One can feel so downtrodden and disempowered that one cannot even imagine a new reality. Brazilian educator Paulo Freire talks about a culture of silence. According to Freire, oppressed people become so powerless that they do not even talk about their oppression so they are silenced. They have no voice and no will.

This can also happen through indoctrination or a colonisation of the mind where people are given negative images of themselves and become dehumanised. This then becomes internalised so that they cannot imagine another way or a new reality. Abolitionist Harriet Tubman wrote, "I would have freed thousands more, if they had known they were slaves." In other words, people did not even realise that being a slave was wrong and evil – such was their level of oppression and marginalisation. Freire advocated *conscientization* – making people aware of their conditions and that another life is possible.

Grooming of young girls for illegal sexual gratification may be a good example of this form of oppression where young women are dehumanised, drugged and degraded to such an extent that they are powerless to extract themselves.

Oppression as Cultural Imperialism

'To experience *cultural imperialism* means to experience how the dominant meanings of a society render the particular perspective of one's group invisible at the same time as they stereotype one's group and mark it out as the Other.' (Young, 1990:59) Cultural imperialism happens when groups develop and apply cultural standards for defining the norm and then impose this inappropriately. So in the West, we might say that the norm is white, male and heterosexual so that even simple things such as parental leave, when meetings are scheduled, ways of socialising may be problematic for women.

Culture can certainly be a source of oppression and this was readily acknowledged by early missionaries – footbinding of women in China or *sati* in

India being obvious examples. There are also more subtle examples such as tribalism in the Majority World or 'old boys' clubs' in the Western world which can deeply embed male power. Atola Longkumer, from India, claims that "discrimination, exclusion, marginalisation and even violence" exist within the church. (Longkumar, 2012:189) She explains how a lack of gender analysis has led to a truncated understanding of the gospel so that an equal Christian community has not been created. This has led to "a position and participatory power that is not very different from the pre-Christian mission days for the Ao women despite education and Christianisation." (Longkumar, 2012:198) This does beg the obvious question as to why Christian mission did not seem to challenge cultural practices that were discriminatory or harmful towards women.

There are all sorts of cultural norms that can work against women from not being allowed to drive in Saudi Arabia, to unjust inheritance laws, to the witness of a woman being worth half that of a man.

Oppression as Violence

This is perhaps the most obvious form of oppression. In the UK, one in four women will experience domestic violence in their lifetime and two women per week are killed by a current or former partner.[10] In the USA, there is a reported rape every 6.2 minutes and one in five women will be raped in her lifetime. Violence against women and girls is defined by the WHO as 'any act of gender-based violence that results in physical, sexual, or psychological harm or suffering to women, including threats of such acts, coercion, or arbitrary deprivations of liberty, whether occurring in public or private life.'[11] The systemic causes of violence against women and girls have social, cultural and religious roots. It also has long history. 'Historical acceptance of the domination and objectification of females is a reality within every global culture and history.' (Gerhardt, 2014:36)

Women worldwide aged 15 through 44 are more likely to die or be maimed because of male violence than because of cancer, malaria, war, and traffic accidents combined. American activist Rebecca Solnit, in her essay on gender-based violence entitled 'The Longest War' wrote the following. I quote her at length because it is so pertinent and powerful,

> If we talked about crimes like these and why they are so common, we'd have to talk about what kinds of profound change this society, or this nation, or nearly every nation needs. If we talked about it, we'd be talking about masculinity, or male roles, or maybe patriarchy, and we don't talk much about that.
>
> Still, the pattern is plain as day. We could talk about this as a global problem, looking at the epidemic of assault, harassment, and rape of women in Cairo's

[10] http://www.nhs.uk/Livewell/abuse/Pages/domestic-violence-help.aspx, accessed 24.06.2015.

[11] http://www.who.int/mediacentre/factsheets/fs239/en/

> Tahrir Square that has taken away the freedom they celebrated during the Arab Spring – and led some men there to form defense teams to help counter it – or the persecution of women in public and private in India from "Eve-teasing" to bride-burning, or "honor killings" in South Asia and the Middle East, or the way that South Africa has become a global rape capital, with an estimated 600,000 rapes last year, or how rape has been used as a tactic and "weapon" of war in Mali, Sudan, and the Congo, as it was in the former Yugoslavia, or the pervasiveness of rape and harassment in Mexico and the femicide in Juarez, or the denial of basic rights for women in Saudi Arabia and the myriad sexual assaults on immigrant domestic workers there, or the way that the Dominique Strauss-Kahn case in the United States revealed what impunity he and others had in France, and it's only for lack of space I'm leaving out Britain and Canada and Italy (with its ex-prime minister known for his orgies with the underaged), Argentina and Australia and so many other countries.[12]

Patriarchy and Sin

Feminist theologians claim that we experience oppression because of patriarchy and sin. Patriarchy is understood to be an all-encompassing ideology which legitimates, normalises and institutionalises oppression of women by men.

> The social, cultural, economic and material conditions of 'patriarchy' effect a fundamental and comprehensive distortion of every sphere of human life: the construction of personal and gendered identities; the relationships between men and women; the construction of meaning and value; our relation to nature, including our own bodies. (McFadyen, 2000:145)

This then becomes pathological and the ideology masquerades as natural and normal; the way things are; the order of reality. The distortions are so deep and so embedded that no one is free of it. Patriarchy is bad for all of us – men and women – it distorts reality for everyone. Moreover, we can become blinded by this as the prevailing culture and fail to see and name this oppression as sin. And then, as feminist theologian Serene Jones writes, 'we must strain hard to see, given the powerfully destructive ways in which oppression structures our thinking and makes even the most profound forms of brokenness seem normal.' (Jones, 2000:109) Oppression works like a blinder preventing us from seeing that we are caught in sin. Therefore, relations of domination begin to abound and women become disempowered and invisible.

Feminist theology critiques a traditional understanding of sin which may help us in the church as we think of a response to this situation of oppression. In 1960, Valerie Saiving Goldstein published a seminal paper entitled, 'The Human Situation: A Feminine View' in which she argued that selfishness and pride might be central problems for men but that it was different for women. Feminist theologians challenge the traditional understanding of sin as pride and idolisation of self. Women's sense of self may not be overabundant and

[12] http://www.tomdispatch.com/post/175641 /tomgram%3A_rebecca_solnit,_the_longest_war, accessed 24.06.2015.

typically, their sense of self is submerged in relationships with others so that women actually exercise self-negation to serve others' needs and interests to the detriment of their own.

> For women the temptation is to succumb to their dependence upon others for identity. This temptation in turn spawns typically "feminine" sins such as exaggerated self-abnegation, the loss of self in socially directed roles, and the refusal to develop one's gifts in service to God and others. (Stewart van Leeuwen, Knoppers, Koch, Schuurman, Sterk, 1993:170)

Therefore, taking pride as the paradigmatic understanding for sin expresses what is typical for men, not for women.

Feminist theologian and psychologist Mary Stewart van Leeuwen offers a compelling analysis of the Fall. She argues that as a result of the Fall, man now suffers from domination and woman suffers from social enmeshment. Man's desire for appropriate dominion, which in its proper form was given originally to both man and woman pre-Fall, is now expressed as a desire for domination. Before the Fall, woman had a desire for intimacy and community which was distorted by sin and so her peculiarly female sin 'is to use the preservation of those relationships as an excuse not to exercise accountable dominion in the first place.' She concludes that what started as 'creational socialability' now becomes 'fallen social enmeshment.' (1990:46) So, women opt out, try to keep the peace at any price and may even avoid developing a strong, inner self. This can then lead to women becoming victims and to situations of unhealthy co-dependency. This analysis has many implications for women. In all contexts and cultures, women must be encouraged to view themselves as responsible human beings and agents, not just objects to be acted upon. It means that women do not need to find their identity in victimhood and that sometimes the harder calling will be to leave that behind. It means that although women may indeed be acted upon unjustly, women must reject self-abnegation and resist any cultural or religious pressures to bind, demean and diminish.

Missional Response

So what is a missional response to all of this? These are difficult issues that work on many levels. Oppression, injustice and silencing of women's voices are bad for all of us – it is not just a women's issue. There has been an increasing recognition of this. In the UK, The Everyday Sexism Project exists to catalogue instances of sexism experienced by women on a day-to-day basis. This is what they say on their website:

> They might be serious or minor, outrageously offensive or so niggling and normalised that you don't even feel able to protest. ... By sharing your story you're showing the world that sexism *does* exist, it *is* faced by women *every day* and it *is* a valid problem to discuss. It is a place to record stories of sexism faced on a daily basis, by ordinary women, in ordinary places. To show that sexism exists in abundance in the UK workplace and that it is very far from being a problem we no longer need to discuss. ... To stand up and say 'this isn't right',

> even if it isn't big or outrageous or shocking. Even if you've got used to thinking that it is 'just the way things are'.[13]

In September 2014, Emma Watson (of *Harry Potter* fame) launched the popular 'HeForShe' campaign against gender inequality. As their website states: "HeForShe is a solidarity movement for gender equality that brings together one half of humanity in support of the other half of humanity, for the benefit of all."[14]

The 'five faces of oppression' analysis is one way of unravelling and understanding the injustice while these particular analyses of sin may help us develop a more nuanced approach to liberation and salvation for women. It may also help us to understand how, in some cases, the church has enslaved women with particular understandings of sin and servanthood over the centuries. If women are continually serving the needs of others, then telling them that they are proud or prideful sinners may not be the best way of allowing women to flourish and find wholeness. If women are diminished and experiencing violence, then their self-confidence and self-esteem will need to be restored and they need comfort and safety.

Now I would like to offer a variety of missional approaches that women have practised and I present these by way of a response to this oppression of women:

- A Missiology of Emptiness and Hiddenness,
- A Missiology of Comforting, Consolation and Healing,
- A Missiology of Hospitality and Relationship,
- A Missiology of Sight, Embrace and Flourishing,
- A Missiology of Resistance

These are all approaches that women are familiar with and these are approaches that enable us to get alongside women. However, all of these approaches do mean walking a slightly perilous road. Each of these approaches (apart from the last one) could, in fact, embed injustice, suffering and social enmeshment so we need to be aware of that in our appropriation of these responses.

A Missiology of Emptiness and Hiddenness

For women, their involvement in mission is often experienced from this point of weakness, sacrifice and invisibility. Women are familiar with approaches that are hidden, less recognised and rarely celebrated. We ALL need to recover these perspectives in our missiology, not just women. Taken to an extreme, these could reinforce unhelpful patterns of domination and submission for women. However, I believe that Jesus' approach was one where he emptied himself for the sake of others, where he sometimes even asked people to keep

[13] http://everydaysexism.com/

[14] http://www.heforshe.org/, accessed 29.6.2015.

his healing miracles secret, where he declared that the first would be last, and told his disciples that we all need to take up our cross to follow him. Jesus' approaches of being hidden, less known and less recognised are Christian approaches in keeping with meekness and humility and that we all (men and women) would do well to emulate.

A Missiology of Comforting, Consolation and Healing

A missiology of comforting draws from the power of the Holy Spirit to comfort, transform and heal – both humanity and creation. The Holy Spirit, also known as the Comforter, is the one who comforts the broken, the afflicted, the suffering. God is a God of consolation who is with the HIV/AIDs sufferers, the abused women, the victims of IS, of war. Women and children are the victims of war and violence. Women struggle on to feed and protect their families, to live in reconciliation and peace, to bind up the wounded, to heal the broken-hearted.

Chung Hyun Kyung claims that Asian women believe "in spite of," – in spite of lack of protection from their fathers and brothers who may beat them or sell them into child marriage or prostitution. She writes, "Some Asian women have found Jesus as the one who really loves and respects them as human beings with dignity, while the other men in their lives have betrayed them." (1992:124) In other words, women find consolation in their relationship with Jesus. They know that Jesus sides with silenced Asian women and can bring liberation and wholeness. Jesus is the one who can bring healing, solace and renewal for women.

A Missiology of Hospitality and Relationship

A missiology of the house or a missiology of the kitchen table could be a necessary corrective to much of our missiology. This conjures up images of intimacy, homeliness, warmth, comfort, rootedness, safety and relationship. Hospitality is a powerful metaphor with which to think about mission. It begins with God and is an essentially outward looking practice and virtue. Hospitality involves listening, learning, seeing the other and negotiation of space by all parties. Generous hospitality can lead to reconciliation and genuine embrace of the other. Again, hospitality is not a simple metaphor and plays out in different ways in different contexts. So while for some it may indeed mean invitation, warmth, sharing of food, relationship; for others it may mean ongoing stress and virtual impoverishment as hospitality is demanded and expected sometimes beyond the resources available.

The whole guest/host conundrum is a fascinating study for Christian mission. Who is the guest and who is the host? This very question is demonstrated and incarnated in the life of Jesus.

Jesus is portrayed as a gracious host, welcoming children, tax collectors, prostitutes and sinners into his presence and therefore offending those who would prefer such guests not to be at His gatherings. But Jesus is also portrayed as vulnerable guest and needy stranger who came to his own but his own did not receive him. (Jn 1:11) Pohl comments that this "intermingling of guest and host roles in the person of Jesus is part of what makes the story of hospitality so compelling for Christians." (1990:17) Think of Jesus on the Emmaus Rd as travelling pilgrim and stranger, recognised as host and who he was in the breaking of bread during a meal involving an act of hospitality. Or think of the Peter and Cornelius story (interestingly, another story involving varieties of food) – who is the host and who is the guest? – who is the insider and who is the outsider? Both offer and receive, both listen and learn, both are challenged and changed by the hospitality of the other. So we can see the importance of not only the ambiguity but also the fluidity and reciprocity/mutuality of the host/guest conundrum. We offer and receive as both guest or stranger and host.

What does this mean for us as we engage in mission? Are we guest or host? Strangers to be welcomed or hosts offering hospitality? And, of course, this is where hospitality as a metaphor for mission becomes so intriguing and compelling.

> Hospitality questions one's way of thinking about oneself and the other as belonging to different spheres; it breaks down categories that isolate. It challenges and confuses margins and centre. Hospitality involves a way of thinking without the presumption of knowing beforehand what is in the mind of the other; dialogue with the other is essential.... To welcome the other means the willingness to enter the world of the other.... (Richard, 2000:12)

Of course, this is the magic of mission and the challenge of the gospel. When we encounter the other as guest or host; insider or outsider (like Peter and Cornelius); when we engage in deep listening, we too are transformed and changed. We learn new things about ourselves and about the gospel. The whole guest/host idea begins to break down and becomes much more fluid and blurry as we learn from and relate to one another in mutual exchange and reciprocity.

A Missiology of Sight, Embrace and Flourishing

The gifts of sight and insight are gifts of the Holy Spirit. Just as the women disciples were the first to see Jesus, our eyes have to be opened to recognise Jesus also. Once we can see Jesus, the Holy Spirit enables us to see the other person. Christian mission requires that we actively see and welcome the guest and stranger in our worlds. A missiology of sight must encourage Christians to acknowledge the identity of the other – the other who is full of potential to be realised in relationship with Christ. The actual and the potential must be seen and acknowledged together. In this encounter with the other, I too am confronted with the truth of myself and all that I am capable of becoming. When I embrace the other, in a small way I begin to die to myself and begin to see myself in the other. John V Taylor comments, "But no less necessary to the Christian mission is the opening of our eyes towards other people. The scales fell from the eyes of the convert in Damascus precisely when he heard one of those whose very lives he had been threatening say, 'Saul, my brother, the Lord Jesus has sent *me to you.* I-Thou." (1972:21)

Flourishing refers not just to human flourishing but to our web of interdependency with all of creation. Feminist theologians have long seen the connection between exploitation of women and the domination of creation and therefore call for a re-imagination of our relationships within all of creation so that flourishing is for all of humanity and all of creation.

- A Missiology of Emptiness and Hiddenness,
- A Missiology of Comforting, Consolation and Healing,
- A Missiology of Hospitality and Relationship,
- A Missiology of Sight, Embrace and Flourishing,

A Missiology of Resistance

All these different missiological approaches are a kind of missiology of resistance. When we can authentically practise these approaches then we are undermining power, resisting domination and opposing oppression. Speaking for the voiceless and empowering the voiceless to speak, exposing and resisting systemic evil is difficult and sometimes dangerous. To engage in a missiology of resistance, we need support; we need a community around us who will support, encourage, pray and stand alongside us.

We are also called to be a prophetic voice. This is part of the conscientization process as we try to understand the forces that alienate and oppress women, that marginalise and silence women, and then to analyse and explain because awareness is the beginning of change. Along with change comes hope – that it does not always have to be like this; that a new world is possible.

This will involve practical, prophetic action also. Elizabeth Gerhardt in her book *The Cross and Gendercide: a Theological Response to Global Violence Against Women and Girls,* explains, 'harmful economic and political policies that do not allow for needed resources for women and their families are a hindrance for women's ability to become independent and to provide for their families.' (2014:157) She explains that poverty, violence and disease constitute a triple threat for women. In most parts of the world, women bear the main responsibility for meeting the basic needs of the family but are often denied access to the basic resources to make this possible such as adequate nutrition, healthcare and education. 60% of the world's hungry are women, two thirds of the world's illiterate people are female, the majority of children not in school are girls, women make up 80% of all refugees and displaced people. The cycle of poverty, violence and disease affects women all over the world. Gerhardt claims that united efforts by churches to understand this and to challenge and shame traditional practices that oppress women will make a difference. She maintains that microfinance can make a real difference in this regard and is a good way for churches to become involved also. This can empower women and give them an opportunity to feed and educate their families.

She cites studies which show 'that microfinance improves not only women's financial situations but their self-confidence and their ability to make decisions that benefit their families.' (2014:161) Improving self-confidence and self-esteem is vital when considering strategies to reduce violence. Poor men may feel equally powerless but cultural expectations and patriarchy will ensure that men exercise dominance within their families. This is true for women everywhere. We see co-dependency and lack of self-esteem in battered wives the world over.

Gerhardt quotes studies showing that as families become more stable, there is less stress in the family, husbands actually respect their wives more and the children have better access to health and education. The Women's Empowerment Programme in Nepal discovered that '68% of women in its programme experience an increase in their decision-making roles in the areas of buying and selling property, sending their daughters to school and health care for their families.' (2014:163) Gerhardt concludes that the most effective programmes are those that are holistic and consider the cultural, political, social and religious contexts. Another example is *28 Too Many* which was started in 2010 by Ann-Marie Wilson as a project to undertake research and provide knowledge and tools to community based organisations working to end FGM in the 28 African countries where it is practised and the diaspora.[15]

Conclusion

Two of the eight United Nations Millennium Development Goals directly concern women: to promote gender equality and empower women (no 3) and to improve maternal health (no 5). The secular world is aware that this is a major issue, which needs a global strategy to resolve. We are the church. We know that without the inspiration of the Holy Spirit and the example of Jesus, global strategies, good and worthwhile as they may be, will not ultimately succeed. This is why gender analysis and an understanding of sin and patriarchy are important so that we can engage in effective measures of resistance against oppression and exploitation. As the church, we are called to 'share the lot of those who suffer and to care for the needy and the marginalized. The Church proclaims the words of hope and comfort of the Gospel, engages in works of compassion and mercy (cf. Luke 4:18-19)' We are called to offer healing, wholeness and newness of life – salvation.

When we can do that effectively, maybe our world will begin to look like this vision of girlhood offered by poet Imtiaz Dharker, a Pakistan born British poet who was awarded the Queen's Gold Medal for English poetry in 2014. Let me conclude with an excerpt from her superb poem, *Night Shift*.

---

[15] http://28toomany.org/

Night Shift
Imtiaz Dharker (2014)
I can see from your name that your mother and father
danced in the streets when you were born
and sent out sugar-sweets to tell the world a gift had come
to them, and they called you Marvellous,
they called you Marvellous, they called you
Marvellous Makanaka.

References

Cadorette, C., et. al. (eds) *Liberation Theology: an Introductory Reader.* Maryknoll: Orbis, 1992.

Chung, Meehyun, 'Mission and Gender Justice from a Korean Protestant Perspective'. pp. 223-246 in *Putting Names with Faces*. Edied by Christine Lienemann-Perrin, Atola Longkumer, Afrie Songco Joye. Nashville:Abingdon, 2012.

Criado-Perez, Caroline, *Do it Like a Woman... and change the world.* London: Portobello, 2015.

Dharker, Imtiaz. *Over the Moon.* Hexham: Bloodaxe, 2014.

Gerhardt, Elizabeth. *The Cross and Gendercide: a Theological Response to Global Violence Against Women and Girls.* Downers Grove: IVP, 2014.

Goldstein, Valerie Saiving, 'The Human Situation: A Feminine View'. *The Journal of Religion*, Vol. 40, No. 2 (April, 1960): 100-112.

Hertig, Young Lee. 'Without a Face: The Nineteenth Century Biblewomen and Twentieth Century *Jeondosa*'. pp. 185 - 199 in *Gospel Bearers, Gender Barriers, Missionary Women in the Twentieth Century.* Edited by Dana Robert. Maryknoll:Orbis, 2002.

Jones, Serene. *Feminist Theory and Christian Theology: Cartographies of Grace*. Augsburg: Fortress, 2000.

Kristof, Nicholas and Sheryl WuDunn.*Half the Sky: Turning Oppression into Opportunities for Women Worldwide.* New York: Knopf, 2009.

Kyung, Chung Hyun 'Who is Jesus for Asian Women?'. pp. 123 - 141 in *Liberation Theology, An Introductory Reader.* Edited by C Cadorette et. al. Maryknoll: Orbis, 1992.

Longkumer, A. 'Tetsur Tesayula: Christian Mission and Gender among the Ao in Northeast India'. pp. 187-206 in *Putting Names with Faces.* Eds Christine Lienemann-Perrin, Atola Longkumar and Afrie Songoo Joye. Nashville: Abingdon, 2012.

McFadyen, Alistair. *Bound to Sin, Abuse, Holocaust and the Christian Doctrine of Sin.* Cambridge: Cambridge University Press, 2000.

Pohl, Christine. *Making Room: Recovering Hospitality as a Christian Tradition.* Eerdmans: Grand Rapids, 1999.

Richard, Lucien. *Living the Hospitality of God.* New York: Paulist Press, 2000.

Saiving Goldstein, Valerie. *The Journal of Religion*, Vol. 40, No. 2 (April 1960); pp. 100-112.

Stewart van Leeuwen, Mary; A. Knoppers, M. Koch, D. Schuurman, H. Sterk. *After Eden: Facing the Challenges of Gender Reconciliation*. Grand Rapids: Eerdmans, 1993.

Stewart van Leeuwen, Mary, *Gender and Grace: Women and Men in a Changing World.* Leicester: IVP, 1990.

Taylor, J V. *The Go-Between God: the Holy Spirit and the Christian Mission.* London: SCM, 1972.
Young, Iris Marion. *Justice and the Politics of Difference.* Princeton:Princeton University Press, 1990.

When Women Speak: A Missiology of Resistance
Response 1

Nicole Ravelo-Hoerson

Cathy Ross certainly needs to be commended for her willingness to attend to past and present omissions in missiological discourse and for her active stance towards mending the omissions. Her approach is significant as it requires being both open and receptive to face repressed issues that have been purposefully allowed to remain under the surface, and it does indeed expand the framework of missiology. Thank you, Cathy, for the clear examples of the many dimensions through which oppression operates! They highlight the fact that women's battles are far from won. BIC's National Women's Day post on Facebook is an illustration of this lack of respect.

Since South Africa's first and free democratic election held on 27 April 1994, changes within South African society have been dramatic. However, while there is much to celebrate, the current situation is sobering. Domestic violence against women is still widespread and rape is on the increase. Pumla Dineo Gqola from the University of Witwatersrand calls it "a South African nightmare". It seems that constitutional advances have generated tremendous backlash. The National Women's Day commemorates 9 August 1956, when over twenty thousand women of all races and ages from all over South Africa, marched together towards the Union Buildings in Pretoria to protest against a legislation aimed at tightening the apartheid government's control over the movement of black women in urban areas. Its main point is to honour the role and the often overlooked contributions of women in building a more equitable South African society. BIC's post to celebrate that day, however, triggered a massive response of tweets and calls of outrage and indignation. It read:

"1 – Look like a girl
2 – Act like a lady
3 – Think like a man
4 – Work like a boss"[1]

Not all men thought that it was offensive to women though. The fact that those men accepted that that post was amusing and called it a joke showed that sexism has become normalised.

To demonstrate that women were not oversensitive, overreacting, or getting worked up about nothing, the deputy news editor at Eyewitness News, Camila Bath, tried to imagine the inverse:

---

[1] http://ewn.co.za/2015/08/11/Bic-under-fire-for-sexist-womens-day-post

" 1 – Look like a boy
2 – Act like a gentleman
3 – Think like a woman
4 – Work like a boss "

In so doing, she pointed out that all South Africans have not reached a level playing field yet.

How do we gather up some of the lessons from Cathy's paper and weave them together into a strategy for a more integrated missiology?

To this end, this response addresses in the first instance a comment that Cathy's paper alludes to, the difference between self-imposed silence and externally imposed silence.

Why Are Women in Seminary Classrooms as well as in Christian Communities so Often Silent?

Of particular concern to me is the self-imposed silence of females in religious settings, especially in evangelical circles. From my personal experiences, it seems to me that the liberation specifically advertised in evangelicalism contradicts some of the lived experiences of women in such circles.

Recently, I taught at a Bible college. Five female students and twelve male students attended the lectures. I used a classroom teaching method that encouraged verbal participation. While all the male students took part, the five female students were silent. They did not utter a word even during the question-answer periods. In so doing, they became invisible members of the classroom. The male students confidently played a dominant role. They knew, they spoke up, and they belonged, while the female students positioned themselves by choice in a supportive role through their lack of speech. My numerous conversations with those female students after the lectures showed that they did not lack topic control and that their silence was a conscious strategy on their part. It was quite revealing that they did not seem to realize that they colluded in their own disenfranchisement and tacitly accepted a subservient position. This lack of female voice, which I have only observed in religious groups, raises the following questions:

- Why are women in seminary classrooms as well as in Christian communities so often silent? Are they quiet in such settings because the particular community values their silence?
- Do they put on gender roles like costumes?
- Do Christian women in various church-related contexts rehearse themselves into voicelessness?
- Do they perform their gender in certain ways because they think certain styles are closely related to being godly or good? Is silence perceived as godly feminity?
- Are we limiting ourselves and each other by such gendered performances? If so, how?

What is problematic here is the tension between self-imposed silence and externally imposed silence.

I grew up in Madagascar believing that my human potential should never be restricted because of my gender. My parents encouraged and promoted in their six children various individual experiences and opinions. My mother, with the strong support of my father, embraced different ways of being a woman in the house and in the work place, which were described as "feminist" by her French friends and colleagues. Her simple answer then was: "If returning to my traditional Malagasy values and wisdom which believe in the full flourishing of both men and women is called feminism, so be it!" She was a pioneering woman in her field. Although my mother did not find the term "feminist" adequate, I claimed it as part of my identity. When I became a Christian in 1977, my intellectual life and my newly found passion for Christ smoothly came together. Connecting the two most powerful ideologies of my life Christianity and feminism, was a natural process. This coming together continues to profoundly shape all the deep textures of my life: living as a wife, living as a childless woman, living in relationship with my extended family, my missionary community as well as my church congregation, spiritual journeying, teaching, evangelizing, writing, researching and mentoring younger people. Of course, I now have a very different consciousness about feminism than I did when I was a naïve young girl living in Madagascar. When I left the wider secular society, I discovered however that many Christian women, especially evangelical ones, struggled to believe that Christianity and feminism could or should exist concurrently in their lives. According to the commonly held opinion then and still now, if one is a "Christian", then one must adhere to certain performances of that identity; if one is a "feminist", then one cannot have a dynamic religious faith because religious faith may be demeaning to women. Hence, to be a woman committed to feminist ideas necessitates a role of assertiveness and aggression, while to be a woman committed to Christ necessitates the role of submitting. I know that women's lives are multiple, mixed, and multifarious, but I often see women who are torn between the supposed contradictions between being a feminist and being a Christian.

Is it possible for Christian women from the West to engage in a missiology of resistance and give a voice to the voiceless in a national and cultural context outside of the West when they themselves have not been able to break free, not of oppressive structures, but of self-imposed silence?

How Do We Lead Women Who Choose to Silence Themselves in Christian Contexts on a Journey towards Gaining Voice?

This brings us to the second point, which is the question: How do we lead women who choose to silence themselves in Christian contexts on a journey towards gaining voice?

I would like to suggest a step, drawn from over thirty years of ministry, which I believe is indispensable as it could motivate the beginning of the journey.

The first step of the journey consists of the genuine acknowledgement of the problem of self-imposed silence and its accompanying ambivalence and contradictions. In my experience, some of the most honest conversations about this issue have arisen out of my own willingness to call myself a feminist and to share what being a feminist means to me and for me in my ministry as an evangelical Christian and a missionary. This self-identification has helped and helps my interlocutors to face their own fear of the "f-word", as Melanie Springer Mock calls it, and its attendant issues – gender roles, women in ministry, and Biblical authority. It encourages them to challenge their belief about themselves, about others, and about God. This process of self-discovery can break down the barriers that hold them back from using their gifts and skills within some Christian communities or in the service of the church. My self-identification may also mean that I have to answer some direct and sometimes personal questions about my own and my husband's feminist and Christian commitment. It can also elicit conversations about gender and women's oppression that are missing in the evangelical context. Indeed, with its connection to the rich history of and discourse on feminism, the term "feminist" belongs to an informed vocabulary which recognises the global world of women's ongoing oppression and understands the complexity of these domains in differing past, present, and future contexts. It can also lead to reasoned and informed responses to caricatures of feminists and misconstrued definitions of feminism, and best of all, it provides opportunities to mentor young women who come to me for personal issues surrounding gender, sexuality, and feminism. Acknowledging the problem of self-imposed silence can be quite unsettling for some women, therefore it is important to accompany them with support, listening ears, feedback, and resources as they strive to be honest with themselves and others, consider and process. Sharing with them stories of other women of faith who have propelled the Christian faith in significant ways, and thus serve as examples to compel a re-examination of feminism's place in Christian communities, can also inspire them to persevere.

While silence can be self-imposed, it can also be imposed externally by religious beliefs and structures as well as by socio-cultural practices.

This brings us to the last point.

How Do We Lead Women Living in Externally Imposed Silence on a Journey to Gaining Voice?

In October 2014, I helped organize a conference in Nairobi, which brought together fifty women from sixteen different African countries. Its theme was designed to facilitate a discussion about the position, problems, progress, and possibilities for women in Christian-Muslim relations. The impetus of that conference was the necessity to address the devaluing and exclusion of African women's voices.

I examined different ministry models and noticed that the degree in which the female MBBs involved were perceived to participate in verbal give-and-takes was considered by most of the delegates as a significant determinant of the quality of the models described.

I also observed that some articulate, confident and outspoken delegates, who described themselves as feminists, seemed to favour discipleship approaches which sought to neutralize, reverse or modify rapidly the converts' traditional conditioning, original socialization and religious programming, and turned the MBBs into active and vocal agents of change instead of passive beneficiaries. They argued that church meetings should include both sexes as soon as possible to reflect the holistic nature of the body of Christ. On the other end of the spectrum, another group of delegates expressed their support for discipleship methods which did not overtly challenge men's realm of power, but allowed new female believers to remain in their traditional domains where they experience security, solidarity, and dignity, and can grow spiritually and develop a voice at their own pace, without the potential of male dominance.

It was clear that there were mixed feelings as to the best way to plant churches to nurture MBBs, at that conference in Nairobi, but all the factions agreed that an effective church planting method should also give female MBBs a voice, a point supported by sociolinguists, anthropologists and missiologists such as Evelyn Hibbert. To that end, Hibbert argues for the possibility of a "gendered approach to church planting in Muslim background contexts". Women need to be empowered with skills, knowledge and confidence to determine the development path they wish to follow and to challenge the entrenched structures, beliefs and practices which hamper them. A gendered approach provides a safe environment in which women can learn, articulate their concerns, develop solutions and explore their God-given potential. Hibbert posits that

> Encouraging women to use and develop their gifts within familiar structures and spheres of influence may not only result in a more mature church, but also help women to have a fulfilling ministry as well as a positive influence on their community. It would also allow men's discipleship to focus on issues that are of particular importance to men. If both men and women are enabled to grow in maturity in their faith and have the opportunity to be fulfilled and affirmed in ministry, they may be more able to engage with each other and act in unison rather than competition or conflict. When both men and women feel secure and confident, they may be more able to sensitively construct new bridges between private and public spaces which reflect the community of Christ as best suits their context. (2015:293)

And as Hibbert explains, empowered women are "silent no more".

> Missionaries to highly gendered societies, especially Muslim societies, need to be open to different patterns of expression of the community of Christ, and to be ready to support meeting structures that are congruent with local patterns. A church is more than a meeting on Sunday and, as such, all the ways the

> community meets and interacts work together to develop the Body of Christ in that context. In this way, different patterns of gendered meetings could allow for the growth of the church, and especially the empowerment of women, in ways that recognize women's leadership and which are consistent with local patterns of gathering and of spiritual activity. (2015:293)

I started this paper with a story from South Africa and I would like to conclude it with a quotation from the South African missiologist David Bosch to help us reflect further on the meaning and importance of a missiology of resistance.

> ...missiology acts as a gadfly in the house of theology, creating unrest and resisting complacency, opposing every ecclesiastical impulse to self-preservation, every desire to stay what we are, every inclination toward provincialism and parochialism, every fragmentation of humanity into regional or ideological blocs, every exploitation of some sectors of humanity by the powerful, every religious, ideological, or cultural imperialism, and every exaltation of the self-sufficiency of the individual over other people or over other parts of creation. (1991:496)

References

http://ewn.co.za/2015/08/11/Bic-under-fire-for-sexist-womens-day-post.

Bosch, David. *Transforming Mission: Paradigm Shift in Theology of Mission.* Maryknoll: Orbis Books, 1991.

Hibbert, Evelyn. 'Considering a gendered approach to church planting in Muslim-background contexts'. *Missiology: An International Review* 43:3 (2015): 286 – 296.

When Women Speak: A Missiology of Resistance Response 2

Karen Shaw

I'm grateful to Cathy Ross for prompting me to bring together my missions background and my concern for the place and treatment of women in the world and among God's people. As I have worked on my own missiology of resistance, I have realized that, like all good missiologies, it should be theologically sound, contextual, and practical.

Theologically Sound

A missiology of resistance must be biblically and theologically sound. It should have *a clear goal, a biblical eschatology*. David Bosch's *Transforming Mission* showed how the church's missiology has been driven by different biblical foci over the centuries. I am increasingly drawn to 1 Peter 4:11 as my biblical basis for ministry among women. "Whoever speaks must do so as one speaking the very words of God; whoever serves must do so with the strength that God supplies, so that God may be glorified in all things through Jesus Christ. To him belong the glory and the power forever and ever. Amen." As someone who has been persistently shushed most of her life in the church, I delight in the idea that women are entrusted with speaking God's own words and ministering by His power, and that, in so doing, we bring glory to God through Jesus. By having this focus in mission, I gain criteria by which I can assess what I do. For example, I can ask if the women I disciple are speaking, and if so, if their words seem to be an echo of divine speech. Is their serving from their own power (or powerlessness), or is it full of divine strength and authority? Is their speech Christocentric and bringing glory to God? You might direct your focus elsewhere: what is important is that we are clear about our end game.

A missiology of resistance would define women (and men), both individually and collectively through *biblical anthropology and ecclesiology*. Unfortunately, in the Arab world the church's understanding of womanhood is at odds with the vision of women speaking as though their words are the very words of God, ministering with God's strength, and thereby bringing God glory. Instead, the popular anthropology and ecclesiology are grounded in local and imported versions of patriarchy. In the MENA region, we are in desperate need of male and female voices presenting a truly biblical understanding of women and men created together as God's co-regents, and the church as the first fruits of restored creation in which there is neither Jew nor Greek, slave nor free, male nor female.

A theology of revelation and a vital pneumatology are essential to a missiology of resistance, for we must define missiologically what we mean by speaking. We cannot resound with the voice of God unless we understand what divine speech is and feel the breath of the Sacred Speaker. The scriptures tell us that by the word of God the universe was created, and that Jesus is that word, God's ultimate communication with humanity. God's word, says the writer to the Hebrews, "is living and active, sharper than any two-edged sword, piercing until it divides soul from spirit, joints from marrow; it is able to judge the thoughts and intentions of the heart." (Hebrews 4:12 NRSV). Pneumatology will prepare us (cognitively, at least) for spiritual warfare, reminding us that our struggle is not ultimately against flesh and blood, but against demonic powers and systems. In Muslim contexts, women and men who follow Jesus need a reliable *doctrine of witness and martyrdom.* This is particularly important for women disciples, many of whom are unused to speaking authoritatively, and many of whom are particularly vulnerable to isolation, violence, and so-called "honour killings" as a result of their witness.

As we saw from Cathy's paper, our *hamartiology* plays an important role in determining our missiology. I appreciated Cathy's pointing out that traditional theologies, written almost exclusively by men, may not grasp adequately women's experience of sin. I personally resonated a great deal with the idea of sin as enmeshment, but struggled to find the idea in Scripture. Perhaps idolatry as woman's primary sin would be more to the point, particularly in an Arab context, and given the severity of both the Biblical and Islamic stances toward idolatry. I have heard Arab believers claim that it is more important for a woman to submit to her husband than to obey Scripture. I have repeatedly seen Arab women more afraid of offending their husbands than of displeasing God. Much of what passes for virtuous feminine submission is in fact androlatry or the cult of family and community, "exchanging the truth about God for a lie and worshipping and serving the creature rather than the Creator." (Romans 1:25 NRSV).

Our *Christology and soteriology* will define the shape our resistance takes: as Christians, that shape must be cruciform. It was through the cross that Jesus overcame the powers, and our resistance will succeed in no other way. In this, we differ from Western secular feminists. Jesus, Himself the very Word of God, knew when to provoke with piercing words of truth and when to be silent and entrust His case to God. The authorities were convinced they had silenced Him, unaware that God had given Him all authority in heaven and on earth, that He was about to commission His disciples to tell His salvation to all nations, or that He was about to pour His Spirit out on His male and female servants and that they would tell God's mighty acts with power in many languages. Women – and men –have eternal power in communication when we speak and live in echo of the word and Spirit of Jesus.

Contextual

Thinking through my own missional theology of resistance has so excited me that I was tempted to start writing a missiology of women's voices for the MENA region. That would have been a mistake, the classic mistake of an arrogant missionary. If I had done so, I would have, in promoting Arab women's voices, silenced them and substituted my own voice. Healthy missiology is contextual. So is healthy resistance. A Lebanese Muslim feminist once complained to me about the cultural imperialism – not of Christian missionaries – but of Western secular feminists who feel they have the right to define for all women the criteria and cultural norms of gender equality. Over and over, I have been surprised that issues which make my blood boil make my Arab sisters shrug, but they weep or lash out over matters that would never have occurred to me. Now I am thinking of getting together theologically astute women from the MENA region and listening to (and perhaps helping them to record) their voices.

What are some of the issues that concern women in my context? Lebanese women have expressed their anger about not being able to pass their citizenship on to their children. They are beginning to speak out against domestic violence. During an election period, they raised their voices against one party's advertising campaign which sought to manipulate women's votes without giving them true representation in Parliament. Muslim women tell about the emotional trauma of living under their husbands' constant threats of divorce or taking another wife. Women of all backgrounds and levels of society complain that they are expected to work full-time *and* do all the housework *and* all the childcare *and* tutoring of their children. They resent how easily one word, *mustarjala* (a women behaving like a man), can instantly silence the most successful, insightful and dynamic of the female sex. Lebanese women express alarm at the growing immorality and secularization of their society. It is as local women hear and speak Jesus into these situations that their voices will be heard with divine authority and grace. Foreigners need to be servants of this process, not masters.

Although local women's agenda and voices must dominate if we are to avoid imposing Western cultural imperialism, there are some unique roles that foreign workers can play, three of which I'll mention here. First, we can be megaphones, amplifying their voices in situations where local women are ignored or patronized, but professional foreign women are not. Second, we can be mirrors, helping women to see themselves and their society by our scholarly reflections. For example, my students find enlightening the research demonstrating that in Mediterranean cultures men react to feeling shamed by aggression and taking charge, women by increasingly submissive behaviors and social conformity.[1] My experience is that this sort of research gives local

---

[1] Shiraev and Levy, 176, L. Abu-Lughod, *Veiled Sentiments* (Berkeley: University of California Press, 1986, A. Blok, "Rams and Billy-goats: A Key to Mediterranean Code

women greater self-understanding and therefore more confidence in their own voices. Third, sometimes we must be prophets pointing out the sin which garbles the voices of the women we are urging to speak. An example that comes readily to mind is the mistreatment by some Lebanese women of their foreign domestic employees: women who advocate their own rights while trampling on the rights of other women lack moral authority. It is imperative, should we take any of these three roles, to do so with humility and quiet tones, listening as well as speaking, and, as Paul says, watching ourselves lest we also be tempted. (Galatians 6:1)

Local women and men who must be the primary mouthpieces of Jesus in local situations. This means that in all of our discipling, from early evangelism to seminary training, we need to teach Bible interpretation and spiritual discernment. Much of the unhealthy teaching which muzzles women comes from poor hermeneutics: interpretations which distort the word of God. Female Arab believers, despite all of the external and internal barriers to speaking out with confidence, will communicate with authority if they know that they are speaking "as though speaking the very words of God." We need Arab women teaching hermeneutics at all levels, for the example of a woman exegete inspires other women and demonstrates to all that God can be heard in a woman's voice.

It is particularly vital at this moment in history that female believers in the MENA region be empowered to speak divine truth. Never before in history have so many Muslims come to believe in Jesus, and for the first time ever, a large number of communities of Muslim-background believers are experimenting with new forms of church. The result of this experimentation will set in concrete the intellectual, relational and cultural foundations of the MENA churches for generations and even centuries to come. As the only woman – a foreigner – on the faculty of the only seminary in the region that gives degrees to MBBs, I am desperate to see local women learning to interpret Word and Spirit, teach in every situation possible and become master-teachers of God's word. The body of Christ in the MENA region is destined for persecution and hardship: to render half of that body mute and powerless is (figuratively speaking) to subject the body of Christ to a stroke just when Crist is seeking to act with power in this part of the world.

Practical

A missiology of resistance must be theologically sound, contextually driven, and it must be taught and modeled practically. My missiology has to be worked out in four ways: teaching women to hear God's voice, teaching women to

---

of Honor," *Man* 16 (1981): 427-440. Although in this instance the researcher has an Arab surname and the authors of the book in which I found mention of this research are Jewish, both resources were published in the West in English, and therefore inaccessible to most of my students.

listen and then speak as though speaking God's own words, exposing women to other women speakers, and helping women find platforms from which women can speak. Rather than theorizing about the practical, let me give examples from my own life and observation.

Teaching women to hear God's voice. One of the courses I have taught at ABTS is entitled *Women from Joshua to 2 Kings*. Students learn both about these extraordinary women and about how to interpret the Bible. Muslim and Christian-background believers are amazed at the number and variety of women in God's word. Most are surprised to learn that in none of these books is the purpose of the author to teach "the role of women." In vain, they search for a way to reduce these biblical heroines and villains to a stereotyped pattern of biblical womanhood. Instead, they find God fulfilling His purposes through these women, just as through the men. Female students watch their male classmates discover, often for the first time, that God wants to teach them through the women of the Bible, and that the whole church, and not just the Tuesday morning women's circle, needs to listen to the heroines of the faith. Women inevitably come out of this course more confident, and men more respectful, than when they entered. Although I teach this at an advanced academic level in a seminary, the same results can be achieved in a simple Bible-storying approach to discipling illiterates.

Teaching women to listen well and to speak with divine authority. As part of a course on the spiritual disciplines, Bassem Melki, the Dean of Students at ABTS, teaches a potent session on silence and speech, simply laying out what the Bible says about how we should use, and refrain from using, our mouths. He then requires the students to fast from speech for 24 hours. Both male and female students find this practical teaching transformational. Through it, they come to recognize the power of both silence and speech, and how often they devalue and squander words. We must not assume that women will have something worthwhile to say, or say it in a godly way, just because they have been allowed a voice. Speaking the very words of God is an art learned over a lifetime. But listening is just as important as speaking. In particular, Christian women and Muslim followers of Jesus who have been hurt by Islam and Muslims need to be taught how to listen well to Muslims.

In addition to formal teaching about speech, the power of women's voices can be augmented by *exposing women to other women speakers* who are articulate, edifying and confident in using the voice God has given them. There are a small but growing number of such women in the region: teachers, *de facto* pastors, leaders of parachurch and other ministries of mercy, and ordinary housewives and working women who are filled with the spirit of God and wisdom. In addition to contemporary voices, we need to hear eloquent voices from the past. Men also need to be become acquainted with these voices, preferably in non-threatening circumstances to begin with, circumstances which may require foresight and care to create, but the effort is worth it. Men who have recognized the voice of God in the words of a sister find it far harder to retain their prejudices.

Helping women find platforms. To be practical in our missiology, we must be creative in finding situations in which women can proclaim God's reign and glory. There are many men and women in the MENA region who are deaf to women's voices, but can see to read. Writing is one potential women's forum in a patriarchal society: books or blogs, articles or advertisements, poetry or prose, logs or letters, stories or Facebook statuses. Many who wouldn't dream of listening to a woman speaker will relish hearing a woman singer, even if she authored the lyrics herself. I affirm vigorously Cathy's recommendation of exploiting hospitality, a traditional Arab virtue, as a forum in which women can both speak and learn, minister and receive. To its shame, the MENA church does not yet ordain women pastors, but that is no excuse for failure to find settings in which to open our mouths in resistance.

Because the sins of pride and idolatry are prevalent, not only at an individual but at a societal level, God's men and women are called to declare His justice at a systemic level. Women in the MENA region have a surprisingly ready podium if they open their mouths to defend of the cause of the poor and oppressed.

While no one should be encouraged to seek *martyrdom*, there is no doubt that it is the pulpit from which God will require some of His precious children to proclaim His grace and saving sacrifice. The words of the martyrs carry tremendous power, and martyrdom is an equal-opportunity dais. If you have not read the poem of 26-year-old Saudi martyr Sara Fatima al-Mutairi, I urge you to do so. Such eloquent resistance! Many thousands of people have been moved by her words.

To Be Continued....

I am the third and final speaker addressing the topic of a missiology of women's voices, but I believe the discussion has just begun. I hope that Cathy, Nicole and I have stimulated you to think deeply about your own missiology of resistance in relation to the silencing of women. As we learn to hear God's voice in this matter and echo it to one another, we become an inspiration and model to women in our own contexts to develop their own missiologies that are theologically sound, contextually poignant, and transformationally practical. We've got a lot of talking to do!

References

Abu-Lughod, Laila, *Veiled Sentiments.* Berkeley: University of California Press, 1986.

A. Blok, "Rams and Billy-goats: A Key to Mediterranean Code of Honor," *Man* 16, 1981.

Bosch, David J. Transforming Mission: Paradigm Shifts in Theology of Mission. Orbis: Maryknoll, 2011.

Shiraev, Eric and David A. Levy, Cross-cultural Psychology: Critical Thinking and Contemporary Applications. Oakland, CA: Pearson, 2004.

Contributors

Miriam Adeney is an anthropologist and missiologist. Her books include Daughters of Islam: Building Bridges with Muslim Women; A Time for Risking: Priorities for Women; and Wealth, Women and God. A professor at Seattle Pacific University, Miriam also serves on the board of Christianity Today International. She works on task forces for the World Evangelical Alliance and the Lausanne Movement.

Eva Bergmann is an independent scholar and church worker, working in Arabic-speaking countries since 2001. Her relationships with Muslim women triggered her research on the attraction of the Islamic revival movement for Muslim women in Syria. Currently she is working with Syrian refugees in the Middle East and teaching Islamics in the context of theological education in Germany.

Bassma Dabbour is a Canadian-Tunisian Christian from Muslim background. Bassma holds a Doctor of Ministry on Leadership. She is the Missiologist and Director of Leadership development of Voice of the Martyrs Canada. With her husband Rev. Riadh Jaballah, they have been serving the NAME and the persecuted church for over two decades. They are blessed parents of three wonderful children Elia, Elina & Elior.

Moyra Dale has lived and worked with her family in the Middle East for over two decades. She worked in adult Arabic literacy and teacher training; and also researched the women's mosque movement. Currently resident in Australia, Moyra continues to write, teach, train, and supervise students, in Islam and crosscultural understanding, with a focus on Muslim women.

Gulnar (Guli) Francis-Dehqani is from Iran, and moved to England with her family following the Islamic Revolution in Iran. She has published in the areas of religious feminism, women's ministry and interfaith studies. Guli has been ordained as an Anglican priest in the Church of England and currently serves as Bishop of Loughborough, UK.

Iris Funk is from Argentina, and has served in North Africa for sixteen years. Working in development, she has worked with both vulnerable children and women, establishing an informal federation of local associations that work with vulnerable women. She is involved in research and advocacy for single mothers in North Africa and their children.

Ida Glaser is academic director of the Centre for Muslim-Christian studies in Oxford, and Associate Staff member at Wycliffe Hall. She previously taught in the areas of Qur'an and Bible and History of Muslim- Christian Dialogue at the University of Edinburgh, and her personal research interests focus on reading the Bible in the context of Islam.

Dwi Maria Handayani is a Langham scholar graduated from Asia Graduate School of Theology, Manila. She serves at Bandung Theological Seminary as program director of the M.Th programme. As a faculty member, she teaches Biblical Study and Sociology. She is also a trainer at Langham Preaching Indonesia and actively speaks in seminars in relation to Muslims and Christian studies.

Cathy Hine has lived and worked in South Asia and the Middle East for more than thirty years, involved in education, development, relief, discipleship and mentoring. Her research interests are women and change in the Muslim context, and women and mission. She was part of Interserve's International Leadership team for nearly ten years. She is currently working to encourage women sharing life with Muslim women, and exploring working alongside women calling for change from within Islam.

Kathryn Kraft is lecturer in International Development at the University of East London, specialising in faith and humanitarianism, NGO management and storytelling in social transformation. She is also the senior research advisor for Faith and Development at World Vision International. Her work has taken her to countries around the world, including more than a decade working with local associations to do research on social issues in the Middle East.

Farhana Nazir is from Pakistan and a lecturer, and Dean of Students, at the Gujranwala Theological Seminary. Farhana is interested in the role of women in leadership in the Church, particularly where Islam shapes the culture. Margaret works among women from many different cultures in Sydney, Australia.

Ruth Nicholls was for many years in South Asia, where she worked alongside national workers who were involved in Bible Correspondence and radio ministry. She has pursued research interests in the use of contextualised liturgies for discipling believers from a Muslim background. Her other interests are Sufism and Folk Islam.

Nicole Ravelo-Hoërson, originally from Madagascar, has been serving God among Muslims in South Africa for many years now. She is a founder member of Christian Concern for Muslims (CCM), actively engaged in rethinking and reconstructing evangelism as a task that calls forth the highest in the creative energies, intellect and imagination of Christians. She also counsels Muslim female victims of spousal abuse, teaches, writes and presents at conferences.

Her current research with the South African Theological Seminary (SATS) focuses on Muslim women in the Western Cape. She also has research interests in the recovery of the therapeutic dimension of the Gospel, apologetics, spirituality, and women's issues.

Cathy Ross has worked in Rwanda, Congo and Uganda before moving into teaching. She is currently Tutor in Contextual Theology at Ripon College, MA Tutor for Pioneer leaders for CMS and Lecturer in Mission at Regent's Park College Oxford. Cathy has published extensively in mission: current research interests are in hospitality, marginalisation, women in leadership and African Migrant Christianity.

Karen Scott, along with her family, has spent many years working in Bangladesh. Through her work in rural health and development programmes, she saw the potential that women have, and has been committed to being a voice for the voiceless. Karen's teaching interests include intercultural studies, the role of the church in society and women and Islam.

Karen Shaw (D. Min.) is Assistant Professor of Cross-Cultural Ministry at Arab Baptist Theological Seminary. An American married to an Australian, Karen lived in the Middle East since 1990. She currently shepherds International Community Church in Beirut, Lebanon. Karen and her husband, Perry, have two adult children, Chris and Phoebe.

Jenny Taylor is a journalist, writer and founder of international media charity, Lapido Media (launched to work with journalists on religious literacy following the bombing of the London Underground in 2007). She has travelled widely in Asia and Africa as editor of Interserve's Go Magazine, and then Head of Media for CMS. Jenny has written and campaigned on women's issues in Islam. Her doctorate from London University's School of Oriental and African Studies examined how Islamic immigration was having an impact on secularisation and inner-city governance.

Sarah Yoon, from South Korea, has been working in the Middle East, along with her family, since 2002. She is actively involved in ministry with local women and discipling believers from a Muslim background. Her research interest has been identity issues for women who follow Jesus from a Muslim background. Sarah is an ordained Pastor.